Praise for *Nothing Short of Joy*

"A masterpiece that will take you out of your comfort zone and into a magical world of joy. I love this book. I love this woman. Read it and reap."
~ **Dr. Wayne Dyer**, internationally renowned self-development speaker and author *The Power of Intention, Excuses Begone!*

"Julie Genovese is an inspiration and a teacher for those who want to heal what can't be cured. So pain, hate and fear lead us to faith, hope and love."
~ **Bernie Siegel, M.D.**, *Faith, Hope and Healing, Love, Magic, and Mudpies*

"Julie Genovese's story is eloquent and moving proof that our spirits are always intact and always whole -- regardless of how things appear physically. Hers is a fascinating and thoroughly readable story of courage and triumph!"
~ **Christiane Northrup, M.D.**, *Secret Pleasures of Menopause, The Wisdom of Menopause, Women's Bodies, Women's Wisdom*

"A magnificent lesson in activating human potential. Julie Genovese proves that we are far more than a body, and the heart is the greatest healer. I want everyone who seeks to grow beyond their conditions to read this book and put Julie's masterful principles into action. Here is a rare and penetrating road map to spiritual freedom."
~ **Alan Cohen**, *Linden's Last Life , A Deep Breath of Life*

"If you have ever wondered what it must be like to have a physically different body, you will relish this compelling memoir. From the very first sentence, Julie draws readers into her extraordinary world with an immediacy that provides an intimate view of her emotional life. The lessons Julie learned that eventually brought her great joy will re[...] You won't be reading about her experie[...] with her."
~ **Susan Page**, *How One of You Can Brin[...] Together* and *Why Talking Is Not Enough*

"Julie Genovese is a master at combining great storytelling with witty humor and profound depth. Her book is a mirror to the soul and a question to the heart. It unveils the feelings behind every sense of "not measuring up" and universalizes the experience so we can all grow from the insights Julie has been gathering all her life."

~ **Jan Phillips**, *The Art of Original Thinking-The Making of a Thought Leader, Divining the Body, Marry Your Muse.*

"Nothing Short of Joy is an amazing story of triumph against all odds! Born with many painful, debilitating limitations, Julie Genovese courageously utilized her spiritual beliefs to create a life of love and joy. Beautifully and eloquently written, her book offers hope, joy and release to people who are suffering in any way!"

~ **Kari Joys, MS**, *Choosing Light-Heartedness*

"Julie's book is an inspiring pick-me-up for the soul and most certainly a read that is nothing short of joy"

~ **Tal Shai**, founder of www.BigDreamGuru.com

nothing short of *Joy*

by
Julie B. Genovese

Behler
PUBLICATIONS
California
USA

Behler Publications
California

Nothing Short of Joy
A Behler Publications Book

Copyright © 2010 by Julie B. Genovese
Cover design by Cathy Scott – www.mbcdesigns.com
Cover photograph courtesy of Rich Russo

Library of Congress Cataloging-in-Publication Data

Genovese, Julie B.
  Nothing short of joy / by Julie B. Genovese.
    p. cm.
  Includes bibliographical references and index.
  ISBN 978-1-933016-59-7 (pbk. : alk. paper) 1. Genovese, Julie B. 2. Dwarfs--United States--Biography. I. Title.
  CT9992.G46A3 2010
  599.9'49--dc22
  [B]
                              2009045421

THIRD PRINTING

ISBN 978-1-933016-59-7
e-book ISBN: 978-1-933016-95-5

Published by Behler Publications, LLC
Lake Forest, California
www.behlerpublications.com

Manufactured in the United States of America

For Mom and Dad

*whose unflappable love, support
and kindness
has never wavered.*

*This book is dedicated to you
with deepest appreciation
and all my love.*

One
Boston White-Coats

Have you learned lessons only from those who admired you,
and were tender with you, and stood aside from you?
Have you not learned great lessons from those
who braced themselves against you,
and disputed passage with you?
~Walt Whitman

My name drifted down through the floorboards, as her footsteps combed the house. Thrashing against my ribcage, my heart just wanted to lift free of the day ahead.

"Julie? Julie!" My mom's voice was growing concerned. "Where are you, sweetheart? It's almost time to go."

I'd never done anything so defiant. *This'll show them,* I thought. *I won't come out, ever. Ever!* The air felt barbed and hot, poking at my eyes and tightening my fists. I punched at the emptiness, a fury rising inside me. I don't want to go! Happiness bounced in the sweet September sky outside, yet I wouldn't relinquish a crumb of my drama below. This is horrible and unfair, I insisted, as fear jammed into my stiff joints. My breath caught when I heard a sudden rustling outside.

"Jule? Are you in there?"

I jumped as Ethan, my older brother, crawled into our secret hideaway under the back porch. "What're you doing?" he asked. "Mom's looking all over for you."

"I'm not going!"

"What do you mean? You *have* to go."

"Do not!"

"Yeah, you do," he said. "Dad'll be so mad if you don't come out right now."

I stared my brother down with a hate that didn't belong to him.

"What? . . . Julie? Say something. Come on . . . cut it out."

I had no words. They had been taken away.

"You can't just sit here." Now he sounded worried.

"They don't care!"

"Who?"

I couldn't admit it. "Leave me alone!"

Even my brother didn't understand, and he was almost eleven. I was only nine. He was smart, and he was . . . like me. He didn't seem to mind the white-coats. He even chatted and laughed with them. How could he stand the way they looked at us and spoke about us? Didn't he feel the same curse? Why wouldn't he join my angry protest? Maybe together our misery had a chance. Maybe it had power. Didn't he hurt too?

When kids teased Ethan, he fired right back at them, angry and fierce. He would yell until they stopped in surprise, or walked away laughing. He wanted to stand up for himself, like my dad. When kids laughed at me, though, I shrank inside and dove out of the way. I wanted to avoid conflict, like my mom. Why wouldn't Ethan stand up to our parents now? Strangely enough, my brother and I never talked about it—how we were different from our other brothers and sisters, how we were different from everyone at school, or about what happened to us in Boston. How could I ask him anything now?

Every hair stood at attention when we heard my dad. "Julie! You come out this minute! This isn't funny anymore. Julie!"

My brother stared at me in dismay and ducked out from under the back porch.

Don't go, Ethan. Why can't we be a team? "Don't you dare tell them where I am," I whispered.

I watched my brother's stiff little body move quickly past the slatted grate, the only thing separating me from Boston. My crooked knees ached from sitting on the hard ground too long. Awkwardly splayed straight out in front of me, my legs refused to sit Indian-style or cross-legged, to kneel, or to slide up softly to my chest. Unwilling to be flexible and fast like the other kids. Unable to run far away.

I'm not going. I won't let them take me there ever again! I clenched my fists until they glowed white, beating the air down again and again.

Time ticked away, destroying my resolve. Ethan was right. I'd be in big trouble if I kept hiding. My dad had lost it over much smaller things, like the night that I whined to my mom about dinner being late. Without words or warning, he flew into the kitchen in a rage, snarling and red-faced. He yanked me over his lap and spanked me so hard that it felt as though my eyes had hit the opposite wall. I ran upstairs, shocked and scared, with him yelling behind me. My mom was quiet. I cried myself to sleep, missing dinner that night.

Did I really want to go on hiding today and risk my dad's temper? Then the car ride would be horrible, and my mom would end up quiet and sad. The thought of all that tension was suddenly more awful than anything else. It's no use. Boston always wins. I could feel its hand over my mouth, ordering me to come. My resistance began to sink in pitiful surrender.

Slowly, I dragged myself from my sanctuary and limped up the back stairs. I'd been promised to those men to poke and prod. I was a broken offering to the gods of medicine.

"There you are, sweetheart." My mom's smile was tired. Silence crowded between us. "Can you please go get ready?"

I slid away from her and pulled myself upstairs. I yanked a pair of jeans over my swollen knees. I sulked, silent for the entire five-hour car trip. Every road sign screamed out my words: *Caution Ahead. Wrong Way. Stop. Please stop.* Approaching Boston, I bit my nails down to raw stubs.

We went into a different building than usual. My mom called this visit "a medical convention." Inside, the fake smiles and plastic toys were the same. Sitting in the waiting area, I watched the parade of kids in casts, braces, and wheelchairs; a little boy with only one leg. Another with shriveled arms and crossed eyes.

An odd-looking girl nervously paced in a corner all alone. What's wrong with her? I looked around but didn't see her parents. I continued watching her as she reached for something on the end table. A pack of cigarettes? My mouth hung slack when she actually lit one. She's a grown-up! Shocked, I hastily looked away. I'd been staring—in the hurtful way I knew too well. Then I noticed a strange little man, dressed in a loose brown suit. Messy and overweight, he was wolfing down donuts. He stood on tiptoe and fed a few coins to the coffee machine. Two small people. Do I look like that? Will I? They lingered near each other but didn't speak. Are they married? Do people like them only marry each other? I glanced over at my parents for clues, but they were chatting calmly.

The phone rang and the receptionist answered cheerfully, "Good morning, Center for Birth Defects."

This was a place for things that didn't work. Defective people who weren't as good. We were ushered into an examination room. My mom smiled at me and put a reassuring hand on my back. I pulled away. She kept smiling.

"I'm Dr. Telsor. This must be Julie."

"Yes, it is," she answered, knowing that I wouldn't.

"She's nine?" he asked, checking his paperwork. The date was September 3, 1972.

My mom nodded. "That's right."

"Why don't we take that shirt off and have a look at her spine," the doctor said as he stared at his clipboard.

I braced myself.

My mom reached for my sleeve. I yanked it away. At slumber parties, I always put on my pajamas in the bathroom while the other girls ran naked in the living room. At home I closed my door. Here, I was expected to undress on command, in front of strangers. I took off my shirt. The doctor started his exam, writing on his clipboard every time he touched me. His silence was heavy, holding me down on the table. All my clothes eventually came off except for my underwear. When the exam was done, I reached for my shirt.

"Oh, stay undressed," the doctor said as he opened the door.

A nervous man with a skinny grin walked in the room. "The technician is here to take some pictures," Dr. Telsor said as he talked to my mom about an important medical journal.

"O-kay, Julie," the skinny grin said. "You are going to be in a very special book so doctors can learn all about you. It will help other children of short stature." He raised his camera and looked through the lens. "Would you like to have your picture taken?"

I looked at my mom in horror. *With nothing on?*

"It will be a big help to the doctors," she started to explain.

How will this help?

"We just want to look at your pretty face," the man said as he got down on one knee, his face now level with mine. The room got smaller. He was way too close. His eyes were pinned on me as he fiddled with his camera. He was really going to do this. She was going to let him.

"Can you look right in here? Gimme a big smile, sweetie." The flashing and clicking and nervous chatter began. "Gimme a big, beautiful smile." I felt cornered and humiliated. Flash. Click, click, click. I was powerless to stop him. Flash. Click, click, click. I smiled and pretended it was normal. "Great!" he said. Flash. Click, click, click. The photographer looked pleased as he got pictures from all sides. I wanted to kick and scream and tear down walls. I wanted to crack his skull with that camera, stab needles into his eyes, rip off his clothing and parade him in the streets. I wanted to fight. I did nothing. The fighting went inside, instead, and waited.

"Julie, can you turn towards the window?" Flash. Click, click, click. "Can you lift your arms up like this? Perfect." Flash, click, click, click. "You're a superstar." I must have been following instructions, though my insides disobeyed. It was so cold. My heart felt freezing cold.

He turned to my mother. "Can Mummy take off those cute panties so we can get her complete backside?"

I looked at her, stunned. She wore that hopeless smile. I had no choice.

I stripped off my last piece of camouflage. It fell softly on the steely, gray floor. He told me to turn around. I did. He told me to turn sideways. I did. *Good listeners get stars in school.* Then he told me to look into the black camera, and I did. Its big glass eye looked back at me and winked.

When we got back to the waiting room, my dad and Ethan were talking to a different doctor. Had they done the same thing to Ethan? Taken his clothes off, taken his picture? Was he measured inch by inch? Had their sentences looped endlessly around him? Why did he seem to be okay? I saw the red balloon animal he was holding. I'd been offered that bribe too.

The doctor talked to me in a baby voice that made my skin crawl. "Would you like to come with me for a little while, Julie?" As if I had any say. Without waiting for my answer, he nodded to my parents and led me away.

"Don't worry, sweetheart, it'll be okay!" my mom called. I looked back at her, and she offered up a sweet smile. "It's for the best," my parents always claimed. "The doctors want to help." *How can that be?* I still had the same pain and stiffness in my legs, I was still the shortest third-grader in school. What did any of it matter? I was still teased. I just wanted to go home.

"We're going right in here." The doctor's toothy smile was the first thing through the double doors. The sight ahead made me gasp. I was abandoned as he joined the sea of white-coats with silver nooses around their necks. Charts and strange pictures hung silent on the walls. Chairs and tables waited in long rows. Bright lights and metal instruments pinched my eyes. So much noise—until they saw me. A hush fell across the room. Forced smiles replaced the clatter. They wanted something.

I stood alone in the front of the room as one of them approached. "Hello, Julie. I'm Dr. Simon." I recognized his Vulcan eyebrows from last year, but I said nothing. I didn't want them to know I was scared. Dr. Simon turned away from me and began to address the group. "One in a hundred thousand births are affected yearly by spondyloepiphyseal dysplasia, a congenital defect. Here we see the proportionate short-statured SED with short trunk and proportionate limbs. This is unlike achondroplasia, which is a disproportionate short-statured dwarfism with normal torso and short limbs." Dr. Simon asked me to turn sideways and raise my arms. "Note the curvature of the spine and pelvic abnormalities."

He paused for a second and then looked me in the eyes. "Would you mind standing up on this table? We just want everyone to be able to see your pretty face."

On the inside I was screaming no, but a yes flew off my tongue. Even though I hated them, I wanted to be good, I was taught to be good, even for the white-coats.

Someone grabbed me under my armpits and lifted me into the air, up on display. Dr. Simon continued, his strange words pressing into my ears as another doctor moved my limbs, turning and twisting them, bending and straightening. His hollow voice magnified my flaws. Clipboards bobbed. Face after face examined me, nodding as they scribbled notes and measurements. They looked so intently, but no one saw.

The exhibition continued as I drifted away, desperate to drown out the labels that were anchoring inside me. Defect; abnormal; deformed; dysplasia; arthritis; dwarfism.

"Would you mind bending forward for me, Julie?" I obeyed. "Note the decreased range of motion of the lumbar spine, narrowed disc spaces, limited flexibility in neck, decreased range of hip rotation and degenerative changes in hips and misaligned knees. There are irregular epiphyses and abnormal growth of the long bones. Out of five older siblings, one brother carries the same diagnosis of spondyloepiphyseal dysplasia. The other four siblings are normal. Mother reports slight motor delays. Patient walked at seventeen months of age."

We just want to look at your pretty face.

When they were done with me, I was brought back to my parents like a lost wallet whose contents had been impersonally scanned. My ID, though, had been left behind. For years I never even knew it was missing.

"She's very well-adjusted." Dr. Simon told my parents, who proceeded to tell him of my many friends, activities, and happy attitude. Apparently, being well-adjusted was a good thing. I wondered if it mattered how I felt, or only how I appeared? I'd been working hard to perfect the part of a well-adjusted person, and often I performed so well I almost fooled myself. But the more people praised how happy I was, the more scared I became. What if they uncovered the lie? Who could love the darkness under the cheerful façade?

"Your children are lucky compared to many that we see. They will most likely lead normal, productive lives." The doctor talked intently to my parents, something about the hospital. I stopped listening, until he turned and poked me in the stomach. "Keep that little tummy trim. Extra weight will cause your joints to wear out more quickly. We wouldn't want that, now would we?" He patted Ethan on the head and shook hands with my parents. At last we could leave.

The car ride home was quiet. Ethan wanted to play "spotting license plates," but I just stared out the window. Why did this seem easier for him? Maybe he also wanted to be good. Maybe he wanted to be a brave example for his little sister. Superman never cried. Batman never whined. Ethan wanted to be strong, like them. Like our dad. Isn't that what the world demanded of boys? No girly feelings allowed if you want to grow up and be a proud man. I was careful not to whine around my dad. Maybe Ethan was being careful too.

The doctors knew what was wrong with Ethan and me. They were always talking about it. My parents knew, but they rarely talked about it. Other children knew, and they pointed at it. Boys knew, and they laughed at it. Boston knew and wanted to change it. Maybe even Ethan knew, but he never admitted it. I didn't want to know.

Two
A Bad Hand

And yet there's One
whose gently holding hands
this Universe falling
can't fall through.
~Maria Rainer Rilke

My artwork was the one thing the kids at school never laughed at. My teachers thought I had a talent for art and my parents treated me like a Picasso sprout. Every doodle was admired, even when I scribbled on one of their phone messages. Even my brothers and sisters were enthusiastic about my drawing and painting.

One afternoon, after staying late to finish a craft project, I headed home alone. Without the usual friends to hide behind, waves of worry echoed out around me. I made it two blocks before I saw them, a magnet of kids materializing from a side street. One was Sammy Gosbin. I wanted to turn and bolt, but I knew that would draw their attention. A rabbit on the run is exciting prey. I crossed the street, hoping they would miss seeing me. But with every nerve on high alert, my fear drew them in like a vacuum.

"Hey, little midget!" Sammy's foul voice called out as he ran across the street. "Where you going in such a hurry?"

Oh God, here he comes. I tried to move faster but my legs were no match for the group. They were at my side in a flash. *Get away from me!*

"Look!" Sammy yelled. He walked next to me on his knees, mimicking my gait. His face was down at my level, spit bubbling at the corner of his mouth. "I'm a dorf too!"

"Look at me!" Another boy got on his knees.

Stop it! Why do you do this?

"How old are you, runt?" one demanded.

My heart wailed in terror and humiliation. *What's happening? Get away!*

"Hey, I said, how old are you, shrimpy?"

I bit down on my agony, staring straight ahead as I moved through the gauntlet.

"Shrimpy! Shrimpy!" They surrounded me with their cruel laughter. It might as well have been a whole schoolyard of kids, closing in, eager to pounce. Turmoil raced through me, spinning me up in their wild taunting. I pushed forward but I couldn't speak. My voice choked on a fear-filled rage. *Get away from me! Leave me alone!*

Sammy's voice mocked me. "Is the little baby gonna cry all the way home?"

Their voices floated to the yards up ahead, so they decided to end the game or get caught. "Bye-bye, wittle midgee!"

"See ya, shrimpy!"

I watched their retreat, making sure they were gone. Adrenaline cycled furiously under my skin as my mind screamed the words that I had not. *I HATE you! I HATE all of you! What's wrong with you? What's wrong with me?* My knees throbbed as I kept up the pace. Two blocks away from my house, I'd never felt farther from home.

My big house was empty except for our hound dog, Pal, who greeted me with delight. I gave him a pat with my shaking hand. He didn't see my flaws. At dinner, my family could tell something was wrong, but no one asked me. We ate our meal, and they talked about everything except for the fact that I was sitting there, silent and sullen.

"What's wrong?" my mom finally asked.

"Nothing," I grunted. I don't think she believed me, but she never pushed. I really, really wanted her to. *Please ask me again! And when I say "I'm fine," don't believe me, don't just accept it. Keep asking!* There was a mountain of tears trapped behind my angry silence, waiting for someone to show me that they could handle the chaos going through my head. Would my dad think I was weak and whiney if I expressed my pain? Would it hurt my mom too much? I longed to unfold the sadness in front of them and have tell me I was okay. But if we talked about how other people saw me, and what others said about me, would they finally see my strangeness, see me differently, and love me less? But if they did ask, really asked, wouldn't it mean that it was okay to talk, that they could handle it, that they knew other people saw me as odd but they didn't? They said nothing, so I said nothing.

At school, in stores, in restaurants, even on vacation, someone was always jeering. Loud, abrasive voices singled me out. Or quiet voices would lower to a whisper as I walked by. Strangers offered pitying smiles. Did my family politely overlook what others saw? Was it love that kept my family from acknowledging my differences, or was it shame? All around me was ridicule, but at home there was silence. The intention to include and protect me had backfired—instead I was shattered by what went unspoken.

Climbing into bed that night, the panic and pain came rushing back. The overwhelming future full of Sammy Gosbins. Tears wore me thin until footsteps sounded outside my door. I muffled my sobs as my mom peeked in. Her voice was gentle as she came in and sat on my bed. "What's the matter, sweetheart? Why didn't you call me?"

I cried harder, not sure I could say anything. "Some boys teased me," I finally squeaked. That was all I could admit, though that day had been worse than the regular taunting I kept to myself. She leaned in to give me a hug, then declared she'd talk to the principal the following day. As if that would help. She'd have given anything to protect me from days like those, but back then I believed there was no way she could.

"Julie, I know it's unfair. You were . . . dealt a bad hand," my mom said softly. Pain was pocketed in her eyes. "But you have a good mind and a generous heart, and those are the important qualities." She went on about my good grades and my nice friends. Her voice was drowned out by the pandemonium in my mind. A bad hand? What did she mean? What exactly was bad about me? She didn't elaborate and my fear wouldn't let me ask. Who dealt me this bad hand? Had God punished me? Punished us? Was it someone's fault? Mine? Hers?

My mother had validated my despair, but she'd also confirmed my fears. Something was very wrong with me. Was it worse than I thought? Too much for her? How could I manage if my parents, my heroes, were as scared as I?

A few weeks later, as my mom tucked me in for the night, she was unusually quiet. "Julie," she started slowly, "remember Dr. Simon telling us about a procedure that would reduce some of your pain and help your hips feel looser?"

I nodded. I had a vague recollection.

"Well, we've set a date in Boston and . . ."

"What?" Instantly I pictured the Vulcan scientist. "No! Don't take me there! Please!"

"Sweetheart, you've dislocated your kneecaps twice in the last few months. And aren't your hips hurting more lately? Isn't it more difficult for you to get around?"

She was right. It was hard to keep up with my friends, especially when my knees were swollen and my hips were tight. Other kids moved effortlessly, out beyond my grasp. I couldn't even reach the ground without something sturdy to lean on. At home, I learned to pick up most things with my toes, but shoes limited me at school. If I dropped my lunch money, I pretended not to notice, hoping someone would pick it up for me. It was better than having to do any arthritic bending in front of the other kids. For years, I preferred to leave coins, pens, and pencils in the hallways of my childhood, rather than leave a defective image in their memory. Or in mine.

"We'll need to stay in the hospital a week or so, but I'll be with you the whole time." She smiled at me, but sorrow crept in around it. "We'll leave July eighteenth. We didn't have a choice in the scheduling. The doctor is very very busy."

"Wait, what about my birthday?"

"We might be home." Then she added quietly, "But probably not."

Shock scorched through me. I turned away, closed my heart and shut her out of my sight. Gently, she pulled the quilt up around me. "I love you," she whispered, as she tucked me back into silence.

"I have to go to the hospital," I told my best friend, Megan.

"What do you mean? When?" Megan asked.

"In a few weeks. My parents are making me. For my knees or something." I wouldn't say the word "hip" because, to me, it was a word associated with women, something I would never really be.

"So you won't have to use your crutches?" Megan asked.

"I don't know."

"Hey, want to come over?"

Spending the day with my best friend soothed almost any pain. We'd met in first grade, and since then, I never imagined life without her. I wanted to be just like her: to look like her, walk like her, laugh like her, and swim like her.

We grabbed our towels and headed for her pool. The turquoise water giggled as we dipped our toes in. Megan dove right into the blue. I tried to mimic her effortless movements. Sometimes, as I glided through the water, I felt like her. I thought I might be like her or the other kids. That's when the world felt great. A dazzling blue sky, splendid sun. Our skin darker, our hair and hearts lighter. Splashing and laughing and pretending. I felt healthy, strong, and almost . . . pretty.

In one swift motion, Megan lifted herself up out of the water and onto the edge of the pool. I had to use the ladder.

"Was my dive right?" I asked the pro.

"You got it. How about this one?" Megan stood with her back to the water, toes balancing on the edge, her hands out in front of her like Frankenstein. Then she leapt. An exquisite curve into the blue. A back dive a dolphin would love. Barely made a splash.

"Neat!" I said.

"Try it, Jule. You can do it."

"Last time I landed on my back."

"You gotta keep trying. You can do it."

Reluctantly, I turned my back to the pool.

"You just have to leap. You'll be okay."

She stood next to me, demonstrating. The sound of her voice disappeared when I saw the reflection of us, side by side, in the sliding glass door. I looked nothing like Megan, with the sun lying happily across her pretty face and smile. Megan was perfect. I was the Frankenstein. Nearly half her size, curved like a cheese doodle, no neck, a big cue ball of a head, legs at funny angles, elbows permanently bent. My confidence sank to the bottom of the pool. How could I be so ugly when I felt so good? Why did I keep forgetting?

I turned away from the reflection. Maybe Dr. Simon could fix me after all.

A month later, as I sat down on my hospital bed in Boston, my heart was in full battle gear. Bars and chains for traction loomed over me.

My mom gazed out the window. "Look, we have a lovely view."

I said nothing. When she spoke, she said nothing real. I wanted her to stare into my eyes and tell me that I was allowed to hurt. Tell me why my body was so bad. Wrestle my pulsing questions out into the open. But her words never ran deep enough to find me. I scowled as she unpacked, wishing my hate could stop this. Wishing my silence would work. Its power had worked on me. Now it was my only weapon.

In the hospital, I never knew what was coming. Or who. A young man in white walked into my hospital room that night. He grinned nervously and told my mother he was going to take a "quick check." Suddenly and indiscreetly, he pulled down the front of my pajama pants and underwear to have a peek. He pushed my loose sleeve up and gazed under my arm, scribbled something on his clipboard, and was gone. It took a minute before I understood that he'd checked for pubic and armpit hair. I had neither, but I felt mortified by these topics that were never discussed at home. *Stop looking at me! I want them all to stop touching me!* I pulled the covers over my head, too ashamed to see my mother's face. Suddenly, I didn't want her sympathy; it would unleash the forbidden tears. So I pushed the pain underwater, as rage swelled up over the sides.

The only time I reached for her that week was when they wheeled me away, drugged and frightened, to the operating room. Dye was injected into my hip joints in order to investigate the degeneration of each ball and socket. After the procedure was done, I awoke in my room, dazed and disoriented. My mom seemed to be floating at a desk in the corner, working on her real estate. Before she noticed I was awake, my hands nervously raced down to check the damage. I found a large Band-Aid on each sore hip. Relieved, I fell back asleep. A few hours later, I opened my eyes to my mother's smile. I jerked my head away and turned towards the hard, cold wall.

"How are you feeling, sweetheart?" She no longer expected an answer. "Dr. Simon said that everything went well. Tomorrow you'll start the traction that will help create space in your hip joints. It should reduce some of your pain. How about a birthday present?"

I wanted to keep up my silence but couldn't resist the bait. "All right," I said, acting like I'd just agreed to eat Brussels sprouts. I tried to hold onto my anger as I ripped open a large, odd-shaped package. But the lollipop tree inside, filled with candy, made it hard to contain my glee.

The following morning, two nurses fitted me in cloth booties with metal soles, wrapped my legs in braces, and hooked me up to the maze of pipes that loomed over the bed. Tugging at my cloth feet were two sandbags, which dangled over the end of my bed. So this was traction. The pain was constant, but not in my legs. Locked in bed in my tiny room, I had no diversions. In the doctor's Godlike eyes, I needed impossible repairs. My safe harbor of family and friends had been ripped away.

I watched TV and waited for a meal break when I was unhooked and allowed to talk on the hall phone or go to the bathroom. If I had to relieve myself sooner, the nurses would offer the gruesome bedpan. Frankly, I would've preferred to implode. My mom and I often watched *The Price is Right*. Usually I liked it. On this particular day, I hated the models and their perfect bodies and strong legs. *Why did I get the stinking rotten egg?* I glared at my mother as she bit her fingernails. Our family all thought she sang, danced, and even looked like Judy Garland. Right then, she looked like Cruella DeVil. Her cheeriness made me want to scream. I hated her. Or was it me I hated?

When the hall phone rang, I was sure they'd free me from traction early if the call was for me. The nurse poked her head in. "It was someone named Megan. I told her you'd call back later when you were out of traction." *What did she say? She's not my mother!* I stared at the nurse. Mom will undo this. Megan is my best friend.

"Just a half hour left," my mom said, as she placed a rainbow-colored gift box on my lap. Inside I found a sparkling ring of two sterling spirals, coiled like a pair of snakes, ready to strike. I loved it, but I said nothing.

Ten days of silence passed while I tried to hold back the doctors, the nurses, the future. If I had enough hate, wouldn't the adults stop pretending? Wouldn't they give me the permission to speak? To feel? Couldn't she change this mess? Nothing was clear in the blackness of that summer stay, except that I turned eleven years old.

As we drove home to New Jersey and through our small suburban town of Lakeside, a long sigh made its way out the open window. Our beautiful, wooded neighborhood was a welcome sight. The white-coats, with their starched smiles and pointy needles, were far away.

My dad, Ethan, and my older sister, Kris, hurried outside to greet us. Their faces sang of home, the place where I could forget what I knew. Where no one pointed out my flaws. No one stared or teased. No one laughed at the body I couldn't control.

That night, before my belated birthday dinner, everyone disappeared upstairs to wrap presents. Birthdays were a special event at our house, and it was a giggly feeling to be the reason for the fussing that night. During dinner, my parents talked briefly about our trip. My mom told everyone how the doctors and nurses had been so nice. I said nothing. The conversation quickly turned to lighter subjects.

After all the gifts were opened, my dad lowered the lights and lit the tall candles. We kids chattered and waited until my brother, Dan, walked out from the kitchen, a proud cake in his hands, his face aglow in the dancing candles. Everyone burst into a spirited round of "Happy Birthday" as my mom's sweet harmony sparkled around us. I blew out the candles, and soaked up the love.

After the festivities were through, I called Megan. I told her about my gifts and then about the huge body cast I had to sleep in at night. How it went from just above my knees, to up under my arms, cut in half like a clam shell, with belts holding it together. It kept my legs spread far apart. The traction had opened up some room between the ball and socket and the cast was an attempt to maintain that space. I was too embarrassed to tell Megan, though, how I woke up every night crying and how my mom gave me sleeping pills. Or how my brother Dan would come and lie next to me so I didn't feel so scared. Megan said I could come spend the night as soon as my parents would let me, but I wondered if I'd be allowed to leave the cast behind.

Talking to Megan made me feel better, like things could go back to normal. At times I knew Megan and I were different, but at age eleven, she was my best friend. We spent long days together exploring the woods, rummaging and playing in her huge basement, inventing games, having sleepovers and laughing until we cried. By the time we were twelve, though, it all changed. Megan was suddenly looking like a fifteen-year-old, mature and attractive. The boys all drooled. I looked about seven, and the boys all laughed. The differences that had never mattered before started to matter in sixth grade—self-consciousness clogged every pore, pressure mounted, cliques formed, bodies blossomed, and friendships changed. Alliances were made and broken in a single lunch period. Megan started spending more time with the cool group.

I watched from the wings, bewildered and limp, wondering what I could do to keep my friend from flying away. I was thrilled when she invited me over to her house one afternoon, until she reached for a pack of her mom's cigarettes. Shocked and scared, I insisted that her mother would *murder* her, she'd get *cancer*, she'd become *addicted* and never be able to stop. She asked if I wanted to try one.

Agony rushed in and out of my lungs as the smoke screen curled around her. With every puff, she was exhaling our friendship. Megan was now rolling way out of my league. She'd just drawn the line to prove it. After that, when Megan and I occasionally passed each other in the hallway and said hello, my heart would leap into her smile. I wanted to talk with her, laugh with her. But she could have any friend. Why would she want me?

I thought that my horrible body was setting me apart again, limiting my future, blocking every happiness. I wanted to follow Megan into her sophisticated world of boys and relationships, bras and heels, make-up and hair styles. But I also didn't want to grow up. I had to pretend to be a kid so I could avoid being a freak. With maturity, the truth would be written all over me in flesh and curves and breasts. I wouldn't be able to hide a woman's shape even if I was still a child's size. My last shield would be destroyed, my denial unveiled. So, as much as I missed her, in truth I was scared to go where Megan went first.

Three
Silver Bay

And which of you by worrying and being anxious
can add one measure to his stature
or to the span of his life?
~Matthew 6:28

The last two weeks of August was always my favorite time
of year because it's when my family took our annual trip to my
grandfather's cottage in Silver Bay, Canada. Surrounded by my
family, I was safe. I belonged. Nowhere else did I feel so good
and, at times, so vulnerable.

A few hours into the long car trip from New Jersey, a
strange smell wafted through the car. The temperature gauge
was high again. "Damn it! We just had it in the shop!" my dad
snapped. Everyone fell silent under the threat of his anger.
Although he was usually good-natured and loving, he was also
an unpredictable pressure cooker. When he started to lose
control, our world never sat quite right.

Car troubles were high on his list of aggravations—also on
the list were his stressful marketing job in New York City,
expenses for our large old house, two kids out of college, two in
college, and two more to go. There were times when a seemingly
trivial event would unleash his fire, like the time he and I went
on an overnight outing with our Indian Princess group, a YMCA
program for fathers and daughters to spend time together while
learning about the environment and Native American culture.
We'd been having a wonderful time until we headed for the
lake, only to find that the teenage lifeguard, who was supposed

to unlock the canoes, was nowhere around. As we waited and waited for the lifeguard, I watched nervously as my father's agitation grew. I was quickly coming undone as his eyes narrowed and his jaw clenched. *Dad, please don't get mad and ruin the day.* But I knew being careless or lazy at your job was unacceptable to him. He often saw life in black or white. Right or wrong. You were with him or you were against him.

When the unsuspecting guard eventually sauntered down to the lake, my dad offered some bitter words and a very threatening posture. The kid tried to dismiss him, which made him more furious. Everything inside me froze as I saw my father's face turn a murderous red. His voice rose up across the lake and terror took me down. I wanted to run. I wanted to scream. *PLEASE Dad, stop! Why get so crazy? Why are you so mad?* But I was frozen silent.

I watched in horror as my dad shoved the guard towards the boathouse. The kid could have overpowered my father, but he let my dad yell and push him until he landed in a stack of life-preservers. One of the other fathers pulled my dad away, but the day was already lost. Fun would no longer be the focus. My singular goal would be to not upset him further. In the hours ahead, I waited in his volatile shadow, walking on egg shells and wiping a smile across my fear. But inside I was always rattled and terrified after one of his blow-ups.

It would take both of us a long while to breathe normally again. Then as quickly as it had left, my dad's kindness and big heart returned. But we didn't talk about his anger that day or any other. Without resolution, these scary outbursts left powerful, tainted impressions on otherwise good times.

As we drove on towards Canada, my dad slowly pulled himself together. This day, there was no blaming or yelling or hours of tension and silence, much to everyone's relief.

At last, the car limped its way over the Peace Bridge into Ontario. As soon as we arrived at the cottage, we headed for the beach. Although it was a short walk down to Lake Erie, and I

had plenty of bodies to hide behind, I still worried. Ethan and
I, together, drew more attention than when we were apart. In
fact, even the doctors were particularly interested in us
because not only was our genetic condition rare, but two
specimens in the same family further beat the odds. My
parents should have considered playing the lottery.

I stayed alert as we walked, always wondering who'd be
watching, who'd intrude. This year I felt extra conspicuous in
my fourteen-year-old body. Even regular clothes couldn't
cover my physical differences, but there was absolutely no
hiding in a swimsuit. I tugged and squirmed, feeling utterly
exposed. Out on the beach, there were no shorts to hide my
crooked legs, puffy knees, and cherub bottom. There was no
shirt to cover my misshapen back, which had become as
curved as the question marks that now defined my world.

Every boy who passed was a dream swaddled in a
potential nightmare. A smile would stir my hopes, a snicker
would stiffen my soul. I spent hours daydreaming about a
boyfriend holding my hand or walking me to school. I needed
a boy to say I was okay. My body didn't seem to bother my
friends, who were all girls. But the boys were another story.
They were either the Sammy Gosbins of the world, or the ones
who admired only the pretty girls like Megan. They didn't
want this body of mine any more than I did. So when friends
chattered about their crushes, I withheld mine. When notes
were passed and juicy rumors spread about who was going
steady, it never involved me.

The following day, my favorite uncle, Shall; his girlfriend,
Valerie; and their two-year-old daughter came to visit us at the
cottage. My little cousin, Kunji, felt like a gift just for me.
When we'd met the summer before, the life shimmering in her
eyes had me lassoed in minutes. Her fun flew around us like
an iridescent dragonfly, circling and defining a world I'd
forgotten. She laughed up and down, ran here and there,
connecting our separateness with her play. It mattered

somehow, deep in her smile, that I was there. As she giggled at my games, unaware of my defects, something important returned.

Then one afternoon little Kunji did something that ripped my mask clear away: she called me Mommy. A cream-colored love lifted up my hope. Holding my hand, she gave me the courage. For the first time, I allowed the dream to speak, very softly, so no one would hear my audacity. Maybe someday? Maybe . . . my own.

We built our annual bonfire on the beach that night, made marshmallow s'mores and sailed up high on a creamcicle moon. As we listened to the water whispering along the shore, my parents were glowing like firelight. We were woven together by their deep love. A night like this with my family was the best I knew of goodness and grace. These faces, these songs and traditions would always remain, even if all else changed. Their permanence was the greatest comfort I knew. I belonged here, and although I felt alone in the outer world, I wasn't alone with them. Life was unpredictable, but with my family I was safe. I was accepted. I wasn't judged or teased, even though I was the baby. I was valuable in their eyes and held up by their smiles.

I thought of the times my sister, Celia, stayed up late with me, night after night, as I finished a big social studies project, and how she had invited me to visit her in Wisconsin for two weeks during the summer. Or when my brother, Ray, patiently sympathized as I complained about the same English teacher that he had disliked, and the way he helped me learn to catch a lacrosse ball. Or how Dan and I imitated cartoons together, and the way he had comforted me while I slept in my body cast. Or how my sister, Kris, always seemed impressed with my artwork, and the way she smiled and waved when I came to her basketball and softball games. Or how Ethan and I would commiserate over homework, and the way he'd let me hang out with him and his friends. My security was deep-rooted in the spirit of each of them: Celia's enthusiasm, Ray's gentle wit,

Dan's sense of fun, Kris's kindness. And Ethan. I'd always have Ethan. "I believe in you, Jule," he wrote once in an apology note after a loud and tiring fight. And I knew he meant it. Because come what may, we were held tight by an unspoken bond.

Celia and Kris strummed their guitars as we sat in our circle of light. We sang our family songs and laughed over the same old stories, as we did every year, guaranteed. Sometimes, people walking along the beach would stop near our campfire to watch and listen. It was one of the rare moments when I wanted to be seen. I wanted them to catch the magic and witness me when I was whole. When I was joy. When our family was one. Because in those moments, open and alive, I felt no darkness around me at all.

The following afternoon, playing a big game of croquet, I was happily out in the lead. Standing alone by the farthest wicket, at the edge of our new neighbor's lawn, I impatiently waited for my next turn. When a car pulled up next door, I glanced over and saw our new neighbor staring at me. Quickly I turned away. I knew that look. I winced when I heard her calling. "Hey little girl!"

I pretended not to hear, but she would have none of it.

"Little girl! Come over here!"

She was an adult. I had to listen. Nervously I stepped closer as the large woman gawked. I'd never met her before, but I recognized the narrow world that housed her. The situation was so familiar, but still a painful surprise. I knew her next question by heart.

"How old are you?" she insisted, giving me a blatant once-over.

Swallowing hard, I said quietly, "Fourteen."

"What?" She laughed. "Are you a midget?"

I lowered my eyes, my chest heaving furiously. She pointed at Ethan and giggled. "Is that your boyfriend?"

A voice cracked the thick spell.

"Leave her alone!" someone shouted. I turned to find my twenty-two-year-old brother, Dan, leaning out from our porch.

The woman looked up indignantly. "I was just talkin' to the little girl!"

"Don't you think my brother and sister get enough crap from other kids?" Dan yelled. "They don't need it from an adult!"

"I didn't mean nothin'!" she bellowed, now intent on my hero. She quickly walked past, brushing me off like a crumb from her double-D chest.

The two voices began to battle on our front step until my mother ran outside and insisted that Dan stop. He threw his hands up and stormed away. My mom apologized to the neighbor, who groused loudly as she lumbered back to her cottage. I stood motionless as the shocking scene reverberated inside my skull. The forbidden had been broached in front of everyone.

I hid in my room for an hour until my mother called us to the table. We had silence for dinner, as my eyes lay cold on my food. I took an occasional peek at Dan, who sat in his own contained fury. He had spoken of my private pain. Who else knew what Ethan and I felt? Dan had opened a bolted door and soothed my loneliness. Something new had begun. I wanted to hug him, hold him, thank him for understanding me. For defending me. If I let it slip by, my heartache would be forced underground again. I had to speak, but my throat was a sour, black knot. I rehearsed words, gathering courage. I looked at my handsome brother, his dark wavy hair disheveled, his brown eyes black.

As I began quietly, "Thank you, Dan, I . . . ," he immediately waved his hand, dismissing me. I sat for a minute, stunned, unsure of what to do. I got up from the table and went off to my room. Crawling into bed, I anxiously waited and hoped for a knock on the door.

An hour went by as I sat and stared out the window. Old cobwebs hung around the frame like tattered curtains. I cried off and on, afraid that no one cared enough to come talk to me, yet just as frightened that someone would. "I was born wrong," I whispered to the dusty windowsill, "and it scares off the people who love me." I had already caused them enough pain. Hidden by myself, my sadness couldn't hurt them anymore. I felt the relief of my predictable cage. *No one understands and no one really cares.* That pledge was easier to cling to than to risk them seeing the real me.

Four
Opposite Twins

Though my soul shall set in darkness
it will rise in perfect light.
We have loved the stars too fondly
to be fearful of the night.
~*Anonymous*

In the fall of 1977, Ethan and I were about to face high school together. My freshman year. His sophomore year. By then, the rest of our brothers and sisters had left home. My oldest sister, Celia, the free-spirited wilderness gal, had become a legal secretary in Chicago. My two older brothers, Ray and Dan, were both in graduate school at the University of Chicago. My sister, Kris, was a freshman at Swarthmore College, and I missed her most of all. She'd been a much-needed referee for Ethan and me. We often fought, about everything—things like which TV show to watch, or whose turn it was to clean the overflowing cat litter. Ethan liked to be the boss, and I liked to ignore him, which made him furious. Kris helped solve arguments, drove us where we needed to go, started dinner when my mom was working late, and generally looked out for us since my parents worked full time.

Each time my older siblings set off on their own, my world felt smaller. I cheered when they came home and I bit my fingernails when they left again. I worried they'd be the only family I'd ever have.

Even though Ethan had dark hair and eyes, and I was blond and blue-eyed, people routinely thought we were twins. I hated looking like my brother. He was stiff and squat and waddled as he walked. Just like me. He was the very reflection I couldn't bear.

Though, we were opposites in some ways. Or at least I wanted to be. Ethan lashed out when kids teased him; I'd run and hide. Ethan was articulate, witty, intellectual; I was quiet, resigned, emotional. He was stubborn about his opinions; I was a compliant people-pleaser. He blamed the world. I blamed myself. He spoke out. I clammed up. Neither of our methods worked particularly well, but it was all that we knew.

Amazingly, sometimes Ethan seemed to forget that he was different. He'd walk through the mall as if he owned the place, oblivious to the usual stares and laughter. I sent sonar wide in every direction, trying to predetermine the problem areas and people. I'd veer away from ogling eyes and stealthily hide behind friends. If kids were hanging around outside a store, to me they were a flashing "Do Not Pass" sign, meant to be avoided at all cost. Not for Ethan. He'd roll on past them, his rounded chest thrust forward like a bowling ball, intent on his strike. Heads would turn in surprise and kids would stare and laughter would boom. He looked so small and pitiful to me. But Ethan sometimes missed the pointing and snickers. I never did. When people noticed my brother, they spotted me too. I hated him for that. Even if he didn't hear their jeers, I noticed them all.

The only way I knew to avoid pain was to shrink and hide. I thought that, for my brother, being unaware was his way to avoid the pain. Or, fighting back was. When Ethan did hear kids heckling him, he would lash out at them, just as our dad would have done—yelling and cursing, delighting the kids with his fury. Bold as he was, he would always fight back. One day I heard the front door slam and the thud of a heavy backpack thrown against the wall, telling me that my brother had had a bad day at school.

"Life sucks," Ethan said as he pushed his thick, dark-rimmed glasses firmly up on his small nose. He ran his hand across his pale forehead, forever trying to straighten his wavy brown hair. "That imbecile Miss Hayden won't give me an extension on my social studies paper. She knows I'm behind because of the surgery, but she doesn't give a crap!" Ethan had been out of school for two months after having his knee surgically straightened by Dr. Simon in Boston.

"Ethan, everyone knows Miss Hayden's an idiot."

"She hands out the grades, though, doesn't she? And she treats that jerk Bruce Randall like a god. He's an asshole—I hate his guts." Bruce Randall tormented Ethan. Sammy Gosbin was an angel in comparison.

"Bruce Randall laughs like a donkey, and he looks like a smiling toad," I said.

"Shut up, Julie! You don't know what he does!" Ethan screamed.

Any other day, I'd have launched full-scale retaliation. Something in Ethan's eyes stopped me. "What did he do?"

"He and Carl Zimmer, they cornered me . . . you know they do whatever the hell they feel like. I'm so goddamned tired of it!"

"Tell the principal . . ."

"They tried to jam my head in the toilet! Okay? But they didn't win," he yelled. "Even though they had me by my ankles, I got a leg loose and kicked Bruce right in the crotch! That made him let go! Then Carl couldn't hold on so they both ran out of bathroom. I swear they'll get theirs one day!" he said in defiance. Then he stormed off, up the stairs, and slammed his bedroom door. I felt sick for my brother. He must have been terrified. Furious. Powerless. No one had ever held me against my will. Sammy Gosbin had once thrown a stick in my wheel spokes and I'd crashed my bike into a hedge. This was so much worse. Were they really going to push his head under the water? What's wrong with people? My throat closed in. *It could happen to me.* The scene haunted me for weeks to come. I wish I had known then about the end of this story, which Ethan shared with me many years later.

A year or so after the toilet incident, Ethan was walking alone in the hallway of our high school when he saw an open locker. As he went over to shut it, he noticed Bruce Randall's name written all over the expensive sports equipment, school textbooks, and notebooks inside. Thoughts of revenge quickly grabbed hold as Ethan remembered the black spray paint in his own locker, which he used for his duties as track and field manager. Ethan had stood there, fighting hard with the uncharacteristic impulses inside him. Then he realized that in order to "get even," he would have to be like Bruce. And my brother knew that was something he would never be. Ethan closed the locker door that day, leaving the temptation, and that particular battle, behind him.

During sophomore year, I continued to work hard in school, trying madly to compensate for my shortcomings. Despite my high grades, and my parents' encouragement, my self-esteem lagged way behind.

I was headed for the cafeteria when Judy Prescott, my friend since kindergarten, saw me. She had an Olive Oyle figure even though she ate like a ravenous cheetah, and a curly frizz of blonde hair. Neither of us quite fit in. There's no way we could have known where she'd be in ten years: modeling, acting, and dating Christopher Reeve. Superman and Olive Oyle. "Jule! Wait up! Did you hear the drama group is doing *The Sound of Music?*" She knew it was one of my favorites. "Mrs. Baron asked me to ask you if you wanted to try out."

"I don't know . . ." I said. The last time I'd tried out for a play was *Bye-Bye Birdie* in sixth grade. Since my mom had been involved in local theater back then, I figured I could get a great part. After many girls had auditioned for Rosie, the lead, Mrs. Swath was ready to move on even though I kept my arm raised high.

"*You* want to try out . . . for Rosie?" she asked.

We stared at each other blankly until Mrs. Swath motioned me to the front. But as I read the lines, I shriveled inside, suddenly remembering that I was defective.

When the casting list came out, my name was at the bottom. "Julie Hobbes: Little Sad Girl." The part had no lines or songs, no voice at all—like me. After that year, as much as I wanted to be on stage, I never risked it again.

"I'd never be picked," I told Judy.

"Mrs. Baron asked for you."

Had my kind math teacher miraculously recognized some latent talent in me?

"She wants us to try out for the kids," Judy said, bursting my bubble.

Now I got it. She needs short people. "Jude, I don't want to play a kid." Judy walked beside me in silence, allowing the unspoken to sink in. She always listened closely to me, as if I might be revealing the secret of life.

Then she said, quietly, "C'mon, Jule. It'll be fun."

I did love this stuff. Maybe I had a chance at the part of the youngest daughter, Gretl.

When auditions began that week, they were utterly nerve-wracking. My voice cracked into pieces on a high note in "Do, A Deer," and I went home wondering if I could even play a kid.

The following afternoon, heart in my throat, I checked the cast list. I got the part of Gretl! Judy got the part of Brigetta, the snotty daughter. She was disappointed, but I said her audition had been great.

Several months later, it was opening night for *The Sound of Music.* Mother Superior entered stage left. It was almost time for us to go on, as Jude and I paced in the wings. Judy looked a bit like a blonde Q-tip in a sailor suit. I was feeling buck naked, worse than when I'd had to strip in front of Gloria Bennett, a member of the stage crew, for a lightning-fast costume change. Mrs. Baron had decided that each vonTrapp kid needed someone to help them change clothes and make it back on stage in time for the next scene. Gloria had been assigned to shuck me like a corn cob, ripping one costume off and throwing a different one on. Gloria had been really nice, but I'd agonized for three sleepless nights. I never willingly let anyone see me undressed, and I was even more mortified now because I needed . . . a bra. I didn't dare ask my mom. Too horribly embarrassing. She had never even had "the talk" with me. I just wanted the awful breasts to go away. Anything associated with maturity was appalling. I knew I couldn't buy a bra myself, either. What would the sales people think?

Waiting off-stage, sudden laughter from the audience left Judy and me chewing off our nails. The scene wasn't supposed to be funny. What if they laugh at me? My sailor suit still doesn't fit right, and I'm a foot shorter than Diane Dawley, playing Marta. Maybe all the fun working on the play was a lie. Maybe I'm not . . . Then Ken, playing Captain von Trapp, blew the whistle, calling the seven kids on stage. We dashed out into the light and stood in our military lineup like popsicles, frozen in terror. I, who hated being inspected by a crowd, was now in front of a packed auditorium. My arms were electrified at my side, my heart crashing against the curtains. The thing that saved me was knowing my family was out there somewhere. They'd be watching with pride and delight.

My breathing came down out of the rafters. I recited my lines and belted out my songs. I was Gretl and, for the first time in my life, I was the correct height for the age. This was an easier role than the one I'd been cast in at birth. Acting young, in order to avoid questions about my stature, had become second nature. Acting happy was the other role I nearly had down pat.

At the final curtain call, my family cheered exuberantly as I took my bow. I felt like a star. The next day, our local newspaper, the *Daily Record*, gave the play a rave review. It even singled me out: "Julie Hobbes, as Gretl, turned in a charming and credible performance." I read it over and over. I had to ask my mom what credible meant, but *charming*—I understood that one.

On Monday, as I got ready for school, I imagined a whole new world. Every bone whispered how things would be different now. Every tendon was reaching for more. Maybe one of the boys I liked would notice the new light in me. I'd bravely sung and danced on stage in front of everyone, hadn't I? Someone thought I was *charming*. I walked with a new perfume of confidence that day. As Judy and I laughed at lunch, I imagined a boy nearby secretly wishing he could have me, a star, for his own. A few girls told us that they loved the play. None of the guys said a word.

Later that spring, we took *The Sound of Music* to Pennsylvania for the Bucks County Playhouse Competition. We won Best Musical Production of 1979 and jumped and hugged in a disbelieving flurry. I looked out over the crowds. For a brief moment while on the stage, I was the star I dreamed about. This audience had seen me win.

Outwardly, my life moved along more smoothly in high school. The Boston doctors had given me a permanent excuse from Phys. Ed. so I no longer had to struggle to keep up with my peers, in that area at least. My friends were solid and silly, tried and true—Judy, Tracy, Simone, Lisa, Renee, Cindy, Lauren, and Claudia. When I saw myself through their eyes, I was free. Megan had gone off to a second private school after she'd been expelled from the first for drinking. Occasionally, when she was home on break, we'd exchange smiles. I swore I could still see our friendship waiting there, sparkling and alive. But after a few words, we'd walk on past and I would put away my missing her.

Although Ethan and I could still be sarcastic and rude to each other, we were getting along better and better. Maybe it was the fact that life had gotten busier in high school and we had less time to fuss at each other. Or maybe we were just growing up. Whatever the reason, we liked hanging out and occasionally we'd get both of our groups of friends together. Although Ethan and I didn't speak about it openly, I could tell that he had his eye on some of my friends, and I had crushes on a few of his. But nothing ever came of either of our fantasies.

My other classmates had outgrown overt teasing, though I was certain it went on behind my back. Strangers still laughed and stared. They called out in parking lots, "Hey midget!" Or stopped me in stores and asked my age, or stared and giggled with their friends. I constantly expected it, although the ridicule from others was no longer necessary to stoke the fire of a shame that I now kept lit all by myself.

In the fall of 1980, my mom drove Ethan to Middlebury College, my parents' and my brother Ray's alma mater, for his freshman year. Later that weekend, when she was expected back home, my mother called to say she would be getting home very late. Hearing the strain in her voice, I asked what had happened. Apparently, Ethan's fears about college had suddenly broken into the open. My chest tightened and my eyes welled up, trying to imagine my small brother under the weight and worry of his new life.

Looking ahead towards college, I felt it too. We'd spent our lives in one small town where people were familiar with us. Would a school full of strangers accept our oddities? Were we capable of making it on our own? But my older siblings had all gone to good universities; we were going to follow suit.

I'd visited Kris at Swarthmore College many times, but living on campus, as she did, sounded so mature. So not me. My guidance counselor encouraged me to apply to Ivy League schools, but I was sure they wouldn't want a defect. I ended up applying to seven good colleges and, to my surprise, was accepted by them all. I decided on Hamilton College.

With the scary change looming ahead, I was feeling wildly unprepared and embarrassingly dependent. As the summer flew by, desperation set in. I needed to talk to someone about my fears, but I had no idea how to admit my insecurities. *Will my* roommates accept me? Will the other students laugh, or dismiss me as someone's little sister? How does college work? How do I write a check? The fearful questions reduced me to a small child in a very big panic. I decided to blame my parents. They're too busy, they don't want to help me, my problems are too overwhelming for them. My deepening fears turned into resentment. Resentment turned into hate. Hate felt like power. If Mom and Dad won't talk to me, I won't talk to them. Ever. So I gave them the meanest cold shoulder I could muster. My eyes rolled whenever they spoke and I'd respond with as few words as possible. I armed myself with enough anger to sever my ties to them and pry myself away from the safety of home.

As it turned out, the transition to Hamilton was far easier than I had ever dreamed. My parents later told me how surprised they were when I waved good-bye to them without tears or the overwhelming concern that had hit Ethan. The campus was friendly and beautiful, and no one pointed out my non-conformities. Maybe college students really were more mature than high school students. My roommates and hallmates became good friends, and the social side of college was worth the endless studying — sort of. I was overwhelmed by the sheer quantity of reading, writing, and homework. I think it was more than I had seen in four years of high school combined.

By the end of my first semester, my parents felt to me like a long-lost treasure. The anger was forgotten. I couldn't wait to spend Christmas at home and sink back into the world where my still-floundering self-esteem felt propped. This holiday get-together, however, was going to change all that. It began with the news that my oldest sister couldn't make it home because of her new boyfriend. The real reason, I later discovered, was that she, Ray, and Dan were steaming mad at my parents. Like three volcanoes, dormant for years, one of them was bound to erupt.

One clue to the upcoming explosion was when I overheard an argument between Dan and Ray. Something about who got more recognition from our parents. Who helped out around the house. Who did more chores. I couldn't understand why my smart, handsome brothers were so angry. I'd idolized them my whole life and here they were complaining like children. Our family rarely discussed problems so I'd never heard anything like this. I thought Ethan and I were the only outcasts — two stunted branches on an otherwise lovely family tree. It had never occurred to me that my other "normal" siblings had their own brand of self doubt.

On Christmas morning, we sat together at the top of the stairs like little kids again. The smell of turkey warmed our memories as we waited for our parents to join in. By three o'clock that afternoon, we were still lounging in our pajamas, just finishing up with gifts. We played cards, tried on new clothes, assembled gadgets, and helped with dinner. In the midst of our celebration, Judy Prescott, who was home on break from Connecticut College, called to wish us a Merry Christmas. I never would have invited her over, though, if I had known what would happen.

Judy and I sat happily in my room sharing tales of our lives away from home. I wondered if my inner transformation was as impressive as her outer one. Her formerly frizzy hair was now in long, blond ringlets. Contacts had replaced her owl glasses, revealing her soft blue eyes. She had landed some modeling jobs and Hollywood would soon be calling. Judy said she liked my new bangs, but I was glad that she didn't mention the make-up. I felt like a girl playing with mother's things. Attempts at self-improvement felt risky; someone might see past them, recognize my insecurity, and realize that I wasn't well-adjusted at all.

For everything I told Judy, I withheld something else. My roommates were great friends, I said, not admitting how terrified I'd been to meet them. I regularly went to fraternity parties, I told her, and danced into the night. But I didn't admit to all the romances that went on in my mind, or how the campus, swarming with bright, young men, held a gazillion secret prospects. How the long list of possibilities kept me in a mad cycle of raised hopes and dashed dreams. The boys were always leering at the pretty girl behind me or the friend next to me. Their eyes told me everything I didn't want to know. My heart had been broken a thousand times, and I'd never even gone on a date. I worried that Judy also believed that I had no chance for a normal life. Maybe no one wanted to divulge the awful truth that I wasn't good enough. If I shared my longings, she might pity my ignorance and steer clear of me. Silence on the subject was preferable to losing her or anyone else.

Over the music on the radio, Judy and I suddenly heard something echoing up the stairway, pushing aside our delight. When I opened my door to listen, I stood in disbelief. Ray and my father were yelling at each other. No one ever argued with our dad, ever. Ray, nine years older than I, wasn't a fighter. I considered him a thoughtful poet with a quiet sense of humor. Had my brother lost his senses? The yelling was becoming more frantic as one tried to drown out the other. As I closed my door, every pore shrank in terror.

Judy and I sat huddled in a panic, staring at each other, speechless. Would she ever come back after this? "I'd better get going, Jule," she whispered.

"Are you nuts?" I pointed towards the only way out, which was down the stairs and into the fray. "You can't walk through that!"

We waited and listened as Ray and my father taunted and threatened each other, banging furious fists on the hall table. I gritted my teeth tight, praying that no one would get hurt. Suddenly my mother's cries pierced the air as she begged them to stop. Then a door slammed. First one set of footsteps dashed up the stairs and then another. Another door slammed. All at once, it was quiet. Judy and I sat motionless. Was it over? Were we safe? I cracked the bedroom door and heard my mother sobbing in her room. *Oh my God.* The hallway looked clear, so Judy and I crept downstairs. The front entrance was empty. Judy sprinted out the door. I started back upstairs to find my mother, but then saw Ray marching out the door with two suitcases in his hands. "Sorry, Jule" he said, and was gone.

I ran to my mom. I felt desperate to offer comfort, but as she cried and cried, I found myself clinging to her like a baby koala instead. I'd never seen her this way, such volumes of grief. "They blame us for everything!" she wailed. "Now Ray's gone, in the middle of Christmas!" The air began to collapse in on us as my thoughts broke in every direction. *Why did Ray leave? Would he ever come back? Would Dad ever be happy again? Would Mom?*

Later that evening, for the first time in our history, we attempted to honestly address our feelings. And my dad's temper. Our parents, wounded and shaken, seemed as unsure as we were about sifting through the emotional rubble. The fear in the room made us distant. Closeness might unleash all the emotions we had long suppressed. The possibility of losing control at this late date stiffened our spines, so we sat like mannequins, trying with all our might to hide our humanness. On any other day, my dad's anger would've been a signal to head for the hills. But the rules were changing and our former safety training was now being called into question.

"So who else here agrees with Ray that all your difficulties in life are our fault?" my dad demanded.

My throat closed. It was inconceivable to confront him with what I'd been feeling, especially as I watched him wringing himself into a bitter fury. We felt an ardent loyalty to my parents. Was the hidden pain worth sacrificing family unity?

Finally, Dan, now twenty-six, answered my dad. "You've both always been supportive and loving when things were good but, when times were hard, we were afraid to approach Dad, and Mom seemed interested in quick resolutions." My father stared at the worn-down rug, body clenched, containing his roar.

"I don't understand," my mom said quietly. "I'm sorry that you feel this way. We certainly have our faults, but we've done our best. I've always let things roll off my shoulders. I assumed you were doing the same. I had no idea . . ." My mother's shock was astonishing to me. Maybe she hadn't known that we wanted to make her happy by pretending to be doing well. But didn't she know how terrified we were of my dad? She had always seemed just as scared to cross him.

Kris quietly agreed with Dan, but sympathized with my parents. "I don't understand why Ray had to leave. I'm so sorry about all of this." It was all she dared to say. We had never criticized our dad at any time. Ethan began speaking, but I couldn't hear any of it over my own terror. I was overwhelmed by dread. Ethan stopped talking when he saw my mom's tears. I was the only one who hadn't spoken. My body trembled at the thought. Would I lose their love? Would Dad ever forgive me? But I couldn't let the opportunity pass by. Finally, I opened my mouth with a vague attempt. "After so many years of being afraid to say anything when we're upset," I said, voice quaking, "we've naturally built up some resentments." It was the most I could eke out. Wild waves of adrenaline coursed through me, drowning out my voice. I sat shaking, sweating, and wondering if my words had just cut a vital lifeline.

After another few minutes in a painful hush, my dad brought our meeting to a sudden halt. "Your silence speaks volumes," he said and stormed out. No one saw my father for the rest of that evening; he remained distant for days.

Seeing our parents suffering twisted our hearts in guilt. We knew they loved us above all else. My dad was an incredibly hard worker and felt tremendous pressure trying to provide for the family he loved. My mom wanted us to be happy and for life to be nice. She wanted to erase problems with a hug and a smile, and often we kids honored both our parents by pretending to be okay. We thought it would keep them proud and spare them further pain. Yet all the hurt and negative feelings didn't go away. They had been crowding underground in protest, and were now coming out in the open.

The foundation of my family, my rock, suddenly felt shaky and vulnerable. Without it intact, profound insecurity began pulling me under. Were we happy? Were we close? Maybe I'd been paddling in a riptide of denial, too scared to question the gospel that I thought kept me afloat.

I'd embraced the "big happy family" ideal, unable to admit my family's shadows. Or my own. Ray and my dad's blow-up abruptly tore away that illusion. Little did I know that with this change would come new growth.

The first few days back at Hamilton, my world felt broken and lost. I couldn't think straight. I couldn't study. I couldn't make sense of what was happening. Until that first phone call from Celia. She knew I'd be floundering. She began to carefully and respectfully break through the old silence, the pain, and the separation. She touched upon my differences. My isolation. Her openness was almost too much to bear. Could I tell her how I really felt? In my desperation, for the first time, I gingerly pulled out the words, admitted the shameful feelings. And even though I hurt, I realized she wanted to share the weight.

Classes at Hamilton slowly relieved some of the confusion as well. When I was busy drawing, in class with Professor Bruce Muirhead, I lost track of time and was able to step out of my worries. The eye-opening discussions in my sociology class, with Professor Ken Wagner, allowed me to better understand the dynamics in my own family. Help was available in every direction.

Dan and Ray began to call and write, sharing their feelings and insights. I was dumbstruck by their comfort and love. Listening to them, I realized my brothers and sisters had their own secret fears and censored feelings. My family wasn't perfect and it was okay. This realization was actually quite freeing. I had never really been alone after all. Ethan's and my differences were not the only issues that had been blanketed. My world opened up when I realized that it wasn't all about me.

Five
Selling Myself Short

Come to the edge, he said.
They said: we are afraid.
Come to the edge, he said.
They came.
He pushed them . . .
and they flew.
~Guillaume Apollinaire

"That was incredibly boring," Josh said as we headed out of class.

"You can say that again. I thought we'd be learning about everyday psychology, not psychosis and catatonia. I wanted to learn about . . . myself," I said.

"Me too," he agreed, to my relief. I didn't want him thinking I needed therapy or anything. "Do you want to study together tonight?"

"Sure." I hoped I didn't look too eager.

"How about in the Johnson Building? We can get a room to ourselves." His suggestive look stopped my heart. I tried to act unfazed.

"Great," I said calmly as he set off for his next class.

I floated to my philosophy class, where dreams of Josh melted all over my books. I went over and over the time we spent together, searching for clues to convince myself that this guy might want—*please God in heaven*—me. At dinner, my plate stared blankly up at me, insisting that I was all wrong and Josh only wanted to be friends. Even so, I headed back to my room to check my hair and make-up a hundred times. I paced around my dorm room, waiting for Josh. Hadn't I seen something in his eyes when we met?

It was September 1982. The first day of my sophomore year was vivid all because of Josh. My parents and I had made a morning car trip from New Jersey to Hamilton College, and on the way I had been bargaining silently with God. Had it worked? I believed in Him . . . except when I didn't. Was I one of His mistakes? Or His punishment? My parents didn't talk much about God or religion, but they lived as if there was something greater. A universe that was wise and purposeful. Perhaps even just, although it didn't seem that way to me. I wanted to believe, though. I wanted to see evidence that Someone was in the driver's seat and that we weren't on a highway to nowhere. That I wasn't an accident. Or one waiting to happen.

God, if You're out there and really care, You know what I want. I've been asking and waiting for such a long time. When will I find a love of my own? Is it even possible? Please, let me find him this year. Please. You were the one who stuck me in this wreck of a body that nobody wants. I'll never find my dreams, unless You intervene. Please . . . please, God. I asked, Or is this all up to me?

As the car climbed the long hill towards campus, the excitement of seeing friends temporarily quelled the sadness. We parked next to my new dorm and started to unpack. I watched out for my roommates, Jamie and Meg. When I heard someone coming down the front stairs, I glanced up and was met by a pair of big blue eyes and a splendid smile. We exchanged "hi's" as I went back to unloading my bags. My heart did delirious cartwheels. *Who was that guy? Was I too obvious? Did I smile too big?*

My parents treated my roommates and me to lunch, then bid us a sweet good-bye. We got busy settling into our two connecting rooms, more space than usual, in a dorm smack in the middle of campus. Most sophomores landed in Bundy, down the steep, unsympathetic-to-arthritis hill. The previous spring I'd pleaded my case to the dean of housing: my knees dislocated easily, so I couldn't navigate a hill every day. The dean took me out of the housing lottery that might have sent me to Bundyville, and I was given my choice of two other rooms.

Standing in the cafeteria line that night, I saw him again, those big blue eyes looking straight at me. What a smile. We said hello, as I continued on in a private state of alarm. For the rest of the meal, I tried to analyze his expression, his smile, his hello. Was he watching as I talked to my friends? Was he just being friendly? I stepped outside my room that night and there he was, walking downstairs.

"We better stop meeting like this," he said.

"Or you have to stop following me. Do you live upstairs?"

"Yeah, me, Bob, and Kevin . . . um, I forget their last names."

Ah, he must be a freshman if he doesn't know his roommates' names. Good news. No pretty little coed has had a chance to snap him up. Yet. "I'm Julie. This is my room."

"I'm Josh Hathaway. I guess I live in the room right above you."

"Then I'll definitely see you around."

"I guess so." He flashed that smile full of butterflies, and I ducked back into my room to exhale.

I had to amass definitive proof that he was interested before I'd risk showing my own interest. Neediness, I thought, would drive anyone away. It was better if everyone believed that I was happy with myself, well-adjusted, and didn't need someone else.

It turned out that Josh and I were in the same psychology class. An omen. When he walked into that first class, my heart lifted as I waved hello. As we continued to see each other in the dorm, or walking to class, my infatuation grew bigger than the quad. He was always on my mind, thoughts of him interrupting my studies, filling my dreams. I was delighted to discover that he was an artist like me. Another omen. My excitement and terror mounted; I worried that I was setting myself up for a brutal fall.

I paced the room, waiting for Josh. I was going to be studying with him in the Johnson Building, alone. Finally, there was a knock at the door. I'd never been picked up for a date before; this felt close enough. "Come on in." I took one last nervous look in the mirror.

"All set?"

"Sure, let's hit the books."

In the Johnson building we found an empty room and spread out our books.

"You're not nervous about this mid-term, are you?" I asked. We were both doing well in class, but he looked as distracted as I was.

"No, it's a matter of memorization and that doesn't take brains, only time. We've got time, right, Julie?"

"Right." I stared nervously at the page in front of me.

Josh was leaning towards me. Before I could find out why, the door flew open. "Sorry! I thought the room was empty. Hi, Josh! Hi, Julie!" It was our peppy dorm-mate. I wanted to slap her pretty face and send her packing.

"Hey, Cyndi," Josh and I said in unison.

"Are you studying for the psych mid-term?" she asked.

"Yeah," Josh said. He looked at me apologetically and asked her if she wanted to join us. Her perfume already had.

"Fabulous." She rushed in with her books pressed against her ample chest. "I don't know how I'm going to pass this exam, it's so confusing!"

Cyndi sat down next to Josh, nearly in his lap, and gave him a wink as she shuffled through her purse. She managed to hold Josh's attention with constant questions. After an hour, I was thrilled to see her go, but the mood had been killed. What was the point in trying to compete with her? Josh was good-looking, funny, and kind. He'd be snapped up by someone who offered the same. We walked back to the dorm after midnight.

"You're so quiet," he said.

"I'm really tired," I lied. Music was blaring from the third floor of our dorm, and a guy hung out of a window, singing.

"It's Cos," Josh said. Craig Costello's antics were famous around our dorm.

"What have you two been up to, hmmm? You better watch out, Julie!" Cos called.

"Shut up," Josh said. "He's drunk."

We walked inside and Josh dropped me at my door. "See you tomorrow," Josh said and ran upstairs. I went into my room, ready to spend another obsessed night reviewing the evening's events.

The next afternoon I sat with my best friend, Trish, in the library. She didn't hesitate to grill me about the time I was spending with Josh. "I think he likes you, Jule."

My stomach did a back flip. I'd never talked about guys with anyone before. Even Trish. "That's ridiculous," I said, busying myself by leafing through notebooks.

"Why?"

"Because."

"Because why?"

"I don't think . . ." I wondered if I could say it and risk her finding out how pathetic I was. "I don't think that—that he'd be interested."

"Why the hell not?"

"I'm just so . . . so different." God, I said it.

"So?"

"Boys want the Cyndi Pipers of the world, not someone . . . like me."

"You've got to be kidding me. She can't hold a candle to you. You're beautiful and good."

I dismissed her instantly. Who was she kidding?

"You seem so confident and happy, I never thought you doubted yourself the way that I do," she continued.

"Surprise."

"Here I've been moaning about a hundred different guys, and getting great advice from you, and all along you've been . . . why didn't you tell me?"

"Too embarrassed," I said quietly.

"I tell you my every insecurity."

"I wish I had your honesty and courage. But you've got a normal . . ." I wanted to say body, but it sounded so childish. "You can have any guy you want."

"Right, that's why they're beating down my door."

"Carlton adored you, but you blew him off. Eddie followed you around, but you didn't like that he couldn't dance, and . . ."

"Okay, I know what you're saying. But you're doing the same with Josh. You act like he's just a friend. I've never seen you so much as bat an eye in his direction."

"I can't. He's too cute and smart . . ."

"So are you! I can't believe you're putting yourself down like this. You've never judged me that way."

I wanted to hug her; instead, I picked at my nail. Trish took on my love life, or lack thereof, as her personal mission. I'd never had a champion before. It felt great. She started making plans the next day. "We're throwing a St. Patrick's Day get-together, inviting Josh and Danny, of course." Danny was her newest heartthrob. "Isn't it a perfect idea?" She reeled off the names of everyone she'd invited and handed me the list. "Who else do you want to invite? How about that cutie David from sociology class? I bet he's got the hots for you, Jule."

"Come on," I mumbled. Trish was the biggest ego booster I'd ever had, but I'd no intention of changing my approach with Josh or anyone else.

That Sunday, Josh was the first through the door for our party. My toes did a pink pirouette. The sight of him, as always, made me giddy.

"Hey, Julie," he said.

"Happy Saint Paddy's," I answered.

"Erin go bra-less!" Trish called, dumping chips into a bowl.

A Jackson Five favorite started and my friend Tim Houlihan grabbed me to dance. We were quite a pair, Tim, the Jolly Green Giant at 6'2", and I, the Little Green Sprout. Almost every weekend we danced together at frat parties. My legs would be nearly crippled by the end of the night, but it was worth it.

Tim swung me around like a small yo-yo, as I saw Trish pull Danny to his feet. Was Josh watching? I didn't dare look. Tim and I retreated for a drink. I avoided the beer, always afraid I'd turn foolish, and got some water. I searched the room for Josh and found him looking straight at me. Plastering a smile on my sweaty face, I walked over to him.

"You're something else." He held up his beer.

"I've always loved to dance."

"Why haven't we danced?"

"I'm game."

"Then you owe me one next weekend. Deal?" he asked.

"Deal," I said nervously.

Crazy Cos was headed towards us, and I seized on the distraction. "You and Trish are the best dancers around," I said.

"You like? I know the hula too. Want to see?" Cos asked.

"I can accompany you." I began singing one of the Hawaiian jingles my dad had taught me and added exaggerated hula hip and hand motions. Josh and Craig laughed. How simple it was to appear at ease, as long as my feelings were tucked away.

"Josh, your orbs are glowing, man. I think it's love," Cos said.

Josh batted his long lashes at me. "Is it love?"

I panicked. "No, it's the sunlight." *God what's wrong with me? Do I have to ruin everything? I'm such a fool!*

Trish and I swapped stories as we cleaned up the mess from the party.

"So, doll face, did you talk much with Josh?"

"A little. Nothing interesting."

She wasn't buying it. "I saw him staring at you and Tim dancing."

"Save your breath. It's not going to work."

"What do you mean?"

Silently, I crumpled up the paper tablecloth.

"What's wrong with you?" she asked.

"That's what I've been asking myself my whole life."

"Jule, you know that's not what I meant. If only you could see yourself as I see you, as everyone sees you."

"I'm not going to risk my friendship with Josh. Anyway, I'm sure that's how he sees me, as a friend." As I picked at an infected hangnail, white puss suddenly was freed.

"I say he's hot for your bod," Trish insisted.

"Right. That'll be the day."

"You're so pretty. Those big blue eyes, your long blond hair, big boobs."

"Oh, God. I especially hate them."

"What? My two don't even make up one of yours."

"Thank your lucky bras."

"You're nuts. Guys love big boobs. It's a known fact."

"They look stupid on my small body. They make me look fat."

"Then stop wearing big sweaters, and start showing off your figure."

"Are you on drugs or something? I'm a stupid, freaking, trash-compacted Kewpie doll!" I'd never said anything like that before. It didn't stop Trish for a second.

"I don't know who sold you this bullshit bill of goods, but I'm telling you that you're beautiful inside and out. I know for a fact that Hamilton doesn't admit Kewpie dolls so drop that excuse right now. You, stupid? Your grades make you a liar on that count. Hell, you're the reason I passed my biology lab. I didn't want to touch a single insect that I was supposed to catch in that swampy glen. You came and nabbed every one without flinching, then stayed up late helping me classify them."

"I meant I'm stupid when it comes to life."

"Remember Reggie? How long did I sob on your shoulder? You made me feel good about myself, even when he treated me like crap."

"Did Danny have fun?" I wanted the spotlight off me.

"He did. Isn't he adorable? He told me he liked my haircut." She ran her hand through her pretty auburn hair. "He's Irish. I think it's an omen."

Sitting in my dorm room a few weeks later, I showed Trish a brochure for the Lacoste School of Art in France. "What do you think, should I do it?"

"It sounds exciting. But I'm selfish, I don't want you to go," she said.

"It's only for a semester. I've never lived anywhere but New Jersey until I came here."

"What about your knee? Is it all right now?" I had dislocated my knee the previous month and had spent two weeks on crutches. It had made it hard to get to my classes.

"It's okay now. That was actually the first time I'd dislocated either knee since I came to Hamilton." I didn't mention, though, that my hips were feeling tighter and ached if I hurried to class or danced on the weekends.

"If you want to know what I really think," Trish said, "I think you should go. Since Nancy has already applied, you'll have company." Nancy Vesley was a good friend and fellow art student. Knowing we could travel together was making my decision easier. I was headed for the south of France. "All my classes will be in art! What a life! Look at these gorgeous pictures of Lacoste."

"It looks amazing," Trish said with a half smile. "But what'll I do without you?"

"You'll manage. Don't go getting married or anything."

"You ask too much. Hey, what about Josh?"

"You're relentless, Patricia Catherine. Anyway, there's nothing there." Ever since our party, I'd been running from him.

"Give it one last shot, Jule. I hate to tell you this, but according to my very reliable sources, Kathleen Bailey has a crush on Josh."

My mood immediately collapsed. Kathleen was everyone's dream girl: natural beauty, nice body, friendly, unpretentious. From the moment I met her, she'd reminded me of Megan McWilliams, my childhood friend. I'd never measure up. I liked Kathleen, but now I was jealous beyond belief.

"Tell me you're kidding."

"No."

"I've got English Lit," I said, wanting to escape. "See you for dinner."

That night I sat at my desk trying to finish a philosophy paper. My poor feet, squeezed into a pair of heels, were successfully distracting me. A friend had invited me to a semiformal dance the following weekend, and I was hoping to stretch the shoes and break their leather spirits by then. I'd only worn them once, at my oldest sister Celia's wedding, and after that evening of dancing, I was sure I'd inflicted permanent nerve damage to my feet. The pain had been worth it, though, for the first wedding in our family.

It had been over a year since the big family fight. My parents had quickly and gracefully recovered from the blow, which had led to other important breakthroughs. I'd grown closer to my brothers and sisters, especially Celia and Dan. They had accepted, even welcomed, my long-guarded insecurities. Our heartfelt letters and phone calls allowed the darkness to begin to lift. Once again, on the heels of a breakdown, hope had come calling.

For Celia's wedding, we'd crammed ourselves like sardines into her small apartment in Chicago, making plans, sharing food and a few precious days. We sang and laughed and told the old family stories and I belonged. I had a home. I had a love that encircled me, accepted me. At the reception, we danced, sang, and laughed, and I'd cheered for Celia and smiled for hours. But it would end too soon. We'd go our separate ways; we'd never be the family we once were. At the reception, I had slipped away to the bathroom to hide my tears. That would become my ritual in the years ahead as each of my siblings found a love and a home of their own, something I was sure would always elude me.

A knock at the door snapped me back to my room.

"It's open," I yelled. In walked a thousand dreams.

"How's the paper going?" Josh asked.

"It stinks, but I'm getting there. What are you up to?"

"Just got back from brunch with Steig and his parents. They're visiting this weekend, so I got a free meal." His friend Tom Steigler was dating Kathleen Bailey's roommate. My heart fell as I made the connection.

"I brought you a donut." He pulled it out from behind his back. "Sorry, the chocolate's smeared. I smuggled it out in a napkin."

"That's so nice. I love donuts."

"I know."

"Want some?" I offered, trying to ignore what his sweet gesture might mean.

"No, thanks. We went to that all-you-can-eat buffet near Colgate. I'm stuffed." He lifted his shirt to pat his stomach. The sight of his abdomen shot desire into high gear, then fear slammed on the brakes. All the years of humiliation and taunting, the stares and laughter. Sammy Gosbin. Frank Hubbers. Boys who had always mocked me.

I got up to grab a napkin and realized that I had on the pink satin pumps with jeans and a t-shirt. I clomped across the room.

"What's with the high heels?" he asked.

"I'm trying to stretch them out for a dance this weekend. Sheer agony, but they're the only pair I have."

"They're sexy."

"Try wearing 'em, believe me, you'd change your mind." My heart blasted off the Richter scale. No one had ever used the word "sexy" in reference to anything remotely associated with me. Grabbing a tissue from my desk, I sat clumsily on the bed. Josh walked over and sat down next to me. I pretended to be busy cleaning the chocolate off my fingers. He was still looking at the shoes.

"They really do hurt. I may be forced to wear ratty sneakers with my dress." I kicked the shoes off in disgust.

"Here. You need a good foot rub." He grabbed my calves and swung them up on his lap.

"No, no! It's not that bad." I was sure he'd be repulsed by my stiff and crooked legs.

"Relax." He held my legs tight. "Sit back and enjoy." He might as well have asked me to levitate. I stared at the solid hands holding my feet, squeezing and touching, stroking back and forth. I could barely keep my breathing in the same room. Excitement and terror vied for control. Any minute, he'd see my true feelings, my obsession. Then he'd pity me, or avoid me, or laugh. I couldn't stand it.

"I know someone who has a crush on you," I blurted out.

He stopped the rubbing and stared at me. "What?" A mix of surprise and nervousness swam in his eyes. "Who?"

"I'm sworn to secrecy."

"Tell me who."

"I won't." Boy, I'd really done it now.

"Tell me." He pushed me down on the bed, his face inches from mine. His breath was warm and his body strong.

"Kathleen Bailey!"

He released my shoulders and moved back in disbelief. "Where did you hear that?"

"Trish is friends with her roommate."

"Are you joking?" He stood and paced in front of me.

"No." I stared at Josh. My sorrow was beyond description. I couldn't think of a thing to say.

"I'd better get to my studying. See you later." He avoided my eyes and opened the door.

"Okay, see you. Thanks again for the donut."

As the door closed behind him, I stared at the wall. *What the hell did I just do?* Falling back on the bed, I felt like the biggest moron ever.

~~~

Finals were over. My room was stripped, everything packed in a trunk and old boxes. The campus was quiet and the dorm nearly empty. Josh had left for home. My parents were due any time. The mood was somber until Trish burst in the open door. "Hey doll face! Guess who I was talking to this morning after my bio exam?"

"The pope." I wasn't in the mood for twenty questions.

"No, that was after my geology exam. Guess again."

"The president."

"All right, forget it. I talked to Cos."

"This is big news?"

"It gets better. Cos said that Josh said he does have a crush on you!"

I stared at her, digesting this oddly distressing news. "Are you sure?"

"Why would Cos lie? Josh told him ages ago when they were out drinking."

"Life rots."

"I thought it'd make you happy."

It did! And it didn't. "I'm headed for France and Kathleen Bailey will be headed right for Josh."

"He can date her until you get back."

"After he's been with her, he won't want . . . me."

"Shut up, you pessimist. You're going to Lacoste, France! Leave this nonsense behind, okay?"

I wished that I could. But I knew Josh would be traveling with me, stuffed in my back pocket. The passport to a life I wanted most.

We rumbled up the steep cobblestone road into Lacoste, as wrought-iron lamps and stone archways welcomed us back through time. The town, a tiny medieval village built on the side of a mountain, lay just below the school, which lay just below the sinister ruins of the Marquis de Sade's chateau. Cresting near the top, we arrived at the school, where the sweeping vista took our breath away. Spread out before us was a French masterpiece: a vast quilt of farmland draped at the feet of lavender mountains. I could barely believe this vision — my daily inspiration for the next four months. Its peace was as tangible as the cobblestones beneath our feet.

In the following weeks, we were immersed in every form of art, as well as the rich culture around us. We sketched inside museums, in oak groves, on rooftops, and at restaurants. We visited the stomping grounds of the many Impressionists who had dipped their brushes in the stunning light of Provence. Doing our "work" — what I loved — lifted an academic weight straight off my shoulders. This colorful new palate was a revelation to my senses. I could feel, touch, and taste the deepest blues, the finest yellows, the hungry reds, the rich purples. Suddenly, art was no longer just a side dish for me. In Lacoste, I discovered it was the main feast.

Other whispers of change stirred inside my cocoon. In this distant French refuge, even my perplexing little body became more bearable. Although my body hadn't been the kindest of dwellings, I began to see that I hadn't been the gentlest of keepers either. I'd rarely appreciated my basic physical self, which functioned admirably well. Instead, I'd usually focused on the troubled parts. Flinging myself out into this new world, beyond my safe perimeters, had paradoxically sent me further inside. Even my struggles, I started to tell myself, might someday serve me. It was a good thing that I had no idea how long that would take.

Judy Prescott, who was studying in England, came to Lacoste one weekend while traveling on break. We hiked our way up a tiny dirt path to see the notorious Marquis de Sade's crumbling chateau. As we arrived on top of the peaceful mountain, the amazing panorama swept in unending circles around us. We stood in motionless awe until the wind picked up and pulled us towards the chateau. We walked through the old ruins feeling somehow like intruders. When the wind suddenly groaned and hummed through an old archway, I was touched by the strangest sensation. It teased my ears with a flash of golden hope. What once was a place of torture now lay open to the heavens, as quiet as a prayer, forever pardoned. Nature had reclaimed her own ground and turned something ugly into something beautiful.

I was swept up in my new world of art for four monumental months and then it was time to say good-bye. After a long five-hour trip to Paris, then a seven-hour flight home to New Jersey, I labored through Newark Airport customs. At last, I spotted my parents at the gate, alive with anticipation. Their happy heads were bobbing back and forth, keeping their eyes on me as the crowd blocked their view. You'd have thought they were trying to catch a glimpse of Doris Day. At that moment, I saw myself in their mirror. I was a starlet, a diamond, even when I usually felt like an ugly stone.

Celia, Ray, and Dan came home that Christmas. It had been two years since Ray had made his angry exodus from the house, which had been followed by a letter-writing campaign from my three siblings, expressing their hurts and resentments. My parents, in the end, kept the doors open. That year, my dad gave the boys what before had been reserved for the girls: a hug. The manly handshake became a thing of the past.

After my semester in France, I couldn't wait to introduce my new self to Hamilton. I felt different. Happier. Trish had said suspiciously little in her postcards to me, except that she had a new crush named Michael. I hadn't heard from Josh. Maybe he'll like the new me, really like me, I told myself. *Even though no one else has.* As the thought quivered inside me, my confidence sank and reminded me of where I really belonged.

It came in the package of that one very odd boy, Ernie Blane. He'd moved to Lakeside in sixth grade, the same year that my friendship with Megan McWilliams had come undone.

Ernie had an abundance of brown hair with a mind of its own. Either he didn't brush it, or he was born with permanent bed-head. His large glasses distorted wide eyes, and his little nose barely had the heft for his bulky black frames. He moved around like a wind-up toy, spoke like one of the Chipmunks, and never worried a day about fitting in. Ernie seemed strangely happy and good-hearted, and he was a whiz at school work. He didn't have a clue, though, about regular sixth-grade things. He didn't know not to screech like a girl when the dodge ball hit him. Or not to burst out in hysterical laughter at a teacher's joke. Even though we weren't friends, I just hated that he was such an easy mark. No matter how often Frank Hubbers and his friends tricked him, Ernie always got sucked back in. Then one day I'd had it.

"Hey, Ern!" Frank called. "Come sit with us, buddy!"

"Oh, hi!" Ernie squeaked, teetering towards them.

"Have a seat, my man," Mitch Howard said. "Any more of those cookies your mommy makes?"

"Want some?" Ernie asked with a smile.

"Of course, we want some, Ern," Frank laughed, as he reached for Ernie's glasses and tried them on.

"Oh, I need those," Ernie giggled nervously.

The glasses were passed down the table, with each boy doing an Ernie impersonation.

"May I have my glasses back, please?" Ernie looked like a baby bird out of its nest.

My friends and I sat helplessly at our table. No one particularly liked Ernie, but this was getting bad.

"Give those back to him," I barked, startling even myself.

The boys turned their heads, pleasantly surprised to find that it was me. Ernie looked blindly in my direction, his head swaying like Stevie Wonder.

"You wanna come get 'em, Hobbles?" Frank asked.

"He's not hurting you, give them back," I said.

"Ooh, someone has the hots for you, Ern."

"I'm getting Mrs. Coals." I stood up to find the lunch monitor.

"Cool your jets, little tattletale." Frank jammed the glasses onto Ernie's face and patted him on the head. "There you go, lover boy. Go get your girlfriend."

Ernie looked over at me and flashed his goofy smile. Now I'd really done it.

Ernie started talking to me more. Looking at me more. I avoided him as much as possible, but it was a small school. Frank made kissing noises when he passed me in the hall. Mitch liked to chant, "Ernest and Julie sittin' in a tree..." One day, Ernie threw a note at me during Math. He wrote, "I have six words I want to ask you!!!!! Meet me after school in the back!!!!! Love Ernie." Oh. My. God. I counted on my fingers. Will-you-go-steady-with-me. Six words. *Oh, no. Please no. It will never end if anyone finds out.* I passed the note to Judy Prescott and watched her tight curls straighten in horror. Jude tore it up and put the tiny pieces in her pocket. After school that day, Judy and I ran for my house. My legs were screaming as I looked back to make sure that Ernie wasn't behind us.

Only another freak would like me. Ever. Ernie was the best I would get. He was me. But I didn't want anything to do with me.

Over Christmas break, Trish broke the news about Josh and his new girlfriend, Kathleen Bailey. My idiocy had practically thrown them together. My breath caught in my throat when I saw Josh again, but something in his manner had changed—I knew he was gone.

A week after my return, I was knocked to my knees by a raging flu. Friends reassured me that it was a common casualty after being abroad. Actually, I knew it was my dream of Josh dying inside. It hurt just to breathe or think.

A letter from Ethan temporarily perked me up. I ripped open the large envelope open but was disappointed to find only a small Post-it from him stuck to something official.

> Hey Jule!
> How's it goin'? I'm waaay behind on my work so I have to make this quick—I wrote to Dr. Abernathy a few weeks ago with a list of questions. Here's a copy of his response. I hope I'm not being pushy or anything, but his answers pertain to you too. Take care!
> Love, Ethan

Adrenaline surged as I peeled off the Post-it and saw the bold letterhead, New England Medical Center. Boston.

> Dear Ethan,
> It was certainly nice hearing from you and learning that you are attending Brown for your Masters. It is a fine university and a pretty one. Your diagnosis is spondyloepiphyseal dysplasia, or SED, a rare form of dwarfism.

I reread the sentence and swallowed hard. Long ago, I'd blocked the doctors' words and sent them away. Kids had always asked, "Are you a dwarf or a midget?" I'd never known the answer for sure until that moment. It identified and negated me—both. I was a . . . I couldn't say it. I was twenty and still could barely think it. What an ugly word. The letter called me back.

> Spondylo refers to the vertebrae, and the epiphyses are the growing part of the bone. The dysplasia means there is something wrong in this area.

It can also affect other bones. What occurs because of
the abnormal bones is that your trunk is relatively
shorter than the rest of your body and is one of the
main causes of your short stature (there are other types
of dysplasias, in which the limbs are short and the
torso is average, such as achondroplasia, which you do
not have.)

*Another type called achondroplasia? That's why I don't look like
them.* Wide-eyed, I continued.

Because the epiphysis of the other bones may be
abnormal, this can result in abnormalities of the hips,
resulting in arthritis of the hips and curving of the
bones. Dr. Simon will probably tell you more about
that since he is an orthopedic specialist. Perhaps the
most serious problem you would have to look forward
to would be arthritis in the joints. The reason for this is
because the joints are not normal and this causes
excessive wear and tear on them, resulting in arthritis.
Some of the surgery that Dr. Simon has performed on
you is an attempt to prevent this from occurring. You
have curvature of the spine, which is associated with
spondylo-epiphyseal dysplasia.

Concerning genetic counseling . . . we do believe
that the type of spondyloepiphyseal dysplasia (SED)
you have is inherited in an autosomal recessive
manner. This means that your mother and father, who
are normal, are carriers of this condition. In other
words they have a normal gene and a recessive gene
for spondyloepiphyseal dysplasia. Statistically, the
chances of your parents having a child with SED
therefore are 1 in 4. Both you and your sister have the
two abnormal genes. However, in order for your
children to be affected, your mate must also carry one
of these abnormal genes. The likelihood that she
would be a carrier is not very high, although possible.

Therefore, most likely all of your children will be normal but a carrier of SED.

If you have any other questions, just let me know. Please give my regards to your parents and to Julie.

Sincerely yours,

Howard L. Abernathy, M.D.

How totally embarrassing, I thought. *Ethan is asking about children. I hope Mom and Dad haven't seen this. It'd break their heart to think Ethan believes he'll ever get married. Or have kids. We're not normal. Why does Ethan always stick his nose where it doesn't belong?*

I was angry and confused, though I didn't really know why. I wanted to burn the letter, rant and rave. Give God the finger. Instead, I folded the letter four times, shoved it in my bottom desk drawer, deep under some old notebooks. I wanted to throw it away, but I couldn't. I thought it told me who I was.

For days, the flu, my brother's letter, and images of Josh haunted me. I lay on my bed surrounded by wadded-up tissues and half-eaten cafeteria meals that Trish had delivered. My throat was so sore it hurt to swallow, so I'd asked Trish not to bring more food. By the third night I realized I'd made a huge mistake. I called Trish, but she wasn't in her room. She was probably at the library. She'd wanted me to go to the college medical center, but I hadn't seen a white-coat in years, and I wasn't going to allow a little virus to send me into their clutches now. On the other hand, Trish had mentioned that the infirmary had sandwiches. Hmm. Starvation versus doctors. It was a tough call, but I finally caved in for the food.

I threw on a coat, yanked a hat over my unwashed hair, and trudged through the deep upstate New York snow, nose running, fever high. I no longer cared what the nurses did to me, as long as there was food involved.

"Why don't you go lie down, darling, and I'll bring you some soup," one nurse said. I climbed into an empty bed. The nurse brought me a steaming bowl. "Eat, then try and get some sleep." As I slurped and sniffled, she rustled around, carefully aiming a high-powered vaporizer at my plugged-up head.

I closed my eyes, which felt like two sizzling fried eggs, and tried to sleep. I thought about Josh. I thought about Lacoste. I thought about my diagnosis, the name for what I was. I fell in and out of a sleepy delirium as the memory of a childhood hospital visit scurried across my mind like a cockroach I'd been trying to squash. It was back in 1974, six days before I'd be turning eleven years old. My mom carried her suitcase, her purse, my duffel bag, my pillow, my knapsack, and my stuffed dog into the hospital. All I hung onto was my heart, hard as stone. A nurse brought us to an examination room, quickly filling it up with questions. Cold stares. Papers to sign. Endless noise. The sharp smells in the place turned my stomach. Then the nurse turned on me. "Okay, Julie, I'm going to need to draw some blood for...."

"What? No!" I screamed. "Nooo!"

"Don't worry, it will only be a pin...."

"Nooooooo!"

The nurse shot a look at my mom. "Julie, you're going to have to...."

"Get away from me! Get away!"

My mother had said we were going to the hospital so Dr. Simon could help me. She hadn't said anything about needles. I never would've come if she'd mentioned needles.

"We might get enough of a sample if I prick her finger," the nurse suggested.

The resulting poke stung, but I'd avoided the big scary needle, and I thought that was the end.

We headed for my room, passing gurneys holding limp and bruised bodies. Lining the corridors were wheelchairs with more crumpled people, tubes running from their noses. They looked sad and defeated. I knew why.

In my room, my mom looked around. "It's very comfortable, don't you think, sweetheart? Look, a TV just for you." But my eyes were set on the two men in white standing nervously outside my door. Their hands were hidden behind their backs. They motioned to my mom. I suddenly knew what they wanted, but before I could begin thrashing, the two men and my mom pinned me down on the bed.

"Please, sweetheart, it will only take a minute," my mom said. "They didn't get enough blood before."

I felt the needle pierce my skin and I shrieked and writhed.

One of the men snapped at me. "If you don't hold still, we might really hurt you."

He had no idea.

I forced my eyes open and looked around the room at the Hamilton Medical Center. It was enemy grounds. My fever was raging, but I got out of bed and left, despite the nurses' valiant efforts to stop me.

Safe in my dorm, I found a note from Trish on my door. "Where the hell are you, doll face?? Stopped by with pizza. Michael and I studying Organic Chem at library (?!?) Details later! Did you break down and go medical? Call me A.S.A.P. xoxo Trish."

Breakdown was right. But the sight of her handwriting made me smile in spite of how miserable I felt. I loved that gal.

I recovered from the flu, but not from Josh. The flu doesn't make you feel like a loser for more than a week or so. Heartaches can last indefinitely. I pretended I was okay in front of Trish. I pretended I was happy for Josh when he told me he was going to Paris for his entire junior year (my senior year). I pretended with every smile I sent his way. A week before finals, I even got to dance with him one starry night. Although I could barely see his face on the dark dance floor, my heart ripped open all over again.

Six
Micro to Macro

In the midst of winter I finally realized
there was in me an invincible summer.
~Albert Camus

The highlight of my last semester at Hamilton College was a surprise visit from my brother and my idol, Dan. When I opened the door of my dorm room one morning, I could barely believe the vision before me. I screamed as we hugged and laughed. Every tedious paper I had to write, every terrible book I had to read, every crush I was desperate to win, every cramp in my tired limbs, was banished in that moment. My relief and joy exploded down the hallway, causing heads to pop out of dorm rooms to check out the excitement. The girls thought he was "dreamy" and wanted to know if he had a girlfriend (he did). The guys admired his self-assured handshake and the way he spoke with such warmth and directness. It wasn't hard to see why everyone admired Dan.

For the last two years of college, he had become one of my dearest allies. When I was at my lowest, his long letters and long phone calls had built up my confidence and hope. We talked about our family, our lives, and our everyday ups and downs. To have him all to myself at Hamilton for two whole days was mind-boggling. He was on his way back to Chicago from a wedding in nearby Syracuse and came to see just *me*! His love and attention felt like everything I needed. I never would've dreamed that, one day, he would withdraw both.

Out at dinner that night, Dan told me about his strange, new macrobiotic diet. "It's not just a diet, Jule, it's a philosophy and a lifestyle. My friend Mike told me about a guy who had pancreatic cancer and the doctors all but signed his death certificate."

"Typical medical madmen," I said, as Dan nodded in agreement.

"As a last-ditch effort, the man tried this diet and cured himself. He's been in remission for six years. That's just one of a million stories like it."

"He thinks the food did it?"

"Yeah. A vegetarian diet, unrefined foods, no processed stuff, no dairy, and no white sugar."

"No sugar? Oh. I don't think I could bear that."

"Jule, it could help with your joints. The books say you can heal practically anything with a holistic approach. I've been doing it for about a month and have more energy than I've had in years."

He did look brilliant and his enthusiasm told me all I needed to know. "How do I start?"

"I knew you'd be game! I saw you have a health food store in town."

"You mean the Whole Food Family? It smells like a dirty sock in there. Everyone makes fun of that place."

"Then they don't know what's good for them. I'll take you there tomorrow."

Western medicine, Dan said, treated the physical body as separate from the emotional and spiritual. The macrobiotic approach held that integrating body, mind, and spirit was the path to healing and wholeness. Given my history with doctors, I was in complete agreement. If macrobiotics was anti-American Medical Association, I was pro-macro.

Dan introduced me to things like tofu, brown rice, and seaweed. I was a dedicated devotee in no time, praying that this food foray would undo the damage in my joints and erase a future of wheelchairs and white-coats. The chance to take control and change my destiny was a colossal thrill. College had opened my eyes to possibilities I'd never dreamed of before— but this could be my miracle. Macrobiotics became my lifeline to a different future—healthy, pain-free, normal. I was in fantasyland, and I liked it there. I even dreamed about growing a few inches. I wanted to believe that macro could cure anything.

Dan's whole-food diet, and my high expectations, brought some wonderful results. By the time graduation rolled around, I felt healthy and full of energy. Life looked more promising than ever. My family, the exclamation point on every chapter of my life, came to Hamilton that spring to see me get my diploma, with honors. Tracy Coan, one of my best friends from high school, also made the trek from New Jersey to upstate New York to see me graduate. The whole enthusiastic crew oo-ed and ah-ed at my senior art exhibit, and then the following day they cheered from their chairs as I crossed the auditorium stage. My parents and I had our differences, but their light had always surrounded me like sunshine, not asking for a thing in return. I had never fully appreciated the gift until then.

That summer, my parents weren't sure what to make of the *nori* seaweed in their kitchen, but they welcomed the strange macrobiotic staples just the same. The only instance when my mom drew the line was when I threw out a plateful of brownies that the neighbor had brought over. Sugar was now an illegal substance in my mind, and the verboten sweets were calling me like a lemming over a cliff. Before I lost all self-control, I cavalierly pitched the brownies into the trash. Kris, too, jumped on the macro bandwagon, and we began talking on the phone regularly trying to figure out where to buy something called *seitan* and whether eating seaweed every day was really necessary.

Kris was now teaching history at a private school in Philadelphia and told me about an opening there for a part-time arts and crafts teacher. I'd never had a real job and had no idea if I could handle one. Would a pack of sixth-graders accept a teacher who was shorter than they were? Nervously, I applied for the position and landed in Philadelphia that September. I thought arts and crafts were self-explanatory, until I met the wealthy girls from the prestigious Smythe Academy.

"When can we make fourteen-karat gold earrings?" whined one, whose father had recently purchased a recreational helicopter.

When I suggested making macramé necklaces instead, my students were appalled. You would've thought I'd insisted the girls walk to school. Or wear white after Labor Day. We settled on collages made from the pages of *Vogue*. The girls cut out collagen-injected lips, eyes laden with mascara, and bodies airbrushed to perfection. That was when I realized I wasn't going to gel with Smythe. What I really wanted was to attend the Kushi Institute, where the principles of macrobiotics were taught. The school was in Brookline, Massachusetts. Near Boston, of all places. God's inside joke. Surely I'd find like-minded people there? Maybe I'd find him.

My mom and dad generously agreed to pay the small tuition, so I turned in my craft apron, said good-bye to Kris, and headed northeast, hoping my parents' old Aspen station wagon would live to see Massachusetts. I stopped in New Jersey at our house in Lakeside, knowing that it would be the last time. My dad had lost his marketing job in New York City and found a new job in Somerset, PA. Saying good-bye to our big old home after twenty years was almost unimaginable. The thought of never breezing through our front door, never coming together around the dining room table, never sleeping under its forgiving roof again, felt like an unbearable loss. The comfort and safety of my home base would be gone for good. So many memories lived in every room, moved down every staircase, and hung on every wall. Would all these memories slowly be erased? The photos of my parents' new house, a modest old colonial, had made me cringe inside. The brick impostor could never take the place of my real home. But after my first visit to Somerset, I was won over. It was smaller but with a similar layout and the old familiar furniture. I sometimes forgot I was no longer in Lakeside.

Once in Brookline, I rented my first room from a pleasant couple in a macrobiotic house. The drawback was that they used only enough heat in their home to keep the water pipes from freezing, claiming it was the healthy way to stay in touch with the seasons. In the dead of a New England winter, it kept me in touch with my thick wool hat and gloves, inside the house and out.

I loved my two semesters at the Kushi Institute, but the house was giving me frostbite. So five months later, when my old high school friend, Lisa Delchamps, moved to Boston, she found a spacious apartment in Somerville with a room—and heat—for me. Soon though, the fun and food and frequent car repairs quickly ate away my funds from teaching, and I knew I had to find a job. I had noticed a "Part-time Help Wanted" sign at Barnaby's Florist, right around the corner from the school. Although I still worried that no one would want a child-sized employee, the storeowner, Shelly, gave me part-time work on the spot. Glory Be.

Waiting for the bus every other morning, engulfed in fumes from the cars whizzing by, I marveled that a nervous small-town girl like me was living in the city. I was proud of myself for being out on my own. I figured out how to parallel park despite a line of honking cars. I learned how to maneuver through several fast-moving rotaries (the maniacal circles with at least five possible exits, which made it way too easy to get whirled off in the wrong direction). I learned how to shovel just enough snow from around my car wheels to get the car out of its parking space on the street; I learned how to gun the engine and spit the car like a watermelon seed over the remaining mounds of snow. I rode the subway downtown and went to the movies by myself. I pushed through my fear and walked out my front door each day into an unfamiliar world. A world I didn't trust. It was terrifying and it was freeing.

At night, I poured over books from the local metaphysical bookstore, Horai-San, where all the Kushi students bought everything from books to pressure cookers. I read about nutrition, meditation, herbs, yoga, natural medicine, spirituality, enlightenment, and everything in between. The new ideas pried my mind open a little more each day. My fears were soothed as I found answers to questions I'd not even asked.

Our family hadn't talked much about religion or spirituality over the years. My older brothers and sisters had gone to Sunday school when they were young, but that had ended when we'd moved from Cranbury, New Jersey, to Lakeside when I was three years old. Years later, I'd heard a story about my dad, who had been a deacon at our Protestant church in Cranbury. The church had held a strawberry festival every spring to raise money for a needy cause, and one year, when a building which housed migrant workers burned to the ground, my dad knew where the money should go. But when he approached the church board, they hemmed and hawed, finally admitting that they didn't want *those* people, who were predominantly African American, around anyway. The money for the project was denied and my dad was incensed. He decided to raise the money independently, and with many friends and neighbors, the necessary ten thousand dollars was collected. A new building went up within the year. My dad never went back to church and never trusted organized religion again.

I had never thought too deeply about religion myself, although I had often prayed long into the night, hoping that Someone was listening. But the books from Horai-San spoke about faith and spirit in an eye-opening way. As I sat alone in my room, I felt tucked into conversations that answered my emptiness. Each new idea quietly untangled my doubts, drawing in grace and inspiration. Life grew larger, the very air seemed crowded with wisdom, the ceiling opened into the sky. Tears of relief turned the pages as I began to recognize myself. These authors, these friends, were reaching down to grab my hand, to lift me up into their vision. They talked to my fears, addressed my confusion, and mirrored a beautiful journey ahead. They reassured my wholeness in a world that had generally left me in pieces. As the old doubts were countered with wondrous possibilities, power and freedom stirred inside me. My heart wanted to gallop straight out of the darkness and into a Light brighter than I'd imagined. It had been patient and wise in its waiting. Even though I had turned back in sorrow, that sorrow couldn't eclipse a Love that would never give up. Settling into the home inside myself was the answer to feeling at peace in the world as well.

Lying in bed one night, I read from *A Course in Miracles*: "How deceived was I to think that what I feared was in the world instead of in my mind." I closed my eyes as I let the old, sad patterns bubble up. It had been four years since I'd seen Josh Hathaway, but the thought of him still ached like poison. I never believed that someone could love...a defect. *I* didn't want me, so why would he? He didn't reject me, I realized, I did it to myself. I refused to believe in the possibility. *No wonder I'm alone. I've been projecting my fear out onto everyone, not realizing it was within. The books and the mystics say I can be free without changing anything but my beliefs about myself.*

I had accepted misery for a long while, focusing on my differences and what I felt was the injustice of my situation. My fragile ego lingered in every stranger's stare and was bruised by every child's taunting. It hid under my old back porch, ran scared through grocery store aisles, trailed after passing cars, and sailed away in open parking lots. Endless distractions kept me in victim mode as I reached out in every direction for the love and approval that waited within.

I was so tired of being afraid and angry. I wanted to start living. Maybe the self-help books were right. If I faced my fears and changed my limiting beliefs, I could lighten up, find inner peace. It sounded easy. But old mantras like "Life isn't fair" and "I was shortchanged" still offered serious resistance. After all, they'd done their job protecting me from the big scary world I now wanted to tackle. *Fool*, I had told myself. *People won't accept you. You'll never be safe.* Powerlessness, I now realized, had become a way of life.

Instead of screaming at the rain, it was time to calm the *inner* storm. I started noticing my habitual negative forecasting. I had thought it was an accurate reflection of the world, but I had made my world reflect my dire predictions. I had so much undoing to do. My journey started in the pages of these books, but I had no idea how long it would take to put the new ideas into practice.

My job at the florist's gave me the opportunity to get out of the books and into the world. Whenever Shelly went across the street for coffee, or off to deliver flowers, I had the store to myself. When I wasn't helping the occasional customer, I'd change the water in the flower buckets, de-thorn roses, or arrange some flowers. While I kept my hands busy with work, my mind too often drifted into the same old wish, that my prince would come—soon. I didn't think I could know real happiness without him. My family accepted me, and my friends accepted me, but they could ignore the strangeness of my body. Could Mr. Right?

Instead of a prince, one day, a thief waltzed through the door. "Open that register, and gimme the cash," the tall, unkempt man growled.

I gawked at what looked like a fat gun wrapped in brown paper. "I'm not allowed to open it when the owner isn't here." The lie just popped out of my mouth.

He slunk over to the register and pawed the button to open the drawer. As he pounced on the cash like a starving animal,

stuffing the bills in his pocket, I stood in disbelief. Then he motioned
to the rear stockroom. "Go back there and don't call the cops." It
wasn't until I turned around and walked that the first fear stung at
my back.

Standing in the stockroom, I waited and listened. When I heard
the door chimes ring, I knew he was gone, and I nervously dialed
411. Then 911. When the police appeared, one officer ran off in the
direction I indicated while the other took a description, which he
relayed to his partner via police radio. In no time, we were listening
to a blow-by-blow description of the chase, as he asked his line-up of
questions. "Was his shirt dark blue or black? What color was his
hair? How tall? How old?"

What I remembered most was the lost look in the man's eyes,
his nervous movements and desperation. I recognized him. The
caged tiger. A fellow inmate in life, nose bent out of shape, life out of
control. I found myself rooting for his freedom.

Shelly walked through the door, quickly looked at the cops,
then at me, then back to them. "What's going on?"

"Are you the owner of this store, ma'am?" the young officer
asked.

"What? Yes, I'm the owner."

"I'm afraid you've been robbed."

"Are you serious? Oh my God! Julie are you okay?"

"I'm fine, really. I'm so sorry about the cash," I said.

Shelly took a deep breath. "I had heard about a string of
robberies in Brookline. Jesus, I shouldn't have left you alone."

The police radio suddenly cut in and then out, the voice
breathless. "Got 'im cornered . . . housing unit on Oak . . . Shit! . . . He
got down the back stairway!"

"Did you lose 'im?" the officer in the store quickly asked.
"O'Hara?"

"He's gone, damn it," the reply crackled.

He got away. The predator and prey had escaped.

The description I'd given fit a man the police had been watching
in Roxbury, the officer told me. "You're free to go now," he added.

"Yes, Julie, please," Shelly insisted, "take the rest of the day off, with pay."

Needing time to think, I agreed. I collected my things and climbed aboard the bus on Harvard Street. *I can't believe I wasn't totally terrified. I'm more afraid of a group of kids than a mugger! I think he felt less control than I did. Was he the face of my own fear?*

I waited to call my parents until I had the story down pat and could deliver it without scaring them senseless. They were not alarmists by any means, but I knew they'd chew off one of their legs if it meant sparing me pain. I didn't want this gnawing away at them. My first call was to Aeva, my psychic friend whom I'd met at Horai-San. I gave her a quick recap.

"The weird part is that I actually felt bad for him," I finished. "Of course, it wasn't my money he took."

"Hey, even an asshole needs understanding. Wait, I'm gettin' an image of him in, like, the Roxbury area, with a cute little blond boy. He's in quite a pickle. Was he tall with black scraggly hair and a scarred face?" she asked, in her strong Boston accent.

"That's him."

"I'll put him on my prayer list. You too, of course, darlin'."

"I wonder if they'll catch him."

"Justice is always served, even if it doesn't look that way to us humans. You understand his struggle because you're startin' to understand your own. You sure have some interesting karma in Boston."

"Yeah. I'm more afraid of doctors than muggers," I said, feeling my left eye twitch.

"Don't judge it, darlin'," Aeva said. "That makes the energy cling to you like a tick to a dog. You were born to stand out, you've just forgotten your Mighty Cherubim status. Yours is the classic ugly duckling story. You've been tryin' to fit into the acceptable duck mold when all along you're really a fuckin' swan."

She made me laugh. "Thanks, Aeva. So no more Boston nightmares for me, right?"

"Not for now, anyway. And now is all we really have."

I called my friends at the Kushi Institute, who seized on the metaphor of my little Hill Street Blues scenario. "Good thing you weren't too yang to attract the bullet!" my worried friend Pamela blurted out. I suddenly understood firsthand the world's addiction to the six o'clock news. Drama can be kind of fun. Tracy, my old high school friend, was ready to throw her one-year-old daughter Casely in the car, drive straight to my door, and drag me home. It made me feel strangely loved. "First you live like a bunch of polar bears in that macro arctic zone," she said, "then, there was that crazy man who called you Beelzebub and followed you for three blocks thumping a Bible. Now you've had a gun stuck up your nose. Can we finally turn in the tofurky salad and resume a normal existence? I propose a freakishly safe little town called Lakeside."

I did, in fact, have frequent bouts of longing for my home town. So when I visited every few months, I stayed with Tracy, her husband, Mark, and Casely, my goddaughter. Whenever I arrived at their house, I exhaled the dirty, crowded city, and breathed in sweet relief. I'd found a new home.

After I hung up with Tracy, I decided I was ready to call my folks. After general pleasantries, I said, "Uh, Dad, are you sitting down?"

"No," he paused. "Should I be?"

"First of all, I'm absolutely fine, but I was held up at the florist this morning."

"What? Held up? Oh, Julie! Are you okay?

I explained the event as if I'd simply spilled a cup of Earl Grey tea, but the ocean of concern in Dad's voice was breaking my calm.

"You're really okay? Are you positive? Wait! Mom just walked in." His speech was ragged as he quickly clued her in. "Oh my baby girl!" she cried as her voice ran and picked up the phone. "Sweetheart?" I could feel her squeezing the receiver, wishing she could sail through the wires and hold me safe.

The robbery hadn't choked me up, but my parents' love sure did. "Hi Mom," I said softly, as the first tears seeped out.

"Oh Julie, I just can't believe it," she murmured sadly. "Thank goodness you're all right!"

"I am. Really. To be honest, I'm almost glad that it happened. I made it, and I'm fine. I'm kind of amazed that it didn't completely rattle me. I can't explain it, but I feel a strange sense of peace. Like there is less to fear out there than I've ever thought."

Seven
Art and Scroll

When you change the way you look at things, the things you look at change.

~Wayne Dyer

I'd spent most of my first year in Boston in a macrobiotic house, the second year in an apartment with Lisa, and the third year with my brother Ethan. After getting his master's degree in teaching from Brown University in Rhode Island, he moved to Boston to find a job, since he had a bunch of old Middlebury College friends already living in the area. When Lisa decided to move in with her boyfriend, I moved in with Ethan. Despite our intermittent fighting as kids, Ethan and I turned out to be great housemates. I had taken him for granted as my brother, without realizing he was one of my dearest friends. Even though our difficulties, our dwarfism, still lay silent between us, sharing the road with him was a comfort and a gift.

We both missed the hubbub of college and our family. Ethan quickly became a bit of a social director for everyone we knew. He organized group trips to restaurants and movies, and a monthly game night for playing cards and backgammon or just hanging out together. Ethan made me laugh, he made me think, and he made me feel at home.

I had recently left Barnaby's Florist and was now working part-time at Horai-San Bookstore, where I took an interest in the hand-painted greeting cards that sold well. Although I hadn't picked up a brush since my brief teaching stint two years before, I decided to pull out my dusty watercolors. Unlike oil and acrylic paints, which could be harnessed and controlled, watercolors had an aqueous mind of their own. It was the reason I'd never particularly liked them. But since they were the most logical medium for making greeting cards, I wanted to give them a chance.

I gazed at my art desk, its unfinished wooden top covered with doodles, paint, phone numbers, and familiar handwriting. My parents had given me this desk when I was twelve. Ethan had written his name on the wood after I'd given him a calligraphy lesson. Celia had drawn a beautiful paisley heart with the words "You gotta have 'art." Tracy had doodled a stick figure that had her frizzy hair. The small drawing of a hound dog had the date when our dog, Pal, left our world. So many memories. Even the sad ones had their place. I sat and cried, feeling my past, so heavy but slipping away. My inner world was changing, leaving room for new colors.

As I gingerly attempted some watercolor washes on my paper, the paint began shifting around on the paper, creating interesting movement that I hadn't anticipated. There was no controlling it, a situation I normally would detest. Instead, I was fascinated. As I tipped the paper back and forth, the water slid around like wind, and my doubts began to drip off the edges. Hours passed. Years dissolved. As the water danced, I felt something inside me start dancing too. It was therapy. It was reunion. Sunrises slipped out of my hands. Turquoise, fuchsia, and daffodil yellow rode across an open sky. They greeted each other in harmony and healing. They spoke to me of joy.

As the paint relaxed into the paper, I grabbed a calligraphy pen and pulled out my fat journal of quotations, exploding with hope. In the two years I'd been in Boston, I'd nearly filled it. Every time I opened that journal, I was home. Colors sang and smiled from deep within the worn pages. Each wise reminder was a stepping stone, a bridge, a promise. On one card, I wrote Richard Bach's words from *Illusions*:

If you want magic,
let go of your armor.
Magic is so much stronger
than steel!

When the calligraphy was done, I sat back and admired my creation. For the first time in a long time, I saw myself in its splashy freedom. After a week of practice, my desk piled high with cards and quotations, I felt alive with the marriage of art and words. Each card was a tiny billboard of faith, a silver trumpeted announcement, a tribute to the authors who celebrated spirit.

I tried to drum up the courage to ask Carol, my new boss, if she would sell them at the bookstore. The thought of putting my work, and a piece of my soul, out into the world sent my previous enthusiasm into a nose dive. *What if people hate my cards? I don't think I could handle it.* Finally, after forcibly setting aside the doubts, I selected ten of my best cards and stuffed them into my backpack. I knew that day only Crystal, another employee, would be in the shop. Maybe I could secretly put the cards out and see what happened.

"Hello, Julie of the sweeping rainbow," Crystal sang out. "How are you on this luscious day of days?" Crystal was a fellow Kushi student and her flamboyant style was the exact reason why the New Age had a flaky reputation. "It was a full moon last night," she cooed, "and we drank sake at our Goddess Circle of Ecstasy. Afterward I was so yin that I was absolutely overpowered by the desire for some salty yang this morning." She held up the bag of barbecue potato chips that she was munching on.

"Those night shade chips have MSG and hydrogenated oil," I said. I actually wanted to devour them in the worst way, but following the macro diet would bring me a miracle, I thought. If I was perfect in my quest, maybe God would undo all the punishment from the past. Then I'd be free from pain.

Losing my willpower meant losing my dream. Then I saw the worried look in Crystal's charcoal eyes. "I'm sorry," I said. "Not very Zen of me to judge, huh? I like those chips too."

Crystal shrugged cheerfully and took off for her break. I seized the chance to make my move. Casually, I wobbled over to a display rack and slipped in my cards.

A few customers streamed in and out, and each time they drew close to my cards, I felt as if they were about to trip a nuclear weapon. A stern-looking woman in a somber green business suit stopped at the card rack and began flipping through the selection like a tax auditor. She wore low sensible shoes and carried a matching bag, both buffed to a harsh shine. She doesn't belong in a groovy store, I mumbled to myself. Suddenly, she spotted my work. I froze in my seat, waiting to be blown to bits.

"These are lovely," she said. "They're new, aren't they?"

"Yes," I coughed, now viewing her as royalty.

"Are they hand-painted? I don't see a signature."

"Well, um, I made those."

"Really? You're very talented! You must sign them. I dabble in watercolor and I know how hard it is. You clearly have it mastered." A huge grin slammed into my face. Her praise lifted me out of my small doubting self.

I started to ring up her purchase as Crystal breezed over, her gauzy red skirt moving like flames across the floor. "Where are the new cards from?"

"You're standing next to the artist," said the customer proudly.

"Holy Mother of Mercy," Crystal said, her Catholic upbringing slipping out like a bra strap. "These are pure light!" Then she threw a massive bear hug around me.

"Can I have your business card?" the customer asked. "I'd love to commission a painting for my girlfriend who's going through an awful divorce."

"I don't have any business cards yet," I said. "But I'll write my telephone number on the receipt."

My first sale walked out the door, leaving me as shiny as her shoes. The woman in green had purchased five of my cards, at three dollars each. A week later she commissioned a painting. I was saturated in every hue of joy. Over the next month, I barely did anything but paint. Carol gladly displayed my cards and encouraged me to contact other stores. I mustered up the nerve to try ZenCyclopedia Books in Cambridge.

"Hi there, are you the owner?" I asked, walking in the door of the bookstore.

"Guilty. What can I do for you?"

I swallowed hard and started the introduction I'd rehearsed. "I'm a local artist and I'm selling hand-painted cards. Would you like to take a look?"

"Sure," he said, as he helped me with my new blue briefcase. He began to dip into the cards as my breath waited on the ceiling. *Do I look away? Walk around? What if he hates them?* I tried to look nonchalant, scanning the store for a distraction, maybe even Mr. Right.

The potent incense reminded me of Crystal and how she smelled like a case of aromatherapy bottles. She and I would be better friends, I thought, if she weren't such a fruitcake. Then again, maybe Crystal felt sorry for me and my cautious steps, my boring turtlenecks and faded jeans. I had the same non-hairstyle forever; Crystal was always changing her cut or color. I wanted to blend in, be accepted. Crystal wanted to burst out, dance free. I was stuck in my ways; she seemed to be attached to nothing.

Come to think of it, there was little wrong with Crystal. My judgment always shot out when I was scared of something, like her uninhibited peace, love, and high colonics. Crystal didn't give a flying fig what other people thought of her. I admired that, but it was a far-fetched notion for me. I had felt different all of my life. Trying hard to be like everyone else had become a full-time job. Standing out often ended in ridicule or disappointment. Like the night before, when Ethan went out to dinner with friends to his favorite Mexican restaurant that I had gone to recently, and two of the waiters immediately homed in on him announcing, "We found a girlfriend for you!" But as soon as they began to describe me, Ethan knew.

"Art and Scroll," the owner said, pulling my thoughts back to the present. "I like it."

"Thanks." I'd worried over my business name for weeks.

I tried to hide my surprise when he bought sixty cards. I tumbled out onto the busy street with a check for $180 in my pocket. The periwinkle sky patted my back, the sunshine held me up like a jewel. I couldn't wait to tell my dad that the briefcase we had bought together was fast at work. *Thank you, God, or angels, if you're listening, I thought. I can work at home and do what I love. Wow.*

The subway car was crowded as it barreled through the dark tunnels to Somerville. I held on tight to my briefcase and to the bar next to me as we all swayed to and fro, trying to act natural. I felt pretty small riding the T, smashed in amongst more substantial bodies. On this day, there was a tall fellow next to me, whose groin was about at my head level.

Someone's powerful perfume suddenly jumped up my nose and settled in for the ride. I figured that the well-dressed woman on my right was the guilty party. She wore a fancy red suit, lustrous jewelry, and what looked like a three-hundred-dollar hairdo. *She's probably headed for her spiffy home in Lancaster where the maid is cooking a lethal roast beef. I guess her day at the office was no match for that perfume. She is still trailing clouds of it.* As my judgments circled like the pearls around her long neck, suddenly the scent became strangely familiar. Then it hit me . . . it was incense from the bookstore. The stink was my own.

My years in Boston were a marvelous awakening. How perfect it was that the place which had affected my childhood so profoundly had redeemed itself in my adulthood. Fate had sent me back into the fray to retrieve a piece of my soul that had been lost twenty years before.

Another year passed in the gray sea of Boston's cars and crowds, but city life really didn't agree with me. By then, I had three Boston clients and had found ten bookstores, from Vermont to Georgia, to buy my cards. I felt the jaws of city life clamping down on my nerves. No wonder my eye has been twitching. Three years was enough. *Why stay here when I can take my card business anywhere?*

I pictured trees, lakes, and the quiet backyards of suburbia. I smiled thinking about a real driveway for my car instead of fighting for meager street parking. I imagined an honest mechanic to take care of my aging Aspen wagon. Lakeside and a family. Tracy, Mark, and Casely were waiting there to catch me. I knew I was moving on again. A month later, Ethan helped me scour the apartment, unearthing my hodgepodge of possessions. He packed up my pots and pans from the kitchen and even vacuumed my old room.

"I'm really going to miss you. We sure had fun," I said.

"You'll be happier in Lakeside, Jule." He gave me a big hug, the only other adult I knew with whom I could stand eye to eye.

My old sputtering car, tired after three New England winters, welcomed me inside. I gazed out at Ethan with twenty-six years of love. My dark "twin" had been there, like a protective shadow, even when we were apart. In the rearview mirror, I could see him lingering in the road, one hand stuffed in his pocket and the other waving. He looked small and vulnerable standing there on that car-lined street. Sometimes he seemed cocky, a little bantam rooster. But everyone who loved him — and that was a lot of us — saw right through the act. His heart was feather-soft. Ethan and I had been fortunate to spend those two years together. Although we didn't know it then, our paths were about to veer far away from each other. As I drove to the end of the street, I took one look back. I waved, beeped my horn, wiped my eyes, and turned that bittersweet corner of my life.

Eight
Lakeside Hibernation

Something was withheld that made us weak...
we found it was ourselves.
~Robert Frost

Although the move to Lakeside kept me busy, I was keenly aware that the strange eye twitch was getting worse. A year before, it had started as a mild flickering under my left eyelid and an annoying fluttering sound in my left ear. Now, whenever I smiled, the facial muscles on the left side would pull so tight that my eye would close tight and my mouth would twist into a sneer. Often my face would get stuck in the contraction so that it looked like I'd had a stroke. I didn't know what to think. Or what to stop thinking.

Unfortunately, my negative focus was giving the problem power and speed. *Didn't I leave the stress of the city behind me? How on earth am I going to meet Mr. Right if my face looks so weird? It's bad enough that I'm different and my body is stiff as a board. Do I have to cope with this too? It looks so ugly. They're going to laugh at the freak all over again.* I unpacked my art supplies, set up my desk, and was ready for work. *Thank goodness I can earn a living and barely be seen*, I thought. I pulled out my quotation book and saw a pink Post-it note that I'd saved after a conversation with Kris a year before.

"Guess who I ran into last night, Jule?" my sister had asked, wearing a Cheshire smile as she hung up the dress from her ten-year high school reunion the night before. Kris was looking more and more like my mom. Gentle smile. Warm brown eyes.

The biggest difference was that her curly hair was now long, pulled back in a ponytail, out of her one-year-old's reach. "Megan McWilliams," she had said. "Remember, she married John Heissenbuttel from my class?" Kris had waited for me to say something but I was speechless. Other friends went in and out of my life without regret, but Megan had remained an invisible scar. I'd never stopped feeling unsettled about the loss. Kris had handed me the pink Post-it. "She wanted you to have her address and phone number. She's living in the Berkshires."

"Did you ask for it?"

"No, Jule. She came up to me. She asked me to give it to you. Are you going to call her?"

"Maybe I'll write first."

My sister nodded in understanding. "She said she'd always felt bad about the way things ended, said you had been her best friend."

A year had passed. I'd wanted to write to Megan but never did. It'd been so many years since I'd seen her. I decided to send one of my handmade cards, a watercolor sky. I wrote in calligraphy a quote from Richard Bach across the sunset. "Meeting again, after moments or lifetimes, is certain for those who are friends." On the inside I wrote that I'd thought about her over the years, and I'd missed her. I said that I'd moved back to New Jersey and added that if she was ever in town at her parents' house, to give me a call. I sealed it and walked right out to the mailbox, fast, before I changed my mind. A month later, the letter came back. "Address Forwarding Expired." I'd waited too long to contact her. My face started its automatic twitching.

Now that I was back in New Jersey, I spent most of my time with the Coans: Tracy, Mark, and their adorable daughter, Casely. Tracy and I had been close ever since middle school, when she'd moved to my neighborhood. Although our friendship had been rocky back then, we were getting along famously now. Tracy had even talked about finding a bigger place for her family, with room enough for me. Sharing the rent would make life easier on all of us. So when she saw an ad for an affordable rental in Lakeside, a situation as common as finding a seamstress in a nudist colony, she pounced. We took one look at the big charming house and were sold. Not only was there plenty of space for her family, but it had a huge attic room that I loved. At first, I had doubts about living with her family, considering our past. Still, if Ethan and I could get past our disagreements, so could two old high school pals. I'd been lonely in my basement apartment. Living with friends again would be fun.

Over the following year, the Coans and I shared meals together, hung out at night, and watched little Casely grow. I had a new family, a home again, and everything I needed. Everything except him. If it weren't for that major deficiency, I wouldn't have ventured out from those safe walls much at all.

Lakeside's natural beauty had nursed and protected me as a child. I'd slowly made my way out into the world, away from its sleepy playpen. Philadelphia and Boston had been overwhelming in comparison. Now I was retreating to the womb, and by moving in with friends, stable and secure, I began my long hibernation.

Back in middle school, my history teacher, Mr. Salvatore, had been vexed by a funny facial twitch that was impossible for us kids to ignore. I'd felt sorry for him sometimes, but after class I laughed right along with my friends when they imitated his jumpy eyes. It was a guilty reprieve to have someone else be the butt of a joke. My class in behavioral science taught me that one. I had taken the class, as my parents recommended, hoping that it would explain why kids teased me and why I couldn't ignore their insults. The textbook was boring, but the class left me believing there were answers out there. So on a Saturday trip to the mall with friends, I slipped off to the bookstore. In the psychology section I found a paperback titled *The Truth*. I flipped through it, my eyes desperate for some balmy relief. The author wrote that anger was actually a cover-up for fear. *Huh?* He said that when someone makes us mad, they are triggering a feeling of powerlessness that's already inside. They're not creating the emotion, they're unleashing it. *Really?* No one had the power to offend, he wrote, unless we allowed it to echo our own self-doubt. No matter what our circumstances, we could find peace within. *No way.*

Could this inner stillness fend off the burning stares and laughter? Could it douse the growing rage inside? The possibility thrilled me. Or was it social suicide to admit that I was messed up on the inside as well as the outside? Seventh grade was not an acceptable time for radical individualism. We worked tirelessly to be alike.

Standing in the bookstore, I worried that someone had noticed the revolutionary writings in my hand. *Will the cashier think I'm crazy?* I also bought a boring teen novel to camouflage *The Truth* and to distract my nosy friends. As it turned out, they thought it was hysterical that I'd bought books at all, and they didn't care to look. But I couldn't wait to get home and break out my manual for happiness. I was ready to transform my life of worry into one of peace.

Although the book was helpful, I was afraid to share the revelations and, after a few weeks, they were quickly overshadowed. When it was *The Truth* versus puberty, truth didn't stand a chance.

Years later, I still remembered that first self-help book. My self-esteem had not gained much momentum since then, still hovering at about a seventh-grade level. As I searched for the courage to be authentic, sometimes it meant being authentically terrified. Ditching my well-honed "I'm okay" act was scary, and speaking up after so many years of silence would take practice. A lot of practice. I began confiding in old friends, at first, sharing bits and pieces of my repressed self. I braved the waters while safe on the phone, where I knew they couldn't see my face in spasm or my nervous nail-picking. I was startled and relieved to find that they too had felt crazed and unlovable. In high school, we'd each worn a plastic smile, masking our common pain, believing it was shamefully ours alone. Trying to appear well-adjusted wasn't only my secret ambition, it was a societal epidemic. Maybe the metaphysicians were right: buried under all the lies and fears, our true spirit waits to be free.

Simone Ramel, who had played Maria in *The Sound of Music*, surprised me the most. Popular, pretty, she seemed to have it all. Even though she was one of my closest friends then, I'd never known how she struggled with her confidence, or that she had difficulty focusing on schoolwork that left her feeling different. She was a hardworking actress like the rest of us.

Was it possible that my fears were not so unusual after all? That most of us had felt separate and alone back in school? It made me want to return to my past and try being myself. So when my old friend, Renee, asked me to be her guest at a wedding of two of our high school classmates, I thought it was an opportunity.

"But you're supposed to take a date," I said, feeling like I was crashing a party.

"The invitation says, 'And Guest.' I'm inviting you as my guest. Brian can't make it, and you'd have more fun. C'mon, we went to high school with them."

I loved weddings, especially the dancing. Maybe if I attended enough of them, the luck would rub off. So I said, "I do. I mean, I'll go." It had been eight years since I had seen many of my classmates.

When Renee and I walked into the church, out of habit I found myself scanning the rows for Mr. Right candidates. That's when I saw him. Not Prince Charming, but the devil himself, Sammy Gosbin. Even though it had happened in grade school, I could still hear his harsh voice.

"Hey, little midget! Where ya going in such a hurry?"

"Shrimpy! Shrimpy! Shrimpy!"

"Julie?" Renee asked. "Where would you like to sit?"

"Oh God, Sammy Gosbin is headed right for us," I gasped, worrying about my twitching face.

Renee looked up and spotted him. "Hello, Sam," she said with a warm smile.

"Hi." Sam looked lost.

"How're you doing?" I asked. *Tortured any kids lately?*

"Are you living in town?" Renee asked.

"No, in Sparta with my brother . . . yeah . . . I lost my license. DWI. I'm looking for work." He glanced at the bouncy blond next to him. "This is my girlfriend, Deirdre."

As we all chatted, I realized that my resentment was nearly gone. Sammy looked kind of sad and vulnerable.

"He used to scare me in high school," Renee whispered as we walked away.

"I thought I was the only one," I said in surprise.

Suddenly I was glad I'd run into him. Bullies are their own worst enemies. They've surely experienced the pain of being humiliated—that's why they can do it so well. Sammy Gosbin's parents had gone through an ugly divorce. We'd heard about his mother's rage and his father's drinking. Sammy had felt powerless too, and he'd gone after others who mirrored that powerlessness. Like me. I'd been a magnet all my life. It was up to me to change my polarity.

So I did meet one of my soul mates that day. Not the one I'd been longing for, but the one I needed at the moment. I'd been bound to Sammy by resentment; ties like that get in the way of love. As I loosened the ancient knots, I felt more alive. That's what soul mates help us do.

Mark, Casely, and I lingered at the table after breakfast. "This has really worked out, hasn't it, Jule? All of us together." Mark gestured as if words couldn't describe our good fortune.

"We sure got lucky on this house," I said. "I don't know where I'd be without you guys."

"We're family, Jule. Someday, when I own my own architectural firm, I'll build Tracy's and my dream house, and design a cool carriage house for you," Mark said with a grin.

I was so touched. He'd made me part of his family and now a little home of my own. But wait. Why wasn't my prince making this sweet offer? Where the hell was he? Worse yet, did Mark think I wouldn't have a husband and a home of my own?

"Who's up for the garage sales?" Tracy joined us, looking eager.

"Juwie, will you wide in the back seat wif me?" Casely pleaded.

"Of course." My answer lit up her little three-year-old face. I felt like a mom, even though I was only her godmother. On our regular lunch and movie dates, she brought wonder and new possibilities out of every dusty corner. The first time it really knocked my socks off was when Casely and I were taking a walk around Birchwood Lake. Every fern and crusty bug was beheld in her hypnotic eyes. Her love threaded right through me and out beyond my restrictive horizons. Small and powerful, with faerie flowers cupped in her hand, she stopped me from forgetting myself. Everywhere she walked, a sweet mist lifted us in grace. That day, just as I was thinking how life was meant to feel this good, a woman passed us with two Shelties. Casely immediately squealed with delight as the dogs sprang around her.

The woman smiled at the three little balls of happiness and then turned to me. "She's beautiful," she said softly, while looking at Casely. "She looks just like you."

Sunshine burst straight out of my eyes. My heart was stunned into silence. The doubts were hushed. The boundaries gone. She thought this adorable green-eyed blond was my daughter? And that maybe I had a husband?

Over the coming year, other people made surprisingly similar comments, and I allowed their assumptions, hoping that if they believed, and I believed, it might come true.

We set off happily for Tracy's garage sales, but my twitching face rebelled. Deep down, I felt nervous out in public, especially around Lakeside. The fear of rejection, which I'd long denied, was now speaking with a megaphone.

Tracy thought she hit the mother lode when she found a dining room set. As she talked with the owner, Casely and I wandered around.

"Julie?" I looked up to find Norma, Mom's old boss. She hugged me and then drilled for a family update. I'd only gotten to Ray when my face went into its spasms. I began to sweat thinking Norma would discover I was actually an insecure wreck. I put my hand up over my eye and looked away, anywhere, desperate to hide my ugliness. I said a quick good-bye and skulked to the car. Casely, my devotee, skipped behind me. She wouldn't have cared if I was covered with chicken pox. *Why do I worry so much what others think?* The earlier conversation with Mark sent me further into my pity party. Did Mark include me in his family because he believed that I'd never have a family of my own? I felt depressed the rest of the day. *Life is so cruel. Why am I being penalized by another visible curse? It's that bad hand again! My best friends feel sorry for me and think they'll have to take care of me. If they can't see my worth, who can?*

Two years into my stay at the Coans's, I began to hate my oasis. Tracy was pregnant with their second baby and I was torn. I didn't want to get pulled further away from a life of my own. Could I leave the nest and live without them? My childish fears stung, then resentment started to burn. My heartache was making me bitter, and I was ready to lash out at anyone who came too close. I knew I needed help, professional help. I decided to check out the local Metaphysical bookstore that sold my cards. While Audrey, the owner, was busy with a customer, I flipped through my own watercolor cards and stopped at a favorite.

The minute I heard my first love story,
I started looking for you,
not knowing how blind that was.
Lovers don't finally meet somewhere.
They're in each other all along.
~Rumi

I dreamed that this private love letter would reach out to my soul mate somewhere, somehow. He'd drop everything just to find me.

"Hi Julie," Audrey said, then introduced me to her customer. "Sylvia Tepper, this is Julie Hobbes, the artist who paints those fabulous watercolor cards. Sylvia has a therapy practice down the hall."

Bing! "What kind of therapy?" I asked.

Sylvia told me about her holistic approach, and I liked her warmth and openness. I could feel the spasms starting, so I asked for her card and escaped. A week later, I sat and babbled to Sylvia about my childhood, excited to talk to someone objective. "I feel I'm at a crossroads and don't know where to turn."

"Inward," she said with a smile.

"Well, I'm trying. I've worked hard to release my fears and feel more secure with myself. But I still quake when I'm out in public. It's getting worse. I always think I'll be ridiculed."

"Your family's silence made it challenging to address the humiliation. You've been continually shocked by people's reactions but didn't have an outlet for that powerful voltage."

I let the validation sink in. It was the first time anyone had said without pity, "I can see why you're afraid. It's okay. I can handle it." I wanted to cry, but my face was busy in spasm.

"Perhaps the twitch is connected," Sylvia said. "The pain you're stuck in is looking for that nonexistent outlet."

"Uh huh. Well, I've been trying to bolster my confidence. Like when I go out, I take a Walkman with headphones, and listen to inspirational tapes and affirmations."

"Good. What are the old beliefs that you want to release?"

"That I'm worth less than everyone else. That I'm a defect." I expected her to cringe, but she was unfazed.

"Even though your family loved you, you saw yourself through the eyes of those who pointed out your differences, since your family was quiet on the subject," Sylvia said gently. "You wanted to know the truth, but were afraid of it as well."

"Yeah. Every time a kid laughs at me, I want to yell, 'What's so bad about me?' Instead, I run and hide."

"Then what?"

"I head home and breathe a sigh of relief."

"Do you allow yourself to feel the hurt and anger?"

"Of course I feel it."

"So you cry, or hit a pillow? Tell a friend?"

I stared at her. "No, I feel it inside, and then I—I move on, I guess."

"Maybe you're missing a step. Perhaps your mind is standing guard over the pain, in a sense, and protecting you from actually feeling the hurt, or the truth."

"But I *am* in pain." *You don't understand.*

"It sounds like you may be routinely running away before the pain hits you full force."

"You're saying it's worse than I already feel?"

"No, not worse. You're much stronger than the pain, but you need to make peace with it. Changing your perspective can be scary. The world is a reflection of what you believe about yourself. As a child, you didn't have the tools to deal with your circumstances, so you made some sad assumptions and disappeared instead. Now your defenses are loyally protecting you from the very pain you need to release. You're on the lookout for the next person who might tug at the sadness and reaffirm the suffering you now expect. In a way, the little girl in you wants to be 'right' about being a defect so you can validate the trauma. The trick is to let yourself look at your beliefs, and allow the pain without judgment. It's just waiting for your acceptance. Then you can let it go."

My acceptance. I thought it had to come from others. "But I've been trying so hard," I whined, wanting her to do the work for me.

"The trying is a bit of a contradiction. Releasing the old lies we have about ourselves happens not when we push, but in moments of allowance and surrender."

"That's so tough to do."

"It may feel strange to give up that control after years of protecting our buried feelings and our beliefs. It's worth the effort, though, and it's part of the journey." She smiled. "And you, my dear, are well on your way."

Nine
Chasing Rainbows

The world breaks everyone
and afterward
we are stronger in the broken places.
~Ernest Hemmingway

It was the spring of 1981 and in one short month I would be graduating from Lakeside High School. As I sat in the sunny school lobby, the month of May was sweetly holding my hands. On the wall in front of me, two of my paintings were hanging in my senior high school art display. The many compliments I'd received were busy tickling daydreams inside me. *At least my art is something I have to offer Hamilton College next fall. Mr. Right has just got to be there. Maybe he'll even be an artist. Maybe —*

"Hi, Jules!" It was Serena Fennel, a harmless Chatty Cathy, always throwing out compliments like birdseed. I wasn't in the mood for her today.

"Whatcha working on?" she asked, unloading all her books onto the table, accidentally knocking my pen to the floor. I ignored it, not wanting to do my bending contortions in front of Serena.

"Oopsie. I'll get that." She leaned over effortlessly. "So Marla DeGrino told me you're going to Hamilton College, congratulations! It's such a great school. You're so so smart."

"Well, I work hard." I shifted uncomfortably.

"You're a super artist too. Is that what you'll do in college?" She stared at me way too hard. I felt like a difficult homework assignment she was trying to read.

"Maybe."

"You're so lucky. At least you have a talent you can fall back on in case, you don't—you know."

I felt a pin slowly being pulled from a hand grenade.

"My mom says it's important, in case I get dumped in a ditch like she was," Serena said. "Dad left when I was three. Mom had to find work and take care of everything. It was so awful."

I bobbed my head mindlessly, trying to untangle the previous comment.

"I mean, that's the only big drawback for you being . . . you know . . . so short. You'll have a tough time finding a husband."

The grenade exploded in shock waves. My eyebrows shot up under my hair. Serena's nonchalance announced my lifelong dread as if it was as trivial as not finding fresh raspberries in winter.

Is this the truth that everyone's afraid to talk about? That I'll be alone? Is it obvious to even a silly girl like Serena?

"Mom says men are dogs," Serena said.

The bell rang and off she ran. I stood up, strangled by her words, and wondering if my legs would hold. Hands shaky, I gathered my books and headed for class.

I stared at the dead frog in front of me as my eager lab partner, Chet Bell, neatly sliced open its soft white stomach with his scalpel. Serena had found my underbelly. Her words cut me open and now echoed around the room, loud and loose. *It'll be tough finding a husband . . . tough finding a husband . . .*

"Cool!" Chet yelled, as he opened the stomach of our deceased amphibian. Minutes before its date with formaldehyde, it had gulped down a horsefly, leaving it undigested. Several boys hustled over to our lab table to peek. One leaned in as I pulled my arms tightly against my body, not wanting anyone brushing too close. They knew what Serena knew. Saw what she saw.

Mrs. Berman wrote our homework on the blackboard, her
diamond ring glowing like a light bulb. She's *married. With her
pretty face and perfect hair, she has it easy. Screw her. Her husband
should tell her about the chalk line on her butt.*

I grinned at my new therapist, Judi Hancox, when I
finished telling the story. Sylvia had since moved to New
Mexico, and my friend Nancy Weber had introduced me to
Judi. I was comfortable with her in an instant. Among Judi's
many healing tools, she was also using a new technique called
Eye Movement Desensitization and Reprocessing, or EMDR.
EMDR was designed to help release negative impressions
stored in the nervous system through the use of bilateral eye
movements, tones, or taps. Studies were showing that it held
great promise in accelerating the therapy process.

Judi was quiet for a moment after she heard my story.
"Do you notice how you sometimes minimize your difficult
experiences?"

"What do you mean?" I asked.

"You end them on a light note. Like the comment about
the chalk. That's a common thread in post-traumatic stress
disorder."

Judi had explained this fancy diagnosis the week before.
She said the disorder often followed a traumatic experience
like military combat. My situation was different, she said, in
that I suffered continual minor shocks instead of one major
event. I told her she was being dramatic.

In the following months, after each session, I would
generally cry all the way home, and then lock myself away.
Maybe it is that post-traumatic thing after all, I thought, as I crept
under my quilt, wracked yet released by sobs. I wanted to curl
up into a fetal ball, although I'd never been able to physically
do that. Something was cracking open and it scared me to
death.

Thankfully, Judi had a deep faith in everyone's ability to heal. When I looked in her eyes, and felt her hope and commitment, nothing seemed as overwhelming as it once had. She saw the horizon. She felt the power in every soul. She honored the beauty in the midst of any ugliness. And as she held the light up for me, I caught glimpses too. There was joy in her wisdom and as it moved me through the changes, my life ahead began to smile and wave me forward.

Judi encouraged me to break out of my shell and socialize again. The thought of putting my fractured self into the action was overwhelming, and I felt defenseless without my old armor intact. The chance to find *him*, though, finally won me over. On my way to a local meditation class, I silently recited my soul mate request to the gods. I'd written it out a hundred times and I'd visualized it a thousand more.

When I arrived, people were already sitting in the lotus position. The sight made me jealous. I couldn't join them on the floor; the only other choice was an old couch piled high with coats. A woman with feathers in her hair said there might be a stool in the back. I found a ratty beach chair. It was either use the chair or sink into the coat-couch. I sat against the wall on my squeaky perch, feeling conspicuous. The smell of incense was potent but even it couldn't cover the smell of mold.

For once, I didn't feel the spastic pressure behind my eye. I scanned the room, checking for Mr. Right. I noticed a guy sitting off by himself, eyes shut, and I was instantly intrigued. How could he sit calmly in a busy, crowded room and not care who was looking at him? The class started and Larry, the director of the massage school, asked everyone to stand in a circle. The quiet fellow stood right next to me. We exchanged smiles and a breeze rippled up my shirt. He was adorable. Thick auburn hair, warm coffee-colored eyes. He was about five feet eight with a slender frame and broad shoulders.

"Turn to the person closest to you and face each other," Larry began. I waited, hoping the mystery man would turn towards me first. He did.

"Hi, I'm Chase."

"What a great name. I'm Julie."

"Julie," he said softly.

"Okay, everybody," Larry called. "We're going to do a heart-to-heart meditation. Take your right hand and place it on your partner's chest. Then put your left hand in your partner's left hand, thus completing the circuit."

"Sounds like Twister," Chase whispered.

This touchy-feely exercise was daunting. Chase offered me his left hand. I tried to look natural as he hesitantly put his right hand on my chest. I wanted to follow suit, but reaching his heart meant standing in a *Heil Hitler* pose. He knelt down in front of me. "Maybe this would make it easier." Now we were eye to eye.

"Thanks," I said. *Prince Charming?* I looked at Larry, hoping that Chase couldn't feel how rapidly my heart was throbbing.

We did a visualization of light coming from our heart chakra and into our partner's. Despite my distraction, the exercise felt great. It was either the exercise, or I was floating on air holding Chase's hand. I felt positively magnetized. When we opened our eyes, he stared at me. It was similar to the shocked looks I got from kids all the time, but his wasn't unkind.

"That felt fantastic," he said.

"Yeah, that was good." I couldn't say how it really felt. Not in polite company.

"You may be little but your spirit is awesome!"

Awesome? He suddenly sounded young, but I was flattered just the same. In our closing circle we all joined hands, and after the final prayer, Chase turned to me but kept my hand in his.

"Why haven't I seen you in class before? Do you live around here?"

"I live in Lakeside." Were these pickup lines? No one had ever thrown one in my direction, so I wasn't sure I'd recognize it. "I know Larry from the massage school."

"Me too! I'm in massage school now."

"I've had a few massages there, but it's expensive."

"Would you like a free one?" he asked. "Fully clothed, of course. We're not allowed to do Swedish massage until we've learned Shiatsu. I'm required to give three Shiatsu massages a week, so you'd be doing me a favor."

I was flabbergasted. I was also intrigued. *Is this possible? Is he interested in me?*

"Seriously? I'd love a massage."

He pulled out his appointment book and asked when I was free.

"I'm self-employed so my schedule's flexible."

"What do you do?"

"I'm an artist."

"Cool! I've never met an artist before." He was sounding young again. "How about this Thursday? I can come to your house, if that's okay."

Thursday was my regular lunch date with Casely. "How about Friday?" I suggested.

"Oh, that's my birthday. My parents will want me around."

"Happy birthday." I hoped he didn't still live at home. "How old will you be?"

"Nineteen."

I tried to cover my surprise.

"Too young?" he said timidly.

"You just seem older. I wasn't into anything like meditation when I was nineteen."

"When was that?"

"Seven years ago."

"That's not so long. So how about tomorrow?"

"Tomorrow?" I was happy that he was making it sooner. "That sounds good. Four o'clock?"

"It's a date," he said.

Oh, the words I'd longed to hear.

"What's your phone number, Julie, in case I need to call?"

he said with a wink. I felt like an overheating radiator. He didn't seem put off by my differences at all. *Amazing.*

When he hugged me at the end of the meeting, silent giggles ducked under my ribcage. I was off and flying into a fabulous new dream. A new me. No one had ever been so forward. He liked me. Someone finally liked me out loud!

I cleaned my room until two in the morning. Chase would have to set up his massage table there so that we could avoid Tracy's watchful eye. I'd tell her he was a friend. She'd think I was crazy to invite him over for a massage, no less. Was I nuts? Desperately nuts. I barely slept that night; adrenaline pulsed through me in wild orange waves. In the morning, I waltzed on air. My face was calm and hadn't gone into its ugly spasm since I'd met Chase. Everything was perfect.

When he pulled into the driveway, I ran to the door, heart in my hands.

"Hi, cutie." He leaned over for a hug. I wanted to jump him right there.

Hastily, I introduced him to my friends and then motioned him upstairs. Tracy immediately realized I was excluding her.

"After you," I said to him, as I stood at the bottom of the stairs. I didn't want him to see me climbing up one leg at a time.

"No, no. Ladies first."

"I'm slow on stairs. I have arthritis in my hips and knees."

"I'm here to help," he said.

He had no idea.

He set up his table in my big attic room and I dragged my stool over to it, ready to get up. This was a monstrous test. I couldn't hide my body now, the very thing I was sure had kept men away. Maybe all the therapy was working after all.

"On my back or on my stomach?" I asked nonchalantly.

"On your stomach, if that's all right. Let me know if anything is uncomfortable, okay?" He started out gently, then moved on to greet each worried muscle.

"It feels wonderful," I said. "So, how did you get interested in metaphysics?"

"I've been practicing karate since I was ten. It was a natural extension of that, I guess."

"My brother Ethan loved his karate lessons. What belt are you?"

"Black belt."

"Wow. I used to watch *Kung Fu*. I had such a crush on David Carradine."

"Really? I'll have to show you some moves when we're done."

Endorphins shot out of me like a thousand fire flies.

"Karate was the one place where I felt accepted," he said. "I was good at it and the other kids respected that. My parents came over from Germany when I was eight. I didn't speak a word of English, so I was on my own a lot. I never fit in."

"Well, I know how that feels. I'm sorry . . . I'm still surprised to hear that normal people felt the way that I did — still do."

Chase stopped massaging. "Normal? There's no such thing. You may be short, and a little more curvy, but you're no less normal than the rest of us. I think inside of you . . . beats the heart of a giant." He started up his kneading again.

Curvy? He said that like it's a good thing. I can't believe he's not put off. What do I do now?

We were quiet for a while.

"Any boyfriends in the picture?" he suddenly asked.

"Uh, no . . . um, just one back in college," I lied, but I imagined Josh. Maybe Chase wouldn't like me if he knew no one else had.

"Oh, college sweethearts. Want to flip over now?"

I turned, feeling even more exposed face up. I was relieved that he didn't ask anything more about Josh. I didn't want to make the lie bigger.

We fell silent again.

"Feeling limber and relaxed?" he asked.

"Absolutely. You have the hands of an angel."

"I guess I'm about done." He turned away from the table and my heart fell off the side. "Do you have to go?" I asked.

"No. I was just getting my water bottle." He put his hand back on mine and stared down at my face. I closed my eyes, pretending to be relaxed. *Can he tell I'm a nervous wreck?*

Suddenly, I felt his lips touch mine gently, and my eyes flew open in disbelief. His face was asking permission, so I reached up to touch his hair and he kissed me again, harder. Everything else disappeared. All I could feel was him: his breath, his tongue, his passion. The intoxication took over, changing me, lifting me. My whole body pulsated, washing away the boundaries. Time stopped. I'd never been closer to heaven on earth. The phone rang and we both jumped. We laughed and went back to each other. A minute later the door opened at the bottom of the stairs.

"Julie?" Tracy's voice was worried. "Phone for you."

"Can you take a message for me, please?"

"Okay. Uh, is everything all right?"

I knew what she was thinking. Date rape. The drama queen was ready to dash up here to save me from this ecstasy.

"We're fine, thanks." *Don't let the door hit you on the way out.*

"You've been up there a while, are you hungry?"

"No, thanks. See you later."

"She's a bit obnoxious," I whispered to Chase.

"No, just protective. A lot like my parents." He quickly looked at his watch. "Whoa, is it really nine o'clock? Man, I'd better go."

"Really?"

"Yeah, I have an hour ride back home. They get bent out of shape when I'm home late." He gathered his gear as I slid off the table, wondering what kind of mess my hair was in. I followed him down the stairs, past the wild, gaping looks of my friends, and out to his car. He put his table in the back and leaned over for a kiss.

"Where do you—where are we going with this . . . do you think?" He'd been so confident, but now he looked as young and inexperienced as I felt.

"I . . . I don't know."

"Me neither," he said with a smile. "Meet me in my dreams? We can take a midnight stroll along the ocean."

My knees started to faint. I was totally wowed.

"Let's find a cabana," he continued, "filled with big soft pillows and melt into each other . . . and stay forever." I threw my arms around him and hugged his waist tightly.

When he drove away, I stood tingling with fuel, feeling twenty-three feet tall. I closed my eyes and took a slow, deep breath. Everything was different. I'd just joined a club that had never before considered me fit. I'd never forget that day. Never.

The air was fresh and saucy. The trees stood proudly cheering for me, bullfrogs jumped for joy. Angels danced in delight. My wish had been granted. Years of waiting and wondering if I was lovable withdrew into the night. Chase's touch had freed me from my confines. The arthritic cage was falling away, a home of pleasure rising in its place. Could I find love behind its walls? For the first time, the answer to my lifelong question was yes.

I stopped myself from calling Chase for two days, trying not to appear needy. In the two months since I'd met him, his interest had waned. We hadn't spent much time together recently. But then I couldn't control myself. I dialed his number.

"Hello?" he answered.

His voice tweaked my smile. He was still out there somewhere. "Hi!" I peeped.

"Hey. I was just thinking I should call you."

"Did you get my message yesterday?" I whined.

"Yes, I've been really busy . . . so how are you, cutie?"

"I'm fine. I just wish—I wish I could see you more."

"We've got meditation on Tuesday. I'll see you then."

That was four days away. I wanted to hold him every day and he didn't feel the same. Was it something I did? Or didn't do?

I went to class early that week, hoping we'd have extra time together. The opening prayer began but Chase hadn't arrived. I eyed the door like a crystal ball, ignoring all else. Finally . . . there he was. Ah. So adorable. The answer to a lifelong prayer. I waved to him, the boy who'd brought the winds of change to my door. The one who—hey, where was he going? I was sure he'd seen me. He sat down next to another woman, smiled at her the way he'd smiled at me. My shoulders caved into my chest. I didn't want it to end. So he wasn't the one—*but please, God, please let me hang onto the magic a little longer.* I sat for the two-hour class in a state of dread. *Please God,* I repeated, as if my begging had magical power.

"Hi!" I said when I found him after class.

"Hey." He got down on his knees and squeezed me tight. I closed my eyes and swallowed the sweet drug. *Please don't let it be over. Please.*

"Do you want to go up Mandarin Mountain on Saturday?" I asked. The mountain didn't actually have a name, but at sunset the hills glowed orange. "We can meditate and watch the eagles again."

"I've got class from twelve to three."

"How about after that?"

"My father wants me to clean the garage this weekend."

"Between classes, work, and your parents, I never get to see you."

"Well, my dad's getting older. Plus, they don't particularly like that I have a girlfriend."

"Girlfriend?" Did he just call me his "girlfriend?" It sounded so foreign but so very nice. I'd never been claimed before. Suddenly, I didn't care what the mystics said about being whole unto myself. To hell with women's lib. I wanted to be someone's

girlfriend. Just when I thought Chase was pulling away, he said something so lovely. His girlfriend. His.

We drove up to my favorite spot on the mountain in time for a spectacular sunset. The sun's brilliance strode across the valley and soared on the eagles' wings. It dove deep into the lake and ducked behind the clouds. The boundlessness held us high on the slope of ourselves, as we greeted the familiar light.

When Chase turned to open his backpack, I scrambled to sit down, not wanting him to see my stiff bending. Normally I couldn't sit on the ground because my hips and knees wouldn't bend at a right angle. But here on the slope, I was able to sit in the grass, legs straight in front of me, feeling almost normal doing what regular people did without a thought. Chase and I sat holding hands and closed our eyes. There, in Nature's daily celebration, I felt connected, alive, and at home. Everything I thought I'd ever wanted, I had that day up on Mandarin Mountain.

Suddenly, Chase got up and grabbed some paper from his backpack.

"What are you doing?" I asked.

"I want to write a poem for you."

"Really? Great!"

I heard him scribbling for awhile as I tried not to watch. Then he turned towards me, looking insecure. He cleared his throat and started to read.

The sky's so deep and wide in your eyes,
Bluer than I deserve
A place so sweet I dare not look
anywhere else on earth.
Can I have the eagle's wings
to soar farther than the view?
If only I could earn, upon my return,
a spirit as grand as you.

I gave a confused smile. "Wow...thank you."

"You don't like it."

"No, I do. It's just that I'm surprised. You don't act like I'm .
.. that important."

"There's so much I want to do and accomplish," he said,
looking towards the valley. "I want to make a difference! I want
to experience everything, but I don't know how to fit it all in."

Whenever he went into this "I" monologue about changing
the world, I'd start feeling like toilet paper on his shoe. Why
didn't he want me along on his grand adventure?

I'd hesitantly told Judi that I was *dating* someone, but acted
like it was no big deal. She didn't buy it for a second, but I was
too uncomfortable to say more. Living it was such a rush.
Talking about it was beyond my scope.

I didn't hear from Chase that next week but managed to
refrain from calling. I wasn't going to ask for his time. Then I
saw him at class and my resolve turned to mush. "Are you ever
going to show me *your* meditation spot?" I asked.

"You mean the park? Well, I only work until three on
Friday. How about then?"

"Sure!"

The park was warm and gentle as Chase and I walked
hand-in-hand around the lake. As we talked about metaphysics,
I pushed away the sadness over having a lot in common and yet
not much of a bond—on his end anyway. I was lost in him just
the same. We headed back to the parking lot as it got dark.

"Want to get in the car and fool around?" he asked in a fake
sexy voice. I scurried like a chipmunk into the back seat of my
old wagon.

"I'll take that as a yes," he said.

I pulled him down on top of me as we laughed and
wrestled. We hadn't slept together yet and I had no intention of
that now. Hmm. Maybe that was a problem for him.

We peeled off clothing, touching and kissing. I'd never
thought someone would want to hold me this way, skin-to-skin,

with so much passion. Suddenly, the interior of the car brightened. A hard rap on the window had us scrambling for our clothes. The front door opened. A piercing light blinded us as the cold air slapped our skin.

A deep voice barged into the night. "What are you doing in there?" As if it weren't obvious. We tried to shield our eyes and bodies.

"It's illegal to be in the park after dark." His flashlight nabbed my face. "How old are you?" I'd heard that question from a thousand puzzled or obnoxious children, but never from a police officer. "I'm twenty-six," I said. I wondered if he'd believe me.

"Are you here of your own accord, Miss?"

"Yes, I am."

"You, Romeo, how old are you?" The light zeroed in on Chase.

"Nineteen," Chase mumbled.

"Get your things and step out of the car." He slammed the door. We pulled on our clothes at lightning speed. The two cops took us to separate cars for questioning. I stared at the filthy floor of the police car in utter humiliation. No one was ever going to believe this. Freed, we slunk back to my car. I looked at the ticket in my hand and the one in Chase's.

"It says 'After hours in Kingston Park and indecent exposure'!" We giggled nervously.

"You flew so fast over the front seat!" I said.

"You jumped a foot when that jerk opened the door!"

The energy fizzled as we drove to Chase's house. In the quiet, I noticed that my car had a strange new rattle. I'd just had it in the shop for new brakes and now, as always, I had to bring it back. I'd inherited my car-karma from my parents and I needed a better mechanic.

I pulled into Chase's driveway and he gave me a quick kiss.

"Good night, you outlaw, you." I expected a smile.

He nodded soberly as if the title fit. The following day I was surprised when Chase called.

"Hi! How did you sleep?" I asked.

"Not too good. How about you?"

"I kept going over what happened. I've never gotten in trouble in my life."

"Me neither."

We talked a little more, then an awkward silence took over. Chase spoke up. "I think it's a sign."

I'd worried over the same thing. "Could be, I guess."

"I don't think we want the same things. I don't want anyone waiting for me to call. I just want adventure and I want to spread the light. I want to fly!"

I wanted to barf. He wanted out.

He prattled on, describing the amazing things he was after. All except me. "When I look into the future, I see an exciting life out there for me," he said. "But I . . . well, I don't see you there."

My body winced and burned. Uncontrolled static pinched my throat. I took a deep breath, trying to calm my senses. "I really don't know what to say—so that's it, then?" I wanted to beg and plead. I felt needy and scared. Too defective. Too different. Too much.

"We'll see each other at class, right?" Chase asked.

"Right," I lied, knowing I couldn't handle that.

As I hung up the phone, lightning ripped through every limb. I saw this coming, but I still wasn't prepared. I crawled under the covers. He'd awakened me from a lonely nightmare that was towering back over me again. I cried and cried, trying to relieve the frantic feelings. I clawed at my tears. I screeched at God. I've been alone so long! *Please don't leave me alone again!* I sobbed even harder, knowing it was already done.

I woke to canary sunshine, a hopeful sky, and an old love song on the radio. I swung my stiff legs over the side of the bed and stared out the window. In the two weeks since Chase had ended it, the "poor me, I'm alone" story had rallied in full force, a self-fulfilling prophecy that I wanted to finally squash. I dressed and put on my favorite earrings from my sister, Celia. I hadn't bothered with any jewelry lately; it would've felt like sprinkling glitter on a pile of dung.

I missed having a part-time boyfriend, even if Chase hadn't been much of one. *Does he miss me a little?* I sent out a girlish prayer that he'd come back, not realizing how that wish would ultimately be granted. *Chase didn't leave because I'm different,* I told myself. *He's young and wants to be free. He wasn't meant to stay. But I'll always be glad for my teenage romance, ten years late.*

I sang along to the radio, trying to imagine someone in love with me. Someone to share the beautiful day, hold my hand, touch my soul. The longing to be accepted was as deep as anything I'd ever known. In spite of all I was learning, I still wondered, *Am I way too strange looking? Too damaged?*

An image of Josh brought waves of regret. Did he ever think of me? I grabbed my address book, intending to call Hamilton College for his number, when an envelope slipped out. "Return to Sender" was stamped across Megan McWilliams's name and address. I'd put this off too long. Maybe what I really needed was a friend. Megan's parents still had a house in town, and their old number was stamped on my brain. I took a deep breath and dialed.

"Hi, this is Julie Hobbes and I . . ."

"Julie? Incredible. Megan was *just* talking about you. This is Megan's sister, Lisa, how are you?"

"Well, hi. I'm good. And you?"

"Fine thanks, let me go get her. She'll be so surprised. Nice talking to you."

Megan's there? Good God, what am I going to say?

"Julie?"

"Megan! Wow, I would've known your voice anywhere!" It was a joy to hear her again.

"I'd have known yours anywhere too. I'm so glad you called."

"I'd no idea you were there. I was actually calling for your address."

"Did your sister Kris tell you that I ran into her at the reunion?" she asked.

"Yeah, but it took me awhile to work up the nerve to contact you."

To my surprise, Megan said she'd wanted to get in touch but doubted I'd want anything to do with her. I was stunned. The popular Megan McWilliams cared about me? "What are you doing in town?"

"The whole family's here because, um, well, my dad has lung cancer. They say it's terminal."

I felt my heart sink. "Oh, no! I'm so sorry. I always liked him so much."

"Both my parents really liked you too. You were an angel compared to the crowd I ended up with. Are you in town? Can you come over?"

"Oh, I don't want to intrude on your family. I don't—"

"Dad'll be so happy to see you. It would cheer him up. Please come over."

"Are you sure this is a good time? I can't—"

"Just come over."

Twenty minutes later, I was driving down Megan's street. As I pulled slowly into her driveway, the old days began soaking in like warm rain. Megan was still a part of me, someone I'd left behind but never lost. I counted back fifteen years since that fateful day with the cigarette, and I smiled, remembering my naïve horror.

I slid out of my car, into my childhood, following the old familiar path to Megan's back door. We had never been allowed to use the front door because of the white carpet. I pushed open the back gate and listened to its intimate creak. The smooth walkway beneath my feet spoke of summer days when Megan and I would slosh from the pool to the house, eyeing our wet footprints as they evaporated like magic from the warm slate. I looked out over the pool where we had steeped like tea bags under the sun. This was the beautiful yard that had been my playground for learning and laughing and, eventually, leaving.

I rang the doorbell. How many times had I stood here as a girl? The door opened, and there she was, exactly as I remembered her: a beauty without having to try. No fancy hairstyle, no make-up, just Megan. Straight brown hair, big brown eyes, five feet tall. A quartz crystal hung around her neck, the only sign of the changes she'd been through. We got along instantly, as though not a day had passed. We talked and talked and discovered that although we'd gone separate ways, we'd stayed on parallel paths: metaphysics, meditation, health food, the lot. Megan was now single with two daughters and searching for her Mr. Right. A year earlier, she'd found a healing path through a Twelve Step Program. She was open and honest about her spiritual journey, which inspired me to risk being the same about mine. A kindred spirit had reappeared, escorting me back to a childhood joy and wholeness. The bond we'd shared made sense now. Our friendship fit into a larger circle, which had found its end, and its beginning, again.

With Megan by my side, I felt reassured that the path ahead would only get easier. Together, we talked and laughed and, with great intensity, we jumped headfirst into the confusion of our past. Megan said that from sixth grade on, she'd felt torn between popular friends and old friends. Sometimes she'd yearned for the innocence she left behind. What really shocked me was that her self-esteem had been as pitiful as mine. We slapped our hearts out on the table and dissected every belief, every circumstance, every time we'd been wracked by pain. We longed for the answers so we could live our dreams. We figured that by dissecting our fears, and keeping our eyes fixed on our life's problems, we could find inner peace. It didn't quite work out that way. While we wanted magic and revelation, our ears were tuned to the discord from our past. The longer we looked at the chaos, the harder it became to see anything else.

Back in Boston, the reintroduction to my spirit had been exhilarating. I'd thought I was finally hearing my soul calling me back home. I believed I had found myself. I was saved. I was free. I was on easy street. I was so mistaken.

There was still a long road ahead. As I journeyed further inside myself, I realized that the real work had only begun. Changing my habits and beliefs and putting my ideals into practice would be harder than I'd imagined. Awareness and truth versus illusions and lies. They duked it out on a daily basis. Actually, I believe my fears were battling themselves. Truth was quietly waiting for me to allow it.

By now, the facial twitch was haunting me every minute of every day. I assumed that it was my fault, that I was wearing all the years of hidden anxiety on my face. Every ten minutes the spasms would revisit the left side of my head, neck, and face, leaving me in an uncontrolled panic. I had to do something. I felt insane enough to give in and see a white-coat.

The neurologist took one look and said blandly, "Hemifacial nerve spasm. You have HFS." He explained that my seventh cranial nerve was being compressed by a blood vessel in my brain near the base of my skull. When he said there was no cure, his voice was devoid of sympathy. Perhaps he'd taken one too many of the muscle relaxers he prescribed for me. He didn't believe the medicine would help, but he had nothing else to offer.

I rarely took medicine and felt ashamed at occasionally swallowing an ibuprofen. I snatched the new drug. Maybe it would destroy my kidneys or liver but, hey, it was better than destroying my hope. The muscle relaxer made me sleepy and as dull as the doctor. The twitching, however, remained lively as a polka band. When my face wasn't in spasm, I dreaded the moments when the spasms would return. I was frantic, enraged, hopeless. Determined to hide and deny the problem, I tried to place myself on everyone's left side so that only the right side of my face could be seen, or I pretended something was in my eye and covered it with my hand. Finally, I started dodging people altogether.

The avoidance tactics left me feeling like a fraud who couldn't face up to the sad truth. I was a confirmed out-of-control freak. I figured I hadn't passed the original lessons in accepting my differences, so God had enrolled me in perpetual summer school. Public Humiliation 101. Get the teachings straight or die trying. As I continued to focus all my attention on my list of problems, like a carnival mirror, the reflection became ever more unstable and distorted. My prince hadn't come calling, my face twitched, and my joints hurt. I blamed everything and everyone. Couldn't someone do *something*? God clearly hated me. What else could explain it? That belief was less threatening than my taking responsibility, which felt too much like taking the blame.

Part of me wanted the Coans, who were a second family to me, to fix everything. When I realized that I had to do it myself, my inner child threw a serious tantrum. *I can't do it alone! Someone else has to help me – someone taller, with limber joints, better looks, money, confidence, and everything else I don't have.* Subconsciously, I placed my impossible assignment on Tracy.

At first, Tracy and I had enjoyed taking care of each other. We shared everything from the mundane to the magical. One minute we were grocery shopping and the next trying to unravel the mysteries of the universe. Like any good codependency, it bonded us like super glue. When Tracy felt insecure, her nurturing became possessiveness. When I felt unstable, I became her judgmental psychologist. Or I'd play the needy child, and she'd be the controlling parent. We switched roles so often we hardly knew who we were.

Long before Tracy moved to Lakeside in seventh grade, my insecurities were already falling all over themselves. One afternoon, Tracy decided to give me a fashion show of her new clothes, a sore subject for me. "So, how do they look?" she asked as she strutted by.

"A bit tight. I can't believe you spent your baby-sitting money on clothes," I said. I pretended to be above such matters, hoping to spoil her cheer.

"New clothes are so much fun," Tracy chirped. "Aren't you getting tired of those old jeans and sneakers?"

I pressed my lips together. *It's hard finding clothes that fit me. Jerk.* "I gotta go."

"Aren't we going to ride bikes? You promised!"

I sighed. "I don't want to ride anymore."

She followed me out the door and jumped on her bike. "Come on," she said, knowing her determination would overcome my will.

"Oh, okay." Without looking at her, I soberly grabbed my blue banana-seat bike. As we rode, my anger wafted away in the breeze, until Tracy broke the silence. "Hey, Jules, let's wear dresses tomorrow! It'll be fun!"

"Fun as the dentist," I yelled as I pedaled away. I hated Tracy for not understanding, though I never gave her the chance. I wouldn't talk openly about my concerns, wanting my friends to think I was confident and that my differences were no big deal. Maybe in return they would be able to convince me.

"How about that raspberry-colored jumper?" Tracy called.

"No, I said!"

"And your blue Bass shoes." She knew my wardrobe better than I did.

I slammed on my brakes. "Give it up, Tracy."

I tried to picture myself wearing that jumper. My curved spine made any dress hike up in the back and dip down in front. Even with Mom's patient alterations, my reflection was a terrible disappointment. No amount of pretty material could make me look like the other kids.

We rode past the school and around the large parking lots. It felt so good to be free in the place where we were usually not.

"Remember how I gave you my last Twinkie the other day?"

"That's bribery!" I yelled as we sped down a hill.

"I'll carry your books home from school tomorrow."

I pedaled faster. Tracy was quiet for awhile, obviously plotting. "I'll give you all my Fritos at lunch," she called.

As we neared my house, I decided to stop. "My legs are sore, Trace. I'm gonna go in, okay?"

She gave me her sad-eyed look, hoping I would cave. If she hung on long enough, history was on her side, and she knew it.

I lumbered up our front stairs, my legs burning from the exercise. "It's not going to work this time, Tracy. Bye."

"Bye. See if I ever do you any favors."

I closed the front door. I knew it wasn't over.

That night, the phone rang. "Hi!" Tracy said enthusiastically. "How ya' doin'?"

"Fine."

"Did you do your homework yet?"

"No, I'm starting now."

"Wanna come over and study?"

"Right. We'll do everything *but* study."

"Oh, man, Jules, you're no fun at all. Then the very least you could do is wear a dress with me."

"You'll never give up. You never do. Fine. I will wear a stupid dress. Happy?" Even over the phone, I could feel her satisfied smile.

I didn't want to wear the dumb jumper, but it did feel good to make Tracy happy. She returned the favor in many ways. She was my devoted watchdog whenever anyone laughed at me. She would place herself right in front of the kids (or adults), glaring at them with her hot Irish eyes until they moved away. We never spoke about it, but I was very thankful for her shield.

The following morning, I did my best with the jumper, and I took time to brush my long hair into a barrette. I clomped downstairs in my blue Bass shoes, ignored Mom's happy gushing, and sailed out the door. My family rarely fussed over clothes, so I was sorely unrehearsed when it came to fashion. I pretended not to care about girlie things, and when I secretly experimented in Mom's barely-touched make-up drawer, I felt ashamed of enjoying the primping that my family saw as shallow.

Running late that morning, due to my extra efforts, I quickened my pace to Tracy's house. With my scratchy tights and a barrette that was pinching my head, I felt wrong all over the place.

When the door opened at Tracy's, there was my devoted pal, my fabulous friend, standing before me in jeans and a blouse.

"Well?" I finally sputtered. "No dress?" As I stormed down the driveway, she tried to explain, saying, "The skirt just didn't feel right this morning."

I ignored my achy knees and speed-walked to school in livid silence.

Between classes, when I saw my traitor friend, I put on my meanest scowl and refused to respond to her hellos. She looked unnerved, and I was glad. Every argument was a chance to turn the tables and regain the control that I thought Tracy held.

Here we were, fifteen years later, and Tracy and I were still in a power struggle. As I regularly confided to her my inner strife, she got to know me better and better. But she always seemed guarded about herself, which over time left me feeling paranoid and hostile. Tracy and I were so alike in ways I hated to admit. Like our habit of finger-pointing. We liked to bark about what others were doing wrong so that no one would notice our own deficiencies. We acted like alpha dogs even though we felt like pups. And we loved sarcasm. Tracy was quick on her feet, with a clever wit and hilarious style, and with my insecurities now out in the open, I wondered if I was making myself a good target. My armadillo façade was now no match for her quick-wittedness. I also knew that the sooner I curbed my own tendency to judge others, the sooner I would feel released from others' judgments. My defensive sarcasm had never eased my pain, it had only served to separate me from my feelings and from others. What I really wanted was to join the game of life, not to stand on the sidelines and judge.

With my old habit of finger-pointing and her sarcasm, our disputes usually ended in a stalemate, and we'd quickly retreat in mutual disgust. Then I'd launch my oldest standby attack; silence with a twist of rage. It felt like power one minute and then utter powerlessness the next. It managed to land both of us feeling worse off than before. Now and again, Tracy would try to lighten the mood or greet me with a smile, but I stubbornly stuck to my gloomy guns. The more I realized that I had let my happiness become dependent on Tracy, the more I hated myself for that dependence. The harder Tracy tried to fix what she had never broken, the more I hated that weakness. The painful catch-22 seemed impossible to break, and resentments started cropping up like ants at a picnic.

"Where are you going?" Tracy asked, as I tried to slip out our back door.

"Out," I said with a steely echo.

"Out where?" She looked hurt.

"The post office, nosy."

"Oh can you get me some stamps? Let me run and get cash." She darted past, pregnant belly leading.

"Tracy! I'm in a hurry." I heard the phone ring, and knew she'd answer it. I felt the heat jabbing in my chest.

"Here." She was breathless.

I grabbed the cash and stormed out. *What am I doing making her rush when the baby is due soon? Why is it that the harder I try to put space between us, the harder she tries to reel me in?*

Months passed and life with the Coans continued to dissolve. There was a momentary ray of light when their adorable baby boy, Zachary, was born. It wasn't long, though, before we retreated into our previous patterns. As often as possible, I made myself scare by running away to Megan's. My life became polarized between her home and the Coans. I was desperate for freedom yet didn't want to grow up. The Coans and I had become a family, and I was acting like the hostile teenager determined, but terrified, to fly the coop.

One of my seemingly incessant facial spasms had just subsided, when I ran into Lin Morel, the wonderful counselor of a monthly support group I'd been attending. I knew I had five minutes to talk before the HFS returned. Lin asked about my crutches, which I was now using most days. I told her about the increasing pain in my hips and knees, and the decreased mobility. But when I felt the pressure building behind my eye, the shame was too much. Despite my loneliness for company, I didn't have the courage to talk to Lin about the spasms, or my fears. My voice was lost somewhere in childhood. I waved good-bye, nervously putting my hand up to cover the left side of my face.

"Julie, wait!" she called after me. "I've got some moolah for you!" I hated to turn back towards her with the spasms in full swing. I lowered my head as Lin pulled out two pads of phony money. She ripped off three thousand-dollar bills and then four hundred-dollar bills. "$3,400 ought to help with the rent. Make sure to put those up where you can see them and affirm your prosperity every day!" I didn't turn around again as I heard her say good-bye.

In my car, I rested my forehead on the wheel and felt a vicious, penetrating scream. *I feel so fucking helpless! It's bad enough that I'm different, but now I can't even smile and look people in the eyes and show them that I'm okay! How can I face people looking like a nervous wreck? No one wants an insecure mess!*

On the way home, I thought about Lin's New Year's Eve party the year before. Our group had sat in a circle, sharing our triumphs and tribulations. I desperately wanted my face to be composed when it was my turn to speak. Sometimes, if I closed my left eye tight for five minutes, forcing it to spasm, the nerve would be calm for another five minutes. I hadn't timed it right that night and the twitching started before I was through speaking. I went into an instant sweat, terrified that everyone saw the ugliness inside me.

Later that night, we were asked to list the issues we wanted to release in the New Year. I could barely keep up with all the drama I'd created, let alone write it down. The HFS, though, was number one on my list, but since I couldn't admit that I had the problem, I certainly didn't want it on paper. Instead I wrote, "I release anger, fear, and judgment. I choose joy."

Next, we wrote a wish list. One woman said she needed a vacation but had no money. Lin suggested that she could win a vacation. So I decided to write: "A free trip to Hawaii." My top priority, of course, had been finding Mr. Right. This also was scary to commit to paper. What if someone read it and scoffed? So I wrote in a scrawl that no one could decipher. After that night, I stashed the affirmations in my wallet, hoping that maybe my dreams would magically materialize when I wasn't looking.

Sitting in the car, I pulled out the crumpled piece of paper to see if I'd made any progress in a year. I scanned my faded writing. *Nothing. Not one stupid thing!* I stuffed it back into its hiding place, as tears won me over again. When I got home, I stomped upstairs and disgustedly threw the phony bills from Lin on my desk. Then I taped them up on my wall, just in case.

Megan had recently fallen in love with an old high school classmate, leaving me even more worried about my own happy ending. On the one hand, I hoped that she'd be really happy this time, and that maybe it was an omen for me. But then I'd panic and want her to be alone again. I begrudged her happiness when I didn't believe in my own. I needed my Wiffle bat. Lin had suggested that I use it to pound on the bed when I felt crazed. I'd thought she was nuts at first, but then, when no one was home, I tried it. It helped—a lot. I always ended up in tears, which showed me the truth that my anger was just a front for hurt and fear.

What if this spiritual stuff is all nonsense? Am I a complete asshole to think I can make more of my life? The HFS, the arthritis, and my ridiculous body are holding me back from everything and everyone. Please, God, are you out there? How long do you think I can hold on? Will life ever go my way?

My bellyaching would have ceased instantly if I'd known what was right around the corner.

Fourteen years earlier, I'd been petrified to leave for college. The only way I'd been able to tear myself from my parents was to find a way to hate them. I whittled down all my anger so that by the time my departure had arrived, I had enough fiery momentum to separate from their warm, safe refuge. Now it was happening again. I felt like a hostage in the Coans' house, wanting to break away, yet terrified to do so. I'd been giving Tracy the cold shoulder for months, trying to sever our confusing ties. Tracy tried to ignore the rift. She wanted to hold on. So did I.

One afternoon, I limped downstairs to grab some lunch and found Tracy cooking in the kitchen.

Casely lit up. "Wanna grilled cheese samich wif me?"

She was impossible to resist. "I'd love that, Caze." Zack was in his high chair. "Hey, Zackie." I said nothing to Tracy.

"Bacon with that sandwich, Missy?" Tracy joked.

"No. I'll make my own."

"No bacon? What are you, one of them tofu-granoli types?"

I just gave her the evil eye. *I would've moved out ages ago if I didn't love these kids so much.* That's what I told myself anyway.

"I think you won some pineapples," Tracy said. She tossed an envelope across the table.

"Caze, it's from the Dole Company in Hawaii," I said. "The water fountains in the Dole factory were filled with pineapple juice when I visited. Isn't that cool?" Her happy grin leapt up and down in my heart.

When I opened the envelope, there was a check on top for $3,120.45. Typical sales ploy. The second check was for $282.35. *Strange amounts.* I scanned the letter for a disclaimer. It said something about stock shares purchased in my name, recently liquidated due to a merger. Stocks? I don't have any. I reread the letter. The checks looked legitimate.

"Trace, I think I just got $3,400 in the mail!"

I stared at the checks. I'd never had a hunk of money handed to me. Except for Lin's phony money. Hey, wait. She'd given me the same amount, minus the pennies. Amazing.

"I'm calling my dad."

My dad told me that he had been contacted by Dole some months back. My grandma, before she died ten years earlier, had purchased shares for each of the grandchildren, buying the most for Ethan and me because of our physical challenges. $3,400 wouldn't go far with doctors these days, but I had no intention of spending it that way. Strangely enough, ultimately, it would lead to a step in that scary direction.

When I hung up, I said a prayer for my wise grandma. She'd always had a generous spirit, and now she had terrific timing. *Is she watching me from the other side?* Maybe I was loved. Maybe I was okay in God's eyes after all. Before the day was over, I knew I was headed to Hawaii. Kris and her husband Greg, who was a lawyer with the Army J.A.G. corps, had been transferred to Oahu. I'd use my Dole funds to visit the home my Hawaiian grandma had adored.

Weeks passed, and my vacation plan was now looking like a permanent move. A clean slate. Hawaii had always been a dream for me. My dad was born and raised on Oahu and had family going back to the missionaries who had settled there. We all thought his Hawaiian roots were wild and colorful after hearing tales of how he had gone to school barefoot, or how he had seen lizards every day, or how he picked his own avocados and mangoes and smelled flowers all year long. Or how he could walk across the hot driveway without flinching, or that if he stood in the sunshine for more than three seconds, he turned bronze. Strangest of all, when my dad was eleven, he and his older brother had stopped to watch missile practice in the harbor below. But it turned out that it was no drill. They unknowingly witnessed the bombing of Pearl Harbor.

Hawaii suddenly held every hope. *Maybe the love of my life is waiting in the tropics! I can always come back to New Jersey if things don't work out. But what could possibly go wrong in paradise?* I piled up magazines, collected calendars, and devoured books on Hawaii. Tropical themes ran through my paintbrush and dripped from my walls. I memorized reruns of *Magnum, P.I.* and *Hawaii 5-0.* I knew I was on the right track. I just had to be.

My future in Hawaii helped ease the pain that had shanghaied my home. I'd initiated a silence between Tracy and me that had turned into an unbearable tension. I could barely wait to wash myself clean. Or so I thought. When moving day came, Mark hauled my guilty boxes downstairs and we silently packed up the car. My heart was feeling such anguish that I could barely remember all the fun we'd once known. I nervously put the last of my things in the front seat. Tracy and I had nothing left to distract us. We didn't know how to say good-bye.

"I guess that's everything," I said, staring at the bloated car.

"Will you call when you get to your parents'?" Tracy asked. She always worried I'd end up as road pizza.

Mark came out of the house with Casely and Zack, their sweet faces reducing me to mush. *Zack will probably forget me. And Casely, innocent in this ugly mess. Will she forget me too?* Tracy probably wouldn't allow me much contact with her. It would be my punishment for this one-sided "divorce." It had been my choice to leave, after all. I reached up to Tracy for a hug, not sure if I had the right. She squeezed me tight, then released me quickly. We wanted to hold on yet needed to let go. I slipped into my car like a criminal, backing out of the pine-scented driveway, trying to see the road through my tears. I wanted to dash back inside, into safety, beg their forgiveness. But it was time to be out on my own. I stole one last glance at the place we had shared, the big stucco home heavy with regret. As I drove away, I opened my mouth and screamed.

Ten
Paradise Found

Live close to the earth
and clear down in your heart.
~Lao Tsu

As I drove the five hours to my parents' house, I cried on and off, sang as loud as my ears could stand, rustled through my pile of snacks—anything to numb the pain. *What the hell am I doing?*

Once in Pennsylvania, though, my enthusiasm for the adventure ahead began to return. I could barely wait to reach Oahu where my troubles would be solved. But when the plane was at last flying me and my new luggage over the Pacific, of course I was dragging the old baggage along as well.

My sister and her three terrific kids gave me a heroine's welcome. My Uncle Ben and Aunt M.M. came to the airport with flashing cameras and flower leis. The fragrance startled sweet-smelling memories. The last time my family had vacationed here, my dad's birthplace, I'd been six. Hawaii felt like a forgotten hearth. This was where I belonged.

I stayed with Kris for six weeks until I settled into a tiny apartment in Makaha, on the dry, less-affluent side of the island. It was forty-five minutes from my sister, but the price and the turquoise pool in the complex finally sold me. Great exercise awaited my aching joints.

During the first night in the new place, every sound made me jump and worry and sweat. The second night was equally as bad. I wanted to run back to Kris's, dive under a quilt and sew myself in. How could I have forgotten how badly I dealt with change? It took so long for me to settle into a new place, but so little to set me back.

The third morning, I sat at my tiny kitchen table trying to plan, to control the day. I'd never lived totally alone before and now I knew why. Paranoia was creeping in. Did the whole building know there was a terrified freak, a perfect target, in apartment 404? I had to find the grocery store but I couldn't use my crutches while shopping, so the trip would be exhausting. My apartment was up three flights of stairs. Carrying my own weight was painful, and with a few groceries it would be that much worse. Who would I turn to if I got into trouble? What if someone made fun of me along the way? My non-aluminum deodorant was helpless against my concerns.

As I made my grocery list, I realized how much Kris and I had eased off the macrobiotics. There were so many conflicting philosophies around diet that it was difficult to find any food that wasn't hotly debated as good by one group and bad by another. The more I'd read about the power of our thoughts and feelings, the more I realized that they were vital food as well. Swallowing feelings of deprivation and inflexibility around macrobiotics was incompatible with my quest for balance and wholeness. There wasn't just one way to health.

No matter where I went, health food stores all seemed the same, I thought. I expected to find like-minded people, feel at ease. Until the incident in Philadelphia, where I'd lived briefly after college. I'd been standing in the aisle of a peaceful health food store, when a man sidled up next to me. Suddenly his voice blasted out at me, loud and pointed. "Are you a *m-midget?* Wow, I've never seen a *midget!* Are you in a circus?" My fists clenched, my throat collapsed. "Look over here!" he called towards the front as I'd slipped away, through the organic produce, over to the vitamins, shaking with terror. No control. No power. No practice in talking about my dwarfism. No words for what I barely understood myself. Without the confidence to speak up, I just wanted to escape. It was no wonder my legs were worn out. It was totally exhausting trying to outrun myself.

As I pulled up to Celestial Natural Foods in Hawaii, I took a deep breath. Along with my dwarfism, the twitching was now in my "unspeakable" category. If someone noticed my oddities, what could I say? What could I do? It made being out in the world a lot of hard work. I sat in the car to let my face do its customary ten minutes of twitching so that the nerve would be exhausted as I walked inside. After getting my groceries and hiding in the aisle while my twitch subsided again, I went up to the counter. As the cashier rang up my groceries, I asked if she knew of any metaphysical groups. She told me that the owner, Susie, would be in tomorrow and she might know. My face was in spasm again, so I scooped up my bags and hurried out. What I really wanted to do was stand in the middle of the store and ask if anyone would be my friend. Instead, I limped back to my lonely apartment.

Although Kris was busy with her family, she was always ready to help. In fact, she'd found a group of artists who hung their work on the outer fence surrounding the Honolulu Zoo, and I joined the organization. Once a week I lugged my artwork downtown, but the exposure was painful, the location even worse. I had to double-park, quickly chuck my gear out of the car, find a legal spot, park the car, and then walk back on crutches. Plus, so many artists vied for business that I barely made enough money to pay rent. Worse yet, I wasn't making friends there or anywhere else.

I spent nights and weekends alone, working on my art. I rarely took advantage of my apartment pool because I thought that sitting by myself would advertise my vulnerability. I tried not to burden Kris with my troubles—I knew she already felt responsible for me, but as often as possible I spent wonderful days with her and her kids. Jude, six; Adeline, four; and Anders, two, were as loving, smart, and kindhearted as their mom. I adored them, but knew I could only depend on them so much.

I thought about the Coans almost every day and held arguments with Tracy in my head. I'd nervously called a few times but had never reached her. I spoke to the answering machine several times, and to Mark, twice. I think he'd been assigned phone duty because Tracy didn't want to hear from me. She didn't respond to my letters or acknowledge my packages for the kids. I'd shunned her back in New Jersey, and she was now snubbing me in return. I deserved it, but it still hurt. I needed my Wiffle bat.

The next day I called the health food shop and Susie Allen, the owner, told me about her "Dream Group." Once a week a few friends got together and analyzed each other's dreams. I gave it a try and it turned out to be great. The hitch was that I lived an hour away. When our sessions ended, I was usually on my own again. Often I'd wait, like a starving kitten, for an invitation to grab a garden burger or go out to the movies. But I would never ask. God forbid I look needy.

On New Year's Eve of 1991, as I sat in front of the TV eating dinner, the phone rang. To my shock, it was Tracy. Hawaii was five hours behind New Jersey, so at midnight her time, after enjoying New Year's drinking, she'd summoned enough nerve to call. The holidays had been tricky since her parents' divorce. We both understood nasty separations. We talked and talked about everything but our problems. As the conversation flowed easily, I realized how much I'd missed her. The only time she got testy was when I asked about the kids. She unabashedly said that she hadn't read any of my letters to Casely because Casely was so scarred by my departure. I tried not to go on the guilt trip she offered. After two hours, we said good-bye. I hoped it wasn't just the drinking that had bridged the ocean between us.

I went out onto my tiny deck and watched the moonlight romancing the waves. Swaying green palms crackled and whispered in the light breeze. The beauty stood in bizarre contrast to my loneliness. When the two existed in the same moment, why did I choose confusion instead of awe? Was the universe a powerful metronome, balancing joy and sorrow, doling out pleasure and pain? Had the rhythmic swaying rocked me into a dark sleep, where I could barely recall the light? Or was it my own choice to swing back and forth in drama as my soul waited in the center?

The following morning, I hobbled down the three flights of stairs and out to the ocean I'd admired the night before. It always made me nervous to stroll alone beyond the apartment property. My town was not the safest place, and my knees and hips were incapable of running should I need to. But it was a new year—I wanted to push beyond my careful boundaries. I walked out to the beach and lowered myself down into a cove of rocks, letting the clear water lap at my legs. Colorful tropical fish rode the small swells like scuba divers. A tiny blue and yellow one bravely approached my foot, pecked my toes gently, then darted off. The honored company felt great—they trusted enough to come close.

My crooked legs were sprawled out in front of me, the water magnifying my swollen knees. Over the years, my kneecaps were no longer flush with my joints, but had gravitated to the sides of my legs. It was as if they were running from their counterpart on the other limb, repulsed by their own reflection. Improperly aligned, they were easy to dislocate. Pulled out of joint by the slightest movement. Just like me.

I splashed water on my tanned arms and face, feeling comforted by the titanic blue bed spread out wide. The outdoors always served to coax me further within. The vastness echoed possibilities, hope, faith: the intangibles that I all too often stuffed under a rock. Just then, I spotted an interesting shell jammed in a crevice in front of me. I inched closer and started to wiggle it loose. When at last it broke free, I was stunned. It wasn't a shell at all; it was a huge inch-and-a-half long tooth. *Amazing! Whose huge jaws did this come out of? A shark? No, they have straight teeth. This one was curved like a—I wasn't sure what. A jungle cat?* I didn't really care. I decided it was an omen. I was in the perpetual omen business, after all. Had to be my angels sending me a sign. Let it be Mr. Right, I thought, as I climbed back up the stairs to my apartment. Please let it be him swimming towards my shores.

It was dusk and the mosquitoes were dive-bombing, so I hobbled fast and was winded when I got to my door. The phone rang as I walked in.

"Is Julie Hobbes there?"

"This is Julie."

"Oh, hi, this is Joe Trafford. I don't know if you remember me. We met at New Light Bookstore a while back."

"New Light in Pennsylvania?"

"Yes! We bought some of your cards."

"Sure, I remember." I had a vague recollection of the owner, a nice-looking older man.

"I was sitting here staring at one of your cards, it's so intense, it blows me away. Your phone number's on the back, and hell, I had to call. You're so talented, the whole package is top-notch."

I hoped he was calling to buy more cards. Beyond that, I was lonely for company and he was oozing with compliments. As we talked, I found out he was an architect and had a house in Pennsylvania but was at his apartment in California. His openness about being a member of Alcoholics Anonymous impressed me. He was forty-four and divorced, and his ex-wife now owned the metaphysical bookstore that sold my cards. The questions became more personal, and I got the idea that he was maybe interested—in me? And he'd seen me in person!

Joe started calling almost every day. His voice felt bluer than the whole sky. After a few weeks of phone calls, he wanted to visit and said he thought he was falling in—then he stopped. "You know what I mean," he said quietly. Glee bubbled up until my whole body felt electrified. The tooth had been an omen.

"Do you know what card made me call you that first time?" he asked one night. "The Rumi quote that starts, 'The minute I heard my first love story, I started looking for you....' Do you remember it?"

"It's one of my favorites," I said, my heart pounding faster. What I was really thinking was, *I made that for YOU! That was a love letter for my prince!* Joe was smart, tender, funny, and into self-improvement. A pure velvet dream. We had found each other at last.

The tooth rode in my pocket as I bustled through the Honolulu Airport and waited at the gate. *This is it!* I wouldn't be hard for Joe to spot, and he said he'd wear a white hat. From what I could remember, he had short white hair and was slim, medium height, and tan. His age was the only drawback in my mind. Oh, and one other small detail. He had started drinking again.

I nervously scanned passengers as they filed past, and was sure one stiff-looking guy with a dirty, off-white hat wasn't Joe. The crowd thinned out until no one was left. *Did he miss the flight? Did he have second thoughts?* My face was twitching wildly so I sat for a few minutes, wondering what to do. I saw the man with the hat talking to a flight attendant. He turned to look back at the gate. *Oh, no. No, no, no. That stranger with the stupid smile is Joe? No way.* The man saw me and waved. I wanted to run. He came over and gave me an awkward hug. He was better-looking than I'd remembered: tan, with Caribbean-blue eyes, but his manner was so unappealing. *What in the world is wrong?*

By the time we got to my apartment, I was still in shock. The conversation was strained and awkward. *What happened to the easy-going guy on the phone? What am I going to do with the stiff?*

That night, on our way out to dinner, I resolved to keep myself open and find the man I'd fallen for on the phone. Was I just scared? After his third drink, I still felt nothing. He was slightly rude to the waitress. He was distant and our conversation was stilted. No matter how hard I tried to imagine getting close to him, I couldn't. And I'd thought I was desperate. Before he landed on Oahu, Joe and I had agreed that he would sleep on my couch. I don't think either of us had thought it would actually turn out that way, but it did.

The next morning I dreaded going out into the living room. I had to say something. We ate breakfast and stared at the TV. He talked about the weather and the beautiful surroundings.

"I don't know what's wrong," I finally blurted out. "Do you?"

"What do you mean?"

"We were excited at the thought of seeing each other and now we barely have anything to say. You don't seem the same as you were on the phone," I said.

"I am." His smile was plastered on. "You're even better in person. Can I take a picture of you right there in the sunlight?"

Oh boy. I was hoping he was feeling as repulsed by me as I was by him. I never thought I'd be in this position.

After sightseeing the next day, nothing changed. He was opinionated and uptight, with an unnerving smile stuck between his cheeks. It seemed to be masking the very authenticity that I was seeking. Where was the depth, the willingness, the open heart? His smile held no joy. Did mine?

Two days later, I could barely stand it. I just wanted the reflection (of myself) to leave. Over dinner, I tried again to talk. "I don't feel the same as I felt before. I'm really sorry."

"We have two more days," he said. "Maybe we should make love."

That little suggestion was the final nail in the coffin.

On Joe's last night, Kris' daughter had a school concert, and I used it as an excuse to get away. I gave him the apartment keys and said I'd pick him up the next day for his flight. The following morning, he called while I was in the shower and told Kris that he was taking a cab to the airport. I felt free. And guilty. That afternoon, when I drove back to my apartment, I stopped at the gate to retrieve my keys. The security guard said I had to go see the building manager in the main office.

"Why?" I asked.

"Looks like you got a summons because of your guest. Drunk and disorderly. He went swimming in the pool last night, nude."

The manager turned out to be understanding and let me off with a warning. I dragged my embarrassment back to the apartment and poured myself into a sad-sack letter to Megan. *I'm so incredibly disappointed and confused and sad. It's so lonely here again. The only thing that makes up for the mess with Joe is realizing that I'm not so desperate after all, willing to take anyone. That was a huge gift from him. Even though the synchronicities had me convinced that he was the answer, omens can be self-created I guess. Or totally misinterpreted. Ugh.*

Trying to think of something positive to tell Megan, I thought of Judy Prescott's visit. One night, the two of us had laughed so hard the security guard had come and told us to put a sock in it! I hated to see Judy go . . . and to be alone again and almost broke. Ironically, I'd been able to pay rent for the last two months because of insurance checks from two odd car accidents. My old car-karma was apparently sending up a new kind of flare. The first time my car was hit, I was packing my art into the car from the Zoo Fence. Then *wham*, an old gal mistakenly went into reverse and backed right into my parked Hyundai. A few weeks later, a drunk on a motorcycle plowed into my car in a parking lot. Luckily (surely angels orchestrated this), only the car body was dented in both cases. I didn't use the money for the dents, since I didn't care how the car looked, I told Megan. If only I had that same attitude about myself.

I continued to add up the plus side: I was living in Hawaii! I'd taken a chance and followed the path the universe had unfurled. I could see the ocean out my living room window and a spectacular sunset every evening. Rainbows, panoramic views, and buckets of sunshine tapped on my windows. So why was I still miserable? The self-help books said if you follow your bliss, you'll find the answers. I'd somehow overlooked the part about *feeling* your bliss instead of arguing with it. I'd been in Hawaii for nine months and found two car accidents, a horrible ant infestation in my apartment, nightmares about Tracy, and year-round mosquitoes. No miracles; no physical rebirth; no fabulous wealth; no wild transformation; and no soul mate. My most loyal friends were my two old crutches. I stopped writing my depressing letter, but the thoughts just kept dog-piling on top of themselves.

I thought that changing my outer circumstances would change the inner me, without realizing it was the other way around. The saving grace was that I followed my dream of living in Hawaii to its conclusion. I wouldn't ever wonder what I was missing. The bubble had burst and the fantasy had dispelled. For now.

A few days after Joe's departure, I drove home from a fun day of swimming with Kris and the kids, my spirits renewed. Suddenly, I spotted a big white egret in the sky — common enough, but still a sheer delight to me. Strangely, its head seemed round, its wings too furry, and it was headed straight for my car. I flinched as its flat face whizzed by the passenger door. Quickly pulling the car over, I scanned the sky, but it was now a speck in the distance. I sat in my boosted-up car seat, catching the breath that beautiful bird had just taken away.

Back at the apartment, I called Susie.

"I saw a snowy white owl!" I told her. "At least, I think it was. Do they live on the islands? It definitely wasn't an egret."

"That's totally cool! Yes, I think they live here, but in my eighteen years on Oahu, I've never seen one. What a neat sign. Which direction was it flying?"

"Towards Honolulu." I thought of the airport for some reason.

"My shaman friend says that you should go in the direction of the bird. Maybe, that means you're moving up here. What does an owl mean to you?" Susie was using our dream group's approach to deciphering a symbol.

"They were my grandmother's favorite."

"She must be watching over you, Jule."

The next morning, I unloaded my art, my table, and all my gear at the Honolulu Zoo, and hung my pictures up on the high fence as I did every week. It was hard work for my small, stiff body. The frames of the paintings clanked against the chain link like tin cups on prison bars. Tourists filtered past as I sat and wrote in my journal, trying to act busy. Allowing strangers to look at my artwork took a lot of endurance and a splash of desperation. The other artists were friendly, but we were all watchful for business. We sat in a row, dry as cereal boxes on a shelf, waiting for a hungry buyer.

"The HFS has created so much shame," I wrote. I retraced my pen over the word "shame" until it was black and blue. "Or is it buried shame that's coming out? Or creating more? The mystics say we often have the cause and effect backwards. Maybe the twitch isn't creating the shame; maybe the past shame has resulted in the twitch." I stared at the words I wanted to believe. If I were responsible for the HFS, then I could cure it too. If the root problem was my past, then I could change the past, and my condition, by loving it.

"They say that God dwells within, giving us the power to create our own reality. If I believe that the HFS is punishment, and live in guilt, my creative spirit will weave whatever story I tell myself, good or bad. The universe doesn't judge my thoughts; it doesn't analyze my choices. It gives me the ability to create in whatever way I believe. Do I like what I've created? Am I really that powerful?"

Glancing up from my journal, I saw an elderly woman making a beeline for me.

"Aloha!" she called out like an old friend, smiling broadly. "How are sales?"

I liked her immediately but wondered how I knew her. "Nothing yet today but I'm still hoping." My life in a nutshell, I thought. This woman, so familiar, was quite beautiful, with her tanned wrinkles and angelic blue eyes. Her white hair was scooped into a loose bun, with soft, loose wisps hula-dancing in the breeze.

"I haven't sold anything in days, but I love it down here, whether I sell anything or not," she mused.

Okay, she's a fellow artist. Why don't I remember her?

"Your rendition of Makapuu Point is the best I've seen. I only do flowers and birds, but I sure appreciate the skill it takes to paint our beautiful Hawaii." She even pronounced the state name correctly, "Hah-vuh-ee," just like my dad.

"How long have you been painting?" I asked. *Please stay and talk.*

"Forever. I'm eighty-three and I had my hip replaced four months ago!" She squatted down to show me the flexibility in her new hip. The hair on my arms stood up and took notice.

"Only four months? My brother, Ethan, had his hips replaced two years ago, and he still can't do that." I didn't add that he never could, and neither could I.

"Doctors know a lot more now than they did even last year."

"I have arthritic hips and knees but I don't want replacements, considering what my brother went through."

"No, no, you'd be fine! Everyone was so wonderful to me while I was in the hospital. I'd do it again in an instant."

What? She made it sound like some kind of vacation. As I listened to her talk, something shifted inside me, leaving an opening where there'd never been one before. Long ago, I'd decided never to entertain medical solutions when it came to my arthritis. I used herbs, nutrition, oils, prayer, visualization, and many alternative therapies I came across. But not traditional doctors. I wasn't nuts. Now, after this one conversation, I felt faith nibbling at my flip-flops, tempting me to step out onto new sand. I was actually considering replacement surgery, and I was almost . . . excited. My fears were slowly eased by this stranger's joy; my anger was soothed by her peace. We talked and talked. Even as my face jittered in spasm, she didn't seem to notice. No one disturbed us for awhile, until a friendly looking tourist approached.

"Hope you don't mind, but I overheard your conversation." He handed me his business card. "I'm a physical therapist, and I wanted to tell you that our patients do wonderfully well with their new joints." The therapist pointed to a man on crutches nearby. "That young fellow is my nephew, and he had his hip replaced six weeks ago after a car accident. Look how well he's doing." I felt a neon lifeline looping around my waist. An orthopedic convention at my tiny art table in the middle of Oahu? I was being bombarded by helpers. Hope had called the troops and in they stormed.

"Everything comes together at the right time," the old gal said, winking.

That night, my direction was clear. I was going home to find Dr. Simon and two brand new hips. As I lay in bed, the jagged mountains out my window sang me into a deep, purple sleep. I was beginning my climb towards higher ground.

The next week, I went to the Zoo Fence excited to share the big news with my white-haired friend, whose name I'd never caught. Thanks to her, I had turned inside-out in a single day. As I set off on my crutches, I asked a few of the artists if they knew her, but no one had a clue about the little old lady. I came to the end of the two blocks without success. I hobbled back to ask Brad, the guy who managed the membership at the fence.

"We've never had an artist that old. You know, too much heavy schlepping," Brad said. *She has to be around. I'll see her next weekend.* Three weeks went by without a sign of her. I seriously began to think she was an angel. How could she be chatting with me one day and then poof into thin air?

A week later, as my plane roared into the cloudless sky, I stared down at the green islands in their blue oyster beds. *Is the pearl down there, or is it really in me?* The return journey felt right, but my spine was tense and twisted in mourning. I hated saying good-bye to Kris and her family. Was I leaving something important behind?

Good-bye, Hawaii. Good-bye, Kris. You made it all worthwhile. I love you. As I looked out over the wing, I thought of my grandmother's owl. A big white bird was flying me home.

Back in New Jersey, I moved into Megan's guest room and further into limbo. A new life stood before me by day. The old life rapped on my dreams every night. I existed somewhere between hope and defeat. Wedged between inspired books and worried journals. Teetering between crutches and a far-off freedom. Unsettled between a friend's generosity and my inability to care for myself. I'd been here before.

"Is it left on Griswald Street?" Megan asked.

"Yes, then right on Palmer," I said.

"Thanks for coming, Jule. It's scary, going to see a medium. I hope he doesn't mind me bringing you."

We grinned nervously at each other as we walked towards the house in Madison, New Jersey. Aemon, the medium from England, answered the door and welcomed us inside his friend's modest home. We chatted for a bit and then he began the session. "I'm getting an older male, has your father passed?"

"Yes," Megan said, slightly astonished.

"He's next to a long brick house with a wood fence. There's a pool behind him."

"That sounds like my house."

Aemon described people and events, even an old family squabble about an heirloom that Megan cherished. Then he talked about her dad's final days. "He wants to thank you for being with him when he died. He's indicating that there were three people in the room, but you made his crossing easier in the last moments."

"My mother and sister were there," Megan sobbed. "I was holding my dad's hand, and I told him I loved him and it was okay to go. I swear that I felt his spirit pass through mine or something. It was so profound."

Aemon waited for a moment as Megan cried. "I have an older female here, a rather impatient sort. I think she's here for you." He pointed at me. "Megan, do you mind if I give a little time to your friend?"

Megan and I exchanged wide-eyed looks. "She's indicating your father's side of the family," Aemon said to me. "Has your father's mother passed?"

I nodded.

"She's been buzzing in the background during this whole reading." Aemon hesitated. "Was she a bit . . . bossy when she was alive?"

I laughed. "Yes."

"There's a smaller male with her who can't get a word in edgewise."

"That must be my Grandpa Bumble! He was shorter than she was, and much quieter."

"Does a dove mean anything to you? Or does someone go by the nickname Dove?"

It didn't ring a bell at first. "Wait! My dad used to take me to Indian Princesses. I picked the name Mourning Dove, Dad picked Thunder Hawk." I found out years later that the dove was not named for the morning dawn, as I'd thought, but for the sad mourning sound it made. It seemed strangely appropriate for me. "My Grandma Bee had made matching suede vests for Dad and me to wear to our powwows. She really loved the idea of our father-daughter outings."

"This is your grandmother's way of giving a reference only you would understand. Your grandmother says you and Megan were discussing a project in the car on the way over here. She's showing me a brush and a pen. Are you a writer? Or an artist?"

Megan and I were amazed. "Megan's a writer and I'm an artist; we were just talking about a writing project in the car."

"She says that both the brush and the writing will be important to you. Now she's directing me west towards California. Wait, she's pointing beyond California over the ocean."

"Hawaii? I just moved back from Oahu where she lived most of her life."

"Was she instrumental in some way with your move? She's taking credit for getting you there."

"She bought some stocks for me before she died, and I used that money to get to Hawaii. Gosh, I'm glad she knows."

"She's talking about a surgery. Did you have surgery?"

"I'm having both hips replaced in a few months and maybe both knees."

"She wants you to know she's watching over you. Now she's saying, 'Washington.' Do you know anyone in Washington?"

"Washington, D.C., or Washington state?"

"She's saying no to both. Is there a Washington, New Jersey?"

"Oh, wow." I stared at Megan. "Chase lives in Washington. That's a guy that I knew awhile back," I told Aemon.

"Your grandmother says you gave him confidence; it wasn't one-sided. She wants to assure you that someone just right for you is on the horizon. It will be after your surgery. She says that you have an enormous heart and not to worry — all that love won't go to waste."

Those words settled around me like the sweetest satin blankie. Aemon had said it. Or Grandma Bee did. Someone thought I was good enough to be loved. Megan thought so too, but I was never sure if she was just being a supportive friend. The words coming from a stranger gave the inconceivable a new life.

Aemon went back to talking to Megan as I sat dumbstruck.
Despite my belief in life after life, it was surreal to hear from the
other side. I felt sad that I'd hardly known my grandmother, and
guilty that I'd never acknowledged her. *Thank you, Grandma Bee!
I thought. Thank you for looking out for me . . . and for Mr. Right. I
just lose hope sometimes. So thank you for everything! Oh, and by the
way, what the heck should I do about Tracy?*

Three months after I'd left for Hawaii, Tracy had finally
broken her silence and sent me a five-page grievance letter. I
was actually glad, though my hands shook as those angry pages
turned on me. She wrote that I was to blame for the entire mess;
I was cold-hearted, selfish, and judgmental. (She was right in
many ways.) She told me I'd used her family and then thrown
them away. (We used each other, I suppose.) Last, but not least,
she said I'd scarred Casely *for life*. Okay, Tracy was still a drama
queen.

When Tracy heard the news that I was moving back, she
talked to me by phone for the second time. She was nippy and
cold and my apologies didn't lift the ugly forecast. Her
punishment was only getting started. I called Tracy again after
settling in at Megan's, but she gave me the runaround about
getting together. By keeping her distance, she wouldn't have to
risk trusting me again. Withholding the kids was her other
stronghold. Typical divorce.

Finally, we were able to agree on a day. When I arrived at
our old house, Casely ran out to greet me, tiny arms and legs
moving in a blur. We shrieked and wrapped each other up in
such joy. How I'd missed her. Tracy walked out holding Zack,
her buffer between us. Awkwardly, I hugged the two. Zack
scrambled down to show me his toy car. Relief loosened every
joint when I saw that I hadn't been forgotten by my godkids.
And not yet forgiven by Tracy. We chatted amiably as I told her
about my surgery plans and my appointment with Dr. Simon.

Although she tried to keep her maternal instincts in check, I could tell it pulled at her heartstrings. It would take time to sort through the issues and rebuild what we had soiled. I hoped a friendship of sixteen years could weather the wait.

Eleven
A Body of Help

Out beyond ideas of wrongdoing and rightdoing, there's a field.
I'll meet you there.
~Rumi

As Megan and I got in the car, our destination five hours away, I could feel Boston like a fossil stamped on my bones. I hadn't left a single footprint in a doctor's office since I was in college, and even then it was only because I'd been desperate for food. I tried to breathe deeply, in and out, in and out. I pictured my angels lining the highway, cheering me on, clapping and jumping and throwing confetti as Megan drove. *I'm not a child any more. I can do this. The doctors don't control me. I don't have to smile for anyone's approval anymore.*

"Do you remember calling me in the hospital when we were in fifth grade?" I asked Megan.

"Yeah, I do. I didn't know it was hard on you. I'm sorry, Jule."

"I didn't tell anyone how I felt. My hips did loosen up a bit after the ten days of traction. For awhile anyway. There must have been many times when Mom and Dad were worried sick for Ethan and me. They loved us so much and I know they wanted us to get the very best care. Boston had the leading genetic specialists at the time. The doctors wanted to monitor Ethan and me while our bones were still growing. Mom and Dad tried to explain it all, but I didn't really listen. I didn't understand." The feelings began to domino as we drove. "Meg, thanks for driving me. I'm really relieved that you'll be there. I—

I don't want to freeze up in Dr. Simon's office and be a tongue-tied kid again."

"Don't worry. Try to picture the doctor as God's mechanic, and the rest will take care of itself."

All it took was the smell of the waiting room to trip my panic button. Adrenaline erupted inside me, and my body set like cement. I took a deep breath and another and another. My stomach flip-flopped as the old feelings crept up my torso. I was trying to face the future with love instead of fear, but I didn't want to go back to this world where I'd felt like a guinea pig. My family's sweet denial had been a welcome yoke compared to the cold medical definitions. Abnormal. Deformed. Where was the truth? Was I an aberration of nature, or a spirit in an uncommon costume?

I signed in and buried my face in a magazine, trying to keep the twitchy facial nerves exhausted so that when my name was called my face would be calm. Instead I called in a headache.

"Julie Hobbes?" the nurse asked.

As I started walking down the hall, I tried to remember a time when I hadn't had pain and stiffness in my legs. Deep down, I thought it was because I hadn't done the right things. I hadn't eaten right. I hadn't lived right. I hadn't exercised and I was plain lazy. My old gym teacher, Mr. Cabot, would've agreed. He seemed annoyed whenever I brought in one of my many gym excuses from mom or from the doctors. I was just soft.

"Come on, Miss Hobbes," he taunted, "exercise is good for you. It'll toughen you up."

The obstacle course looked harmless that day so, despite my note from home, I caved. The first obstacle was a set of three-foot-high parallel bars, with a gray mat thrown over them like a saddle. *Did Mr. Cabot say go over those bars? He must have meant go under them.* When it was my turn, I started to go underneath.

The coach's whistle pierced the air. "Nice try, Hobbes, but we don't tolerate cheaters! Go over it! Come on now, show some guts!"

I couldn't buckle under now that everyone was watching. Maybe if I ran hard enough and flung myself high enough, I could claw my way over the top. I took off with a bang, my little legs pumping. What felt like my best sprint was actually a decrepit trot. I tried to leap, but hit the mat and slid to the floor like a flattened cartoon character.

Furious at the giggles from my classmates, I gathered my courage for a second try. "All right, Miss Hobbes. Go under it if that's the best you can do."

Mr. Cabot liked the kids who were fit and fast. In that one way, we were in agreement. I'd have given anything to live in the skin of a normal kid. Towards the end of class, we had to line up in rows, and Frank Hubbers was jerking single hairs out of my head while we stood in line. I whirled around, holding up my fists. Frank said, "C'mon, little Hobbles, I'll give you one free shot."

All at once, I'd had it. My furious fist lunged at Frank. I heard the clunk of his jaw, saw his head jolt back. Frank grabbed his chin in shock. Frank and I had to walk an extra lap that day, but Frank stopped pulling my hair. It was a fair trade. After school, I walked home with my friend Diane Ousterling, who wanted every detail. "What did he do when you nailed him in the nuts?"

"No, in the chin!" I said in disgust. What other rumors were out there?

"He deserved it, Jule. He's such a bully." She saw my scowl. "You're gonna get taller some time. Mom says you won't but I told her you will! You will, right?"

I was stupefied. "Of course I will. I'm just growing slower than everyone else," I lied. I hated her for bringing it up. I knew I'd never look my peers in the eyes. The doctors had said I might reach four feet tall. Maybe Diane wouldn't want to be my friend if she knew I'd always be different.

The door of the examination room opened and my heart stopped. I wanted to run under the back porch as I turned to face my old foe. A white-coat walked towards me, his hand extended. "Hello, Julie, it's been a long time."

"Hi," I said in amazement, as he shook my hand. *This can't be him. What happened to the evil Vulcan?* He turned to Megan, with a gentle smile for her as well.

"I hear you're having difficulty with your hips," Dr. Simon began.

"Yes. They're painful and really stiff." His jet-black hair and scary, pointy eyebrows of my memory were now a pleasant, cottony gray. He had sympathetic blue eyes. Yesterday, I'd have sworn on a stack of Bibles that he had dark, lifeless orbs.

He motioned for me to sit on the table, and he quietly started his exam, carefully moving my legs, checking the structure and the range of motion, just as he had done some twenty years before. I never would have recognized him, but something deep inside now remembered him very well. He finished his exam and looked at my X-rays. "The arthritis is very advanced, as I'm sure you know." His soft-spoken manner threw my memories for a loop. I remembered that he had been quiet, but I thought it was due to insensitivity, not shyness. "My recommendation is to have both hips replaced," he said. "Your knees are worn out as well, but I think we should correct the hip joints first."

"I figured that's what had to be done."

At the end of my appointment, surgery was scheduled for September, two months off.

I felt strangely free and light. I could see Dr. Simon for who he was, and not who I had imagined him to be. I realized that, as a girl, I'd needed an enemy to fight. The doctors had served as a handy repository for the confusion and pain. Their focus on my body had felt hostile and judgmental, even when it was well-meaning. Now the choice to change that focus was mine.

As Megan and I drove home to New Jersey, I imagined my angels cheering, laughing, and cleaning up the darkness I was leaving behind.

The next two months were long and difficult as I prepared for my hospital stay. But the day before I was to leave for Boston, I got a phone call. The surgery had been canceled.

"*Why?*" my dad asked me on the phone.

"The policy you have for me covers only 80 percent of the hospital costs. The hospital wants a $25,000 deposit *up front!*"

"What? Why didn't the hospital know this long ago? This is ludicrous!"

"I know! I can't turn back *now*," I said through tears.

"Julie, Mom and I will meet you and Megan in Boston, okay?"

"But the woman *said* we needed all that money and—"

"We might be able to scrape together enough to satisfy them."

Hope was revived. Perhaps it would be okay after all. *Thank God I can always count on my parents*, I thought.

But the hospital wouldn't budge on the full $25,000 deposit. In Boston, they told me to apply for disability in New Jersey. As we drove home, my doubts were tripled. Later that week, when I entered the mind-boggling Social Security maze, questions swirled in my mind. *Would I qualify? Did I deserve state aid?* My parents had never treated Ethan and me as if we were handicapped. Their positive expectations had given us determination and strength. Was it weakness to ask for help now? Was it failure? At the Social Security office, and over the phone, I repeatedly spelled the Latin name, *spondyloepiphyseal dysplasia*. I hadn't been able to spit out the word "dwarf" when I had first telephoned the office. No one had used the expression when I was growing up, and never once had it found a home on my tongue. Dwarf. It sounded like an ugly troll. *Dwarf.* It was an alien echo at the bottom of an empty well.

"Stupid name tag," I vented to Megan.

"Exactly. It's just a label, like eggplant or carrot. You're not the label. You're a person. A talented, beautiful person who happens to be little."

I looked away, unable to bear the compliment. "People who have cancer don't say, 'I'm a cancer.' They say, 'I *have* cancer.' I *have* dwarfism." Somehow this rationale lessened the blow. "Anyway, I've got to get on with the application and interviews," I told Megan. "I've got to learn how to talk about my...dwarfism," I said with a gulp. "I have a huge list of phone calls to find all my medical information. Got to prove my needy case and all."

"Let me know if I can help," Megan said and was gone.

Dr. Abernathy, one of the specialists I had seen regularly as a child, was the first doctor I had to contact. I rehearsed my introduction, and dialed the number.

"Hello, Center for Birth Defects," the pleasant voice answered.

My throat constricted, airless. *Defect.* I slammed the phone down and sat trembling. I'd forgotten that name. *Defect.* I lay back on my bed, closed my eyes, and broke into tears. I saw myself as a young girl, standing there high on a table, the doctors staring and probing. I saw the camera flashing over and over, capturing my naked, flawed body. The agony flooded back. *We just want to look at your pretty face.*

I had always believed that I'd been uncooperative with my parents and the doctors. I thought I'd made it clear how horrible I felt. But I hadn't. I'd smiled. *Could I have done it differently? Could I have screamed no at the top of my lungs?* The regrets and the blame made me sob even harder. Why did it hurt so many years later? Then I realized that I was still hiding my feelings. Still worrying over what others thought of me. Still saying yes when I wanted to say no.

Ten years earlier, my brother Dan had swooped in, introducing me to the world of macrobiotics. Together we had skipped merrily away from the allopathic sovereignty. One alternative therapy had led to another, offering ongoing hope. I'd read about amazing physical transformations through holistic treatments, prayer, laughter. I didn't want to give up on that dream. *Have I lost my faith? Did I ever have enough?*

Friends were surprised when they heard the news of my surgeries. My silence over the years had kept many of them in the dark about the severity of my problems, just as I'd intended. For the most part, I'd kept the "poor me" hidden from others, but now I began to wonder if that suppression wasn't part of the reason my life had followed this course. Had I quietly dug myself into a pit, waiting for others to notice how deep it was? Only with others' permission did I grant myself permission to feel my pain. The lifelong denial was like a twenty-nine-year-old war raging inside. Not exactly a hospitable place for healing.

It took four months of calls and endless automated phone prompts. Four months of digging up medical records, climbing the walls, faxing this and sending that, going for doctors' evaluations, filling out paperwork, pleading my case, talking about my...dwarfism. I spent plenty of time punishing the bed with my Wiffle bat. But the maze had an end: I was declared disabled and awarded Medicaid and a small monthly check. A victory. The grand prize was two tickets to surgery. Two hips. Two knees. Yikes.

I sat at the kitchen table at Megan's as I reread the tear-stained disability letter. Opting for a hardcore medical solution was the toughest concession. How ironic that I'd spent enormous time and energy fighting for access to the white-coats that I'd fought all my life to avoid. Suddenly, the full circle from one extreme to the other made me smile through my tears. Maybe yin and yang could shake hands at last.

A date was set with Dr. Steven Fried, the New Jersey surgeon recommended by Dr. Simon. First, my hips would be replaced. Only a week later, they'd replace my knees. I had a month to prepare. I ate well and took herbs and vitamins. I meditated. I drank special teas and researched homeopathics for post-surgical healing. I repeated affirmations. I visualized angels. I made inspirational tapes for before and after surgery. I prayed. I talked to my friends and family for support. I read. I wrote letters of encouragement to myself and asked Megan to mail them to me during the two-week hospital stay. I did everything I could think of to smooth the way. Everything except forgive. The skeletons I'd been dragging around were about to make an appearance, exposing the past I hadn't yet put to rest.

I was shaken up, confused, exposed—an open wound. As my surgery date neared, fears morphed into anger, and I turned on Megan. I'd spun another codependent web and, naturally, it was the first place I went to dump my grievances. It had become an ugly habit, first with my parents, and then with Tracy. Megan was on bed rest with her third pregnancy. A sitting duck. I found fault in everything Megan did. I chanted the quiet angry mantras of my past. *She's just like Tracy. Just like Mom and Dad. How could they love the real me? Weak, defective, unlovable me. Why give Megan anything if she can't save me?* I stopped helping with her kids, stopped talking to her. I tried to convince myself that she was walking away from my suffering.

The morning of the surgery, I was calm on the surface. The HFS twitching was the only sign of the terrified tornado underneath. Forms were signed as we sat and waited. I changed into a hospital gown and fidgeted some more. It took ten jabs before the IV finally got started. The nurse insisted that I had veins like angel hair. Great, even my veins were defective. Thankfully, I had my mom and dad to lean on, and I knew they would be waiting for me when I was done.

An aide wheeled me down hallways and packed elevators, exposing me and my twitch, my oversized gown, and my glamorous hair net to everyone. In the holding area I was treated to an embarrassing shave of my short and curlies. After I was completely stripped, pricked, snipped, and prepped, I was taken to the operating room. Bright lights in a sharp sea of chrome stabbed at my eyes. Adrenaline alarms sounded in every direction.

I didn't recognize the doctor or his nurse behind their masks until Dr. Fried spoke. "Morning, Julie. Are you ready?"

"I guess so." I clung to his familiar voice.

Then I recognized his wonderful nurse, Donna, by the friendly crinkling around her eyes.

"Hello, Julie," she said sweetly, as she patted my hand.

"You'll do just fine," the doctor assured me. "You're in good hands here."

They shifted me over to the operating table, where my body would be sliced open, my bones sawed in two, and the defective pieces thrown away. My eyes closed as I said a prayer to Grandma Bee and the angels.

"Hi, Julie, I'm your anesthesiologist. We're starting the medication into your IV. You might feel a slight burning, but it will subside."

I nodded. Everything went black.

Muffled sounds surrounded me but my eyes refused to open. I heard a startled voice say, "She's awake."

Someone spoke in my ear. "Julie, this is Dr. Fried. Everything went smoothly. It took longer than expected but you have two new hips. You can rest in the recovery room now."

I tried to respond but the drugs locked me down.

"Lift her all together. One-two-three!" Excruciating pain flooded my body as they lifted me off the table and onto a gurney. My head snapped back as I tried to shriek. The pain jettisoned me back into the darkness.

What's happening? In a slow-motion shock I tried desperately to move. *I can't breathe. Help!* Struggling to open my eyes, I wanted to get my bearings. *Open. Open.* The battle overwhelmed me again and again. Years passed through me as I sank in the powerlessness. At last I saw the white ceiling. Then the room. Next, the bed and my immobilized legs. *Oh my God—the pain! Someone please help!* I twisted at my waist slightly. The pain spiked deep. My legs felt massive and crushed. I tried to call out, but no sound came. *What are these tubes coming out of my mouth?* My hands were tied to the bed rails. Nurses whisked by as I faded in and out, desperate for human contact. Suddenly, I felt someone touch my arm—at last! Such relief. When I turned, all I found was an automatic blood pressure machine. The cuff squeezed my bicep then released it. *Someone please help me.*

Two nurses stopped near my gurney. "Bob's home, glued to the damn TV. He lives and dies with those Giants."

"I'm a football widow too. Glad I had work today so I didn't have to listen to him yell at the screen."

One backed up, inadvertently brushing my handcuffed hand. When I grabbed her lab coat with two fingers, she turned to see what she was snagged on. "Hello there, blue eyes. How are you feeling?"

I turned my finger and pointed towards the tubes.

"Those keep your lungs working during surgery. The doctor had a difficult time with the intubation, so he left them in, just in case."

I tugged at my bound hands, silently asking why.

"We didn't want you pulling those tubes out before you were fully awake." She untied my hands. I clung to her coat, pleading with her not to go. "I'll be right back."

An eternity passed. At last a young technician came over. "I'll take those tubes out for you, okay? Keep your head back on the pillow. I'll count to three. Are you ready?"

I nodded. Yes.

"One-two-three," and he yanked at my insides. I gagged and spluttered as the tubes made their way out of my lungs. I felt I'd vomited glass. "The pain...." my whisper rasped.

"The tubes probably scratched your throat up pretty good when they went in."

"No, my legs," I croaked.

"I'll have to get a nurse." He was gone.

I waited in agony. I hailed a different nurse and grabbed her hand. "The pain is so bad," I hacked out.

"I'm afraid I can't give you any pain meds until your blood pressure comes up. It dropped dangerously low during surgery and medication could drop it farther."

Tears filled my eyes. "Please stay here with me. When can I see my family?" I whimpered.

"Once your pressure comes up, we'll take you to your room. Let me see if I can find someone to sit with you."

Reluctantly, I released my death grip on her hand. I waited and waited. I tried to sleep but the blistering pain kept hauling me back. *I can't get away from it! Help!* "Nurse?!" I whined as loud as I could, "Can I have some water?" Someone offered me two ice chips. "Can I have pain medication yet? Can I see my parents? *Please!*"

She walked around to the blood pressure machine. "It shouldn't be long now. I'll see what the doctor prescribed."

There was nothing to distract me from the madness and confusion in my body. Wake up! it wailed. *You're ripped clear through! You're bleeding everywhere!* My brain, my legs, my every synapse was screaming orders to run or die or move or roar! Do something quick! But I could only lie there, not knowing how I'd make it through the next agonizing minute. *What's happening? Help me!* Finally, a nurse arrived, pushing a machine in front of her. "I'll start a morphine drip into your IV." My fingers and toes began to fidget in wild anticipation. *Will it knock me out? Please God just knock me out!*

As an aide wheeled me through the hospital corridors, a clock said it was nine at night. Surgery had been at eight in the morning. I hadn't just imagined the endless wait in recovery.

When I was wheeled into my room, my parents jumped up. "Oh Julie, we were so worried!"

I was too exhausted to sob, but a few tears dashed out to see them.

My mom's voice was gentle and loving. "We kept asking where you were."

"I went to the nurses' desk every half hour," my dad said with his protective hand on my brow. "Oh, Julie."

Visiting hours were over and my parents had to fend off two nurses to spend a few minutes with me before they had to leave. The morphine was helping to cradle the pain, but despair was creeping in. I greedily sucked on melting ice chips, closed my eyes, and prayed for sleep. My stomach started to churn. Before I could buzz the nurse, I threw up all over myself.

In the following days, I woke up each morning at three o'clock. I'd hit the morphine pump and feel the burn, but the drugs weren't helping me sleep. I'd doze off and then be shocked back into consciousness. I shook constantly. I was nauseated and couldn't eat. I ached for company and dreamed of daylight when I could call someone and end my isolation.

The third morning, the nurses didn't question Tracy when she whisked in before visiting hours. After my wrenching phone call at six that morning, Tracy was on a mission of mercy. It had been such a relief to hear her voice. I cried and complained, hoping she would forgive me. She already had. We talked about the fear and shame of needing each other. Under the pressure of our various troubles, we had caved and blamed the other. Blamed the mirror. Nothing new. She was pregnant and nauseated too, but that couldn't stop her from making the forty-five minute car ride after I called. She brought a variety of treats, trying to perk up my appetite and spirits. The greatest help, though, was knowing we had survived a storm. She sailed to the rescue again, and I forgave myself for needing her. The pattern still existed but the dam had broken loose. The good in our friendship was swimming back to our side.

My mom came to visit that day just in time for physical therapy, where they bent my hips in gritty determination, despite my tears. They walked my fresh incisions up and down the halls until I lost strength. I wasn't improving according to schedule. *What's wrong with me? Is this what I get for losing faith, for giving in to the doctors?* The myriad tests that were run to diagnose the constant shaking, the nausea, and the inability to sleep brought no answers. They saw nothing. My fear was invisible.

When evening came, and my mom left, I cried and shook, terrified of facing another night alone. During the day, panic was held at bay, but when the sunlight faded and visitors went home, it yanked me deep into its coils. I was taken back to the operating table. I screamed no, but they took me anyway. They were going to cut off my long monkey toes. They held me down and just as they began to slice, I snapped awake from the nightmare. I was panting so hard, ready to throw up. "Please can someone help me to the bathroom? Quickly?" I said into the intercom.

A kind nurse walked in as I started to cry. "We're amazed at how well you're doin', sweetie," the nurse said, as she gently walked me to the bathroom.

"Really?" I thought the nurses saw me as an annoying baby.

"Sure, look at you walking with two new hips. Most patients here only have one replaced at a time." She pulled the bathroom door partially shut, as I stood over the toilet trembling. I could hear the nurse changing my sheets. I'd been bleeding like I'd had a child. As she helped me back to my clean bed she answered the question I'd been afraid to ask. "Even if it's not that time of the month," she said, "the ladies just tend to bleed anyway." I asked the nurse to stay, but she had work to do. I lay in the dark, my face in a tight spasm. *So this is rebirth.*

Shaking, freezing cold, I was tightly wrapped in a wet sheet. *Why have the nurses left me this way?* Then I realized I was in the middle of a dark road. As a car sped too close to my mummified body, I couldn't move out of its way. Another car careened by as the rain pelted my skin. I wanted to scream but couldn't breathe. My heart was pounding like a pile driver when I jerked awake. The sheets were soaked with sweat. I buzzed for the tired nurse. My reality had turned into a litany of nightmares. All my life, I'd tried to run from the darkness. This time, I was going straight through it.

My hip recovery was slowed by the degeneration in my knees, but the thought of bilateral knee surgery was unthinkable. "Your knees are severely misaligned, in need of a lot of reconstruction," my doctor said. "In order for the hips to heal in proper alignment, your knees need to be addressed. The sooner the better." The complete recovery for all the joints would take two years. I knew I had to get on with it. Three months after my first surgeries, I dove back in for two new knees.

"Don't leave me alone in recovery again, please. Please." I begged my surgeon, who wanted to reassure me but made no promises. If I hadn't been so dazed, I might have recognized my feelings of powerlessness as a consequence of my own fear, not a cause or a curse of my dwarfism.

The double knee surgery threw me right back into pain and fear. The bandages on my left leg, which had been wrapped too tight in the operating room, left me with no feeling in my ankle or foot. The doctors hoped the nerve damage was temporary, but in the meantime, I had to wear a brace so that I could walk.

I pushed hard through the pain of the tough rehab, all the while noticing that other patients seemed to be managing quite well. They didn't leave a heaving ball of sweat and toil behind them. *What's the matter with me?* Deep down I realized that the other patients had had only one knee replaced. But that fact didn't deter me from seeing the extra effort required of me as evidence of my innate weakness. I pushed and worked and forced every move in a counterproductive attack. The true work, which I ignored, was in learning to let go.

After two difficult weeks in the hospital, the day came when I could sign release forms and go. The team of residents who had been following my case came in for one last group hug. Generally they talked to each other about me instead of to me. Except today. I was leaving.

"You're bionic now, Julie," the handsome one laughed.

"No more hospital food, huh? Let us know if you need a new shoulder or two," joked another.

"All the best to you," the quiet one offered.

The group of clipboards moved to the next bed. *New shoulders? Why joke about joint replacements with arthritis patients?*

Ahead of me were more weeks of rehab, sleepless nights, and a deep pain that drugs couldn't console. I couldn't feel my foot for four months, and when the nerves did begin to heal, the pain was horrible. The combined experience of four surgeries—even though successful—was overwhelming. In the following weeks, I was an emotional train wreck, derailed by the smallest tasks, overloaded with lifelong luggage. I could not seem to muster the strength to stay positive. In my head I still cycled the old tapes of victimhood. *I'm useless. I can't do it by myself. Isn't it obvious to everyone by now?*

Nine months passed as I bounced like a child between Megan's place, my parents', and the Coans' home. During that time, as I healed slowly, Tracy and Megan both gave birth to beautiful baby girls, Sophie and Mary. My friends had what I desperately wanted, but what I didn't think I could have.

Tracy helped me scrape together money from some card sales so I could rent a room in a woman's house in nearby Denville. I joined a health club and learned to use the Nautilus equipment. To my complete surprise, I realized that exercise could be fun. I was able to work my legs without dislocating a knee or having my hips stuck at right angles. Endorphins, the body's natural happy drug, began to flood my system as I proudly walked on my treadmill to freedom.

As my strength and confidence grew, I was coming to terms with other things as well. Tracy was surprised when I asked if she'd go with me to a Little People's convention in Atlantic City that summer. Up until then, I didn't even want to be a Little Person, let alone hang out with them. But I felt ready to look myself in the eyes. To know I had never really been alone.

At the convention, Tracy, who was 5'8", towered over the rest of us. At 4'4", I was average height, and for the first time in my life, I felt tall and leggy. It was disconcerting to look down at some of the kind people I met. *Is this what the tall world feels while talking with me?*

Despite the two nice men who asked me to dance, and one who asked for my phone number, my spirits started to droop. As the evening wore on, I felt displaced and defensive. I used the convenient rationalization that many of the people had achondroplasia, and their bodies were differently proportioned than mine. They looked more like each other than me. Right. The truth was that I didn't want a mirror so clear and vivid after all. I walked away, disgusted with myself. Tracy told me to give it time. In the end, she was right. The change was coming.

That October, I flew to California for Ethan's wedding. Both Ethan and Dan had converted to Catholicism two years earlier, after which I had seen less and less of them. I felt at odds with their new conservative opinions, and they were equally disappointed in my liberal ones. As I flew across the country, I made a conscious decision to put the conflict behind me, determined to show my support for Ethan, no matter what our differences were.

While Ethan and his fiancée were busy with wedding details, the rest of our family visited the Golden Gate Bridge and walked among the regal redwoods. It was fantastic to be with them, and even the spasms couldn't dim the magic. We laughed together, ate together, and practiced the songs we were going to

sing at the reception. Celia, Ray, Dan, and Kris were already
married, and after four weddings, we knew how to celebrate
with abandon. When the reception was over, though, I'd always
find a bathroom stall to cry in. Without so much as a date, let
alone a boyfriend, when would it ever be my turn?

The Latin mass was long, and the stone church was cold
and damp. But as soon as the priest pronounced Ethan and
Heidi husband and wife, warm tears rolled down our chilly
cheeks. Ethan had done it. My dark twin had made it out of the
long, lonely winter. I glanced down the pew, looking for my
parents' beaming faces, but I stopped at Ray. He was crying
with the rest of us. I'd never seen him shed a tear. I realized
something: my siblings had been saddled with a different pain--
something like survivor's guilt. Maybe it had been just as hard
for them to watch Ethan and me when they had been spared our
particular struggle.

Unpacking from Ethan's wedding, I glanced at my
calendar. Nancy and Dick Weber were running their annual
holistic health fair, and I'd volunteered to help. I'd met Nancy
Weber five years earlier at her local meditation group, and we'd
been friends ever since. This year I was feeling particularly eager
since, for the first time, my legs were straight and strong. I
hadn't gained much flexibility after the surgeries, which was a
huge disappointment because I'd had such high hopes of being
able to do deep knee bends, to kneel or sit on the floor, or to just
skip and run. But as hard as the therapists and I had tried to
force my new joints to bend beyond ninety degrees—and we
really went at it like gangbusters—my new joints wouldn't
budge. The doctor had warned that they might never achieve
full range of motion after such invasive reconstructive surgery.
Apparently, my joints were listening. At least the deep daily
pain was gone, and *that* was a very worthwhile trade.

As I drove to a meeting of the volunteers for the fair, I
visualized my prince and let myself *feel* the joy and excitement of
my dream coming true. The self-help gurus said that if I wanted

the love, the fun, and the heavenly relief of finding a partner, I had to feel it right into my reality. I had been practicing for years but, lately, I no longer ended the fantasy feeling sad about the missing man. I ended it with excitement. With belief. Maybe I was getting the hang of it after all. I was raising my vibration by becoming the answer to my own question.

I made sure that by the time I got to Nancy's meeting, my twitching eye was temporarily out of steam. *I can't smile at my soul mate with my face in a pinched sneer.* Hugging friends, I scanned the room, searching, as always, for him. I spotted an unfamiliar guy sitting on the couch. *A wedding band. Drat.*

As Nancy assigned tasks, my attention kept orbiting back to the man on the couch. His voice was warm and kind. He had a strong angular jaw, raven-black hair, and a well-trimmed beard and mustache. He was muscular and around five foot seven. At the end of the meeting, I heard him mention his elbow surgery. I was interested in hospital stories, so I grabbed the excuse and jumped into the conversation. Although Bill was funny and engaging, I tried to dismiss the attraction. *How pathetic am I, imagining a spark between us?* I thought.

Two days later, I drove to the fair. When I saw Bill standing with the other volunteers, my feet steered themselves right over to him. We talked until it was time to scatter to our jobs. I worked for an hour at the registration table then went to check on a workshop in another building. The beautiful October day hugged me with its warmth. A blue sky smiled in every direction. I strolled around the corner and there he was, with a pretty woman sitting next to him. Jealousy flashed through me. *Don't get hooked into that age-old nonsense*, I told myself. I said hi and walked on, feeling the day flittering in my soul, walking tall on new legs. I checked for tickets at a workshop and chatted with Laura, the presenter. When her eyes glanced past me, I turned to look, and found Bill leaning casually in the doorway. My jaw dropped at his feet.

"Hi. Are you done with your workshop?" I asked.

"Yeah. I came to see how *you're* doing."

He had come to find me.

We sat on a bench and talked for awhile. I sat on his left, trying to hide the twitch. I told him a little about my surgeries, my daily workout and my slow rehab. He got down on the floor to show me some stretches from his bodybuilding days. Sprawling out in the college hallway didn't seem to bother him. He was difficult to resist. *That ring. What am I thinking?*

Then I discovered it came from his second time down the aisle.

"It's pretty much over," he said. "Still hard to accept, though."

I felt a selfish spark of hope. "I'm sorry...have you two tried therapy?"

"She won't go. Ever since our son died a year ago, she barely talks to me."

"How old was your son? What happened?"

"He was born with heart and lung problems. He only lived a day. I held him as he died," Bill said softly.

"I'm so sorry. Wow. How do you get over something like that?"

"I don't know. My wife assigning me to our basement apartment hasn't helped. She's always on the phone with a guy from work, says he's only a friend. I'm not so sure."

I liked his candor but I was suspicious. Was I a sap falling for a con artist's story? Maybe he used these soap operas to cover terrible secrets. Could anyone interested in me have both oars in the water anyway? He shared details I'd never volunteer, like the fact that he had Crohn's disease, an autoimmune problem that attacks the intestines. When he was twenty-five, the doctors didn't think he'd live another year. He'd radically changed his diet and outlook and had proved them wrong.

"You've been through the wringer," I said. "What are you going to do now?"

"Pick up the pieces. As soon as my elbows are healed, I'll get back to work. Move out of the house."

When we walked back to the main building, Bill went off to help with a workshop and Nancy asked if I'd give art lessons in the childcare room. Generally, I wouldn't have been brave enough to confront a bunch of children, but I was feeling confident. Really confident. After an hour with the kids, I retreated to the lunch area. Bill found me. "Where've you been?" he asked.

"Nancy grabbed me for arts and crafts. It was great."

"I didn't want to leave without saying good-bye."

"You have to leave? I had so much fun talking with you," I said.

"Me too." He leaned over for a hug. "Here, I wrote down my phone number. Give me a call if you have any questions about those exercises I showed you—or for any reason."

"I definitely will," I said. "Talk to you soon."

I looked at the writing on the rumpled napkin. *He gave me his number!* I ignored the inner voice that said I was a desperate idiot, and instead basked in the excitement. *I'll wait a week to call him.*

"Now there's a good guy," Dick said as he hauled a stack of chairs past me. "He used to be crew chief for the Porsche racing team. Very talented. Been my mechanic for years."

A week passed with Bill splicing in and out of my thoughts. I finally picked up the phone and dialed.

"Hi, it's Julie, from the festival last weekend. How are you?"

"Hey, how are you doing? It's great to hear from you!"

Really? We chatted, but then came the blow.

"My wife and I are doing better."

"Oh, that's great." I hoped that I'd hidden my disappointment.

"Turns out she met you at one of Nancy's meditation classes."

He described me to her?

"I'm driving out to Arizona next week to visit Ariel, my daughter from my first marriage."

"How old is Ariel?" I asked. I knew so little about this man, and yet I'd let myself dream.

"She's nine." I loved the timbre of his voice and his easy laugh. "I miss her like you wouldn't believe. Look, when I get back from Arizona, we'll have you over for dinner. I love to cook."

A guy who likes the kitchen. How fantastic. I doubted that the dinner would happen but agreed. We chatted for an hour and I hung up, feeling down. Why pursue this situation? Still, I was proud I'd followed through. I tried to put him out of my mind, but after a month, a dinner with Bill and his wife didn't look so bad. Could we be friends? I decided to call.

"Hi, Bill? It's Julie again."

"Hi! I was just thinking of you. I was hoping you'd call. I was getting ready to call Nancy for your number."

Really? We chatted like old friends. Eventually, he told me that his wife's male "friend" had moved into the house while he was in Arizona, and Bill wanted out. I had hardly absorbed this startling news when he surprised me further.

"What are you doing tonight?"

"Tonight? Uh, nothing really."

"Do you want to have dinner? I could bring over my special shish-kabobs and pasta with homemade pesto."

"Sure," I said, as my skin rippled with questions. *Is this a date?* I hung up in a frenzy, my fears screeching like a cat in a bathtub. *How many times have my romantic notions been wrong? Every time.* Then I'd picture Bill and the sirens in my head couldn't obliterate the tweak of joy. Providence was pushing me out of my safety net. The times when I risked my heart didn't hurt as much as the times when I didn't. Like with Josh. I knew I had to leap. *I'll have Bill sit on my right or do the cover-and-pretend-my-eye-itches routine to try to disguise the blasted twitching.*

Apparently, he accepts my dwarfism; I don't want to test him with the HFS. Aside from that, he'll see the real me. If he's the one, I don't have to hide.

Bill arrived with a big brown bag of food and an even bigger smile. We reheated the dinner he'd prepared, and we ate, never at a loss for words. He was the richness of a deep chocolate mousse. The magic of tropical moonlight. We sat close on my couch and when our talking quieted, Bill held out his arms. I wrapped myself around him, resting my head on his warm chest. Doubt and delight rocketed through me. We melted together, entwined for a long while, such a sweet peace. And a deep hunger. I felt delirious from the excitement and wild anticipation. *What now?*

When at last I felt brave enough to look up at him, he leaned down and kissed me softly. Exhilarating waves of fear and pleasure crashed inside. The room burst into colorful flames. As we breathed each other in, I felt released by his strength and passion. Luscious kissing and hands full of heat swept me away to an intoxicating place. He pulled me closer to him, and out beyond us both.

Later that evening, as I watched his car disappear down the road, I took a deep, slow breath and smiled. The desperation was gone. For the moment anyway. The fearful girl who had yearned for everyone's love but her own was growing up. In my long wait to find him, I'd come closer to myself. That love remained even after he left that night.

In the following weeks, Bill and I saw each other almost every day. I watched cautiously to see if, and how, he'd handle his divorce. He talked about his feelings and trusted me with his sorrow. When his elbows were healed, the doctor released Bill to work. He found a job as a master mechanic at Saturn, rented an apartment, sold his van, and bought a smaller car. Although his progress was reassuring, I was on a rocky roller coaster ride. The wisdom I'd always heard but never truly believed was now ringing true: whatever you most desire in your life is often the thing you have most feared. Love was finally knocking at my door, even as I was finding nervous reasons to slam it shut.

It's the classic rebound, right? A recipe for disaster! Can I trust him? What about his past? I must be crazy. Desperate. Blind! Will he come to his senses and flick me aside? Will his wife beg him to come home? The possibilities kept me on guard. Even though we had been together for a month, and he regularly stayed over, we hadn't slept together. I wanted him in every way, but I was so afraid he was going to leave.

"How is it," I asked him on the phone one night, "that you're able to trust love again after two failed marriages?"

"I don't know exactly. Well, partly because they weren't a complete loss. I have a terrific daughter and . . ."

"I'm sorry, I didn't mean . . ."

"It's okay. I do feel like I failed sometimes, but I know that I'm bound to get it right one of these days."

I admired his faith and courage. Why take the past and lob it into the future, as I so often did?

The next morning, I took a break from painting to retrieve the mail. A colorful envelope from Celia greeted me, as well as a letter from my dad. I opened the phone bill first, saving the good stuff for last. I was surprised that I owed $100, twice the usual amount. I quickly discovered the mistake, an eleven-minute call to Florida for a whopping $45. I called the phone company to explain the error but the operator informed me, snickering, that the call was a 900 number—a sex line.

"A *what?* I've never called one of those numbers in my life!" No doubt an excuse she'd heard before.

"I had it electronically traced. It came from your residence," she said firmly.

Getting nowhere with her, I hung up. *The phone company's in for a fight . . .* Then it hit me. Bill. On a few occasions, I'd left him at the house alone. A sickening feeling punctured my stomach. *I've been duped by a lecherous deviant! What a fool I've been!* The rage and hurt pummeled my crimson face. *How could I have been so naive?*

It was four o'clock. Bill was coming for dinner at six. I paced and cried, wanting to rip him limb from limb and then kick him out the door. When Bill arrived, I was waiting, anxious to deliver the blow. He greeted me with his warm smile. I coldly handed him the bill and began to rant and rave, watching his face for signs of guilt. He stared at the bill, dumbstruck; then he pulled a time card from his wallet.

"I was at work that day, see?" he said calmly.

Then it dawned on me that he'd started his new job that week and hadn't been alone in my house.

"The operator insisted it was from my line," I said defensively. I scanned the bill. Now I saw a call to my friend Lisa on her birthday. The time of the two calls overlapped by several minutes. The phone company had indeed made a mistake. Bill was vindicated, but I kept staring at him, thoroughly stuck in my anger. Was this feeling a sign that I shouldn't be with him? The omen business was such a tricky one to manage.

"I need time alone. I'm going to a meditation class at Nancy's tonight," I said.

"What about dinner?"

"I'm not hungry."

"Do you want to meet back here for dessert? I'll go pick up some..."

I waved him off.

I cried as I drove to Nancy's. During our meditation, my feelings came clean. Fears had been triggered that were there long before Bill: the fear of investing my heart, the fear of rejection, the fear of my sexuality. Wait. What could be more perfect then a mistaken charge to a sex number! Maybe it was no accident. Angels work at the phone company, don't they?

After class, I rushed home, hoping Bill would be waiting after all. *Please be there. Please be there.*

And there he was, sitting on the front step. Waiting just for me.

"Hi," he said quietly and handed me a box of chocolate-dipped strawberries, a small stuffed animal, and a card.

God, I felt like a jerk. "Why are you giving me gifts when I'm the one who owes you an apology?"

"Because I don't blame you for doubting me. My past relationships suck."

"No, it's me. I'm so sorry." I avoided his eyes; the forgiving look in them was too much. "I accused you and then dumped on you even after I realized the mistake. I was angry at myself...for being afraid. For not trusting you. Or me."

"It's all right. So—I guess this was our first fight."

"But you didn't argue."

"It takes a lot to tip me over."

"Not me. I'm like that little teapot who gets all steamed up."

"Good thing I love tea," he said.

I leaned on him for a hug before the tears poured out.

Despite a lifetime of extreme modesty, I was finally feeling more at home in my cherubic birthday suit. Bill wasn't turned off by my differences, and being around him felt exciting and natural. It was time to drop my fear and my ridiculous notion of virtue; the chastity belt had to go.

"I'm going to the pharmacy on my way from work, need anything?" he asked on the phone.

Here was my opportunity. "Hmm, there's one thing I can think of," I meowed in my best *Playboy* tone.

He paused. "Really?" Bill had never pushed me on the subject.

"No glove, no love," I said.

"Are you sure?"

"You better hurry before I change my mind."

"I'm on my way," he laughed. It was only one o'clock in the afternoon.

I was anxious and excited for the rest of the day. The relationship had been going so well. Would tonight change anything? When I answered the door that evening, Bill stood on the front steps with a goofy smile and a little brown bag from the pharmacy. We laughed like guilty kids. I was glad he wasn't acting like the smooth operator.

We ate dinner and talked about everything but the little brown bag. Bill was usually open about sex; now he was quiet. I felt positively aglow but wondered what to do. A further bond might leave our hearts out on the line, allowing a dark seriousness to eclipse the fun. We watched television, bathing in a roomful of pheromones. Finally, I realized that my fiery Italian was trying to be a gentleman. I decided not to be a lady and I jumped him. The boundaries fell away as we began our romp into the night. There was unexpected lightness in the air, and as we laughed and relaxed, we smoothed out the hours in pleasure. When the dawn woke us, still entwined, we greedily kissed the new day. And the next. And the one after that. The following weeks were filled with romance and fun. The insecurity over my dwarfism, I thought, was far behind me.

Twelve
Small World

Lift up your eyes
and look on one another in innocence,
born of complete forgiveness
of each other's illusions.
~A Course in Miracles

My art business was picking up as two big calligraphy jobs fell in my lap. Bill encouraged me to advertise in one of the expensive bridal magazines and as soon as the ad appeared, the jobs flowed in steadily. Between the increased calligraphy work and time with Bill, I cut back on my trips to the gym from six days a week to three. After a set of exercises at the knee press one day, I bent over to stretch out my hips before moving on to the stair stepper. Suddenly, a pair of sneakers planted themselves on the worn brown carpet in front of me. I paused, still bent, hoping the onlooker would retreat to another machine. The feet didn't budge, so I looked up. *Whoa.* "Hi there, cutie! How are you?" Chase asked brightly.

I was shocked but managed to return his hug.

"Good, thanks." Actually I was a sweaty mess.

"What a cool coincidence. 'Course, there's no such thing!" he laughed. "I've been teaching yoga here for the last six months. You?"

"I've been coming here for over a year."

"Strange that we never ran into each other . . . so what else have you been up to?"

"Well, I had both my hips and both knees replaced." Had he noticed the nine-inch red scars running down my knees?

"All four? Man." He squatted down in front of me so that we were eye to eye. He'd always been sweet that way. "Now you're pumping iron." His smile was so appealing. I tried not to feel whatever it was that I was feeling.

"I'm trying to get more flexibility."

"It looks very good on you." He stared uncomfortably long.

I felt pressure behind my eye signaling the twitch. "You know, I'd better get back to my exercises before my muscles get cold."

"It's really good to see you. Hey, do you want to have lunch sometime?"

"Uh, okay." I thought about Bill.

"How about Wednesday at noon; I don't have any classes."

"This Wednesday? I think I'm free."

"It's set." He spoke into a handheld recorder. "Date with Julie, Wednesday at noon." Then back to me. "I'm teaching at the massage school. Do you want to meet there or here?"

"I'm closer to the school."

"Great. See you then!"

"Bye."

Hmm. Why did I bump into him now of all times? I wondered. Do I need closure . . . or do I want to know if he still cares? Maybe he's an old dream that could turn into a nightmare.

"You're quiet," Bill said at dinner. "How's the calligraphy going?"

"One bride wants hydrangeas watercolored on each envelope and gold calligraphy. I mean, *hydrangeas?* Not an easy flower to do quickly. I've tried to steer her away from the metallic ink. It's such a mess."

"You've got to charge more for complicated flowers or that ink. Did you finish your price list? People will take one look at

your paintings and want custom artwork. If you have your
prices ready, you won't undersell yourself."

He knew me well already. "You're right," I said. "I have to
do that. Bill, uh, you'll never believe who I ran into at the gym
today. Chase."

"Really?" His fork hung in midair for a second.

"We're having lunch on Wednesday. I hope you don't
mind." I studied his face.

His answer was somewhat hesitant. "Okay, do whatever
you need to do."

"I think I need some closure or something. It's weird it's
happening now, when I'm so happy with you. I think the angels
are helping me clean up unfinished business."

"As long as you're not swabbing the decks of me," he said
with a smile.

I called Tracy the morning before my lunch with Chase.

"Order red wine," she commanded.

"You know I don't like it."

"Not to drink, you idiot, to fling at him."

Tracy had never liked Chase four years earlier and was
questioning my sanity now. He was flighty. He hated making
plans. He was always running. What was he now, twenty-four?

"Do you have an appointment?" the receptionist asked
when I got to the massage school.

"No, I'm here to meet a friend for lunch."

Fifteen minutes ticked by as I twitched in my seat, keeping
one eye on the door. It was a familiar feeling.

At twelve forty-five, the receptionist gave me a sympathetic
look. "Do you need the phone?"

"Is Chase around?" I asked, feeling ridiculous.

"He doesn't have any clients today. May I call him for
you?"

"I guess so, thanks."

She dialed the phone. "Chase? This is Rita at the massage
school. You have a lunch date who's been waiting for almost an

hour . . . yes, one moment." She lowered her voice to a whisper, "He wants to talk to you, dear."

"Thanks." I felt like the old ball and chain again.

I picked up the phone. "Hey, there."

"Oh man, Julie, I'm so sorry! I lost that stupid cassette player and I forgot everything I'd put on it."

Airhead. "I guess I wasn't high on your list."

"No, that's not it. I've just been really busy. I've got so much going on and can't keep everything straight."

Tell your same story, walking, I thought.

"That's why I bought the recorder, but then I don't know what happened to it."

I laughed out loud. *Angels probably hid it for me.*

"You're really hating me right now, aren't you?"

"No, it's no problem. Maybe another time," I lied.

"Promise?"

"Who knows. I'll talk to you later."

"Wait, I don't have your number."

"I'll call you. Rita has your number." *We've all got your number, bub.*

I hung up and thanked Rita, who looked satisfied with the conclusion. I walked back to my car as thoughts of Bill stood up and cheered.

May seemed especially beautiful that year as I waited outside for Bill to pick me up. The air was buttery warm. Daffodils popped up all around the yard. I think the crocuses were singing love songs to the bees. And Mother Nature cupped the sky in laughter, spinning me in her expanse. As I sat there drinking in the day, the glory grew richer, wider. I felt folded into the mix like honey, buzzing with vision and possibilities. The earth was reborn and I was in love. Then the insistent facial twitching barged in, and *wham*—I fell all out of step. It slammed my eye shut and pulled at the edge of my mouth; if I tried to smile, I looked like a growling dog. It woke me at night and triggered headaches. If it would only go away, I told myself, everything would be ideal.

I forced my left eye shut tight for ten minutes in order to exhaust the nerves, so that when Bill arrived, I could smile without any contortion. It was Friday and we were heading to his apartment for the weekend. Recently, Bill had suggested we move in together. The thrill had squeezed me tighter than he had. But I worried that if it didn't work out we'd have the anguish of separating our belongings as well as our hearts. As much as I loved him, I didn't want to jump in too soon. I also wanted to meet his daughter, Ariel, first. We were to pick her up from the airport the next day.

"Julie's an artist," Bill had told Ariel on the phone a few weeks before. "Maybe you two can paint together when you get here."

That had made me cringe. He so wanted us to get along. Would I be one more woman in the way of her dad? Not to mention, a very different one.

"I think you may be taller than she is," I'd heard Bill say. "She's a dwarf."

That had stopped me cold. I'd never heard that phrase from Bill's mouth or from anyone who knew me well. He had said it so sweetly, though, as if he were describing the color of my hair. I'd forced myself to use the word, "dwarf," when we were together, hoping to get used to it. It hadn't worked for me yet. Apparently, it had become second nature to Bill.

We drove to the airport to get Ariel, my stomach in a tangled knot. Divorce could be brutal on everyone. I felt I was stepping into a disaster zone without a first-aid kit. Bill told me how he regretted agreeing to let his ex-wife move out of the state five years earlier. Months after they left, as it became more difficult to see his daughter, he had realized his mistake. At the airport, Bill hurried past the flight attendant to grab Ariel. They were a joyful sight. As they hugged and laughed, Ariel looked over her dad's shoulders and said, "Hi, Julie!" Phew. She took me in without a hitch.

Although I had seen pictures, she was even prettier in person. Already a half-foot taller than I was, she had dark blond hair and chocolatey cat eyes that twinkled like her dad's.

The week together was wonderful, and disappeared in a flash. Back at the airport, Ariel and Bill exchanged sad smiles, hating to say good-bye again. Only allowed to be with one parent at a time, her young soul was torn down the middle. The difficulty might mold her in a way I hated to envision. Then again, life's hardest knocks can transform into the greatest gifts.

Driving home from the airport, Bill was unusually quiet, and his eyes glistened with tears. "She doesn't have the life she deserves. Saying good-bye is the roughest part of all."

Between trying to see over the cart or reach things on the shelves, grocery shopping had long been an enormous chore for me. I was a magnet for curious children, and if I didn't get caught in line with snickering kids, then I would bump into several in the aisle. Shopping with Bill, though, had turned the grocery store into a walk in the park.

"Salmon looks fresh, how about I grill some tonight?" Bill asked.

I'd never liked seafood until Bill cooked flounder the week before.

"You're the Italian Scallion. I'll give it a whirl."

The fishmonger weighed the salmon. "Shrimp is on sale," he said, smiling at me. "Does your daughter like shrimp?"

I usually overlooked these blunders, just as my friends and family had.

"She's not my daughter," Bill laughed. "This is my girlfriend!"

Both the fishmonger and I were as wide-eyed as the fish in the case. Bill remained unfazed, though, and that meant the world to me.

Ten months later, we moved my clothes, my art table, my books, and my heart into his apartment. I was sailing so high above my old life that I thought sadness would never visit again. Happiness had settled squarely on my shoulders, and no weight could ever be as heavy as those I'd left behind.

I wanted to tell Ethan and Dan about my new address, but because of their Catholic conversions, I knew it wouldn't be welcome news. Ethan, whose car once touted the bumper sticker "Question Authority" had since replaced it with "Abortion is Murder." We lived within miles of each other, but we were worlds apart. I hoped that some day my left and their right could find common ground. I sent them a note to say that I was sorry that they wouldn't agree with my decision to live with Bill, but that we were very happy. Ethan called two days later.

"Hi, E!" I said. I was surprised to hear his voice.

"Hi." His tone was somber. "I got your letter and . . . I know you're not going to want to hear this, but I'd be betraying what's right if I didn't tell you. Living with someone before marriage is wrong. It's a sin."

"O-kay," I said slowly. "I obviously don't agree. The Catholic Church doesn't hold a monopoly on truth, Ethan."

"Yes, it does."

"If it works for you, fine, but this is my life and I . . ."

"What if you get pregnant?"

"What? You know that's really none of your business."

"You're my sister, and I love you! Is Bill going to get his previous marriage annulled? If he doesn't, and you marry, Dan and I can't come to the wedding. Have you thought about that?" I could feel his anger chewing through the receiver like a determined bulldog.

I sat in stunned silence as he lectured on. "I'm hanging up if you don't put a lid on it," I told him.

His tirade continued and I hung up, disgusted and shaking. I took the phone off the hook. Ethan would try calling back. And I locked the door. I didn't know him anymore. That night, I cried when I told Bill. I cried more when a letter came from Dan two weeks later. My older brother wrote that he would always love me and could continue seeing me, alone, but would not allow his children to be around Bill and me as a couple. He believed that since Bill was born Catholic, he was still married to his ex-wife in the Church's eyes. Well, two ex-wives. So I was an adulteress. The law, and a few divorce papers, didn't count. To them it was black and white. Right or wrong. You were with the Church or you were against it. *Don't my brothers have any faith in me? I'm thirty-two years old! Are they afraid for my salvation? Or for their own? Will I ever see them again?*

Talking to Megan on the phone, I told her that the angry letters I'd written to Ethan and Dan weren't helping me find resolution. Retaliation never does. Blame never does. In the big picture, my brothers weren't responsible for my feelings. I was. I needed to stop the constant arguing in my mind. I needed to stop talking about "what they did" to everyone who asked about them. The fury I felt was just a cover-up for fear. Another reason to claim "victimhood." I'd started doubting myself ever since their harsh decree, because, even though I felt at times that I'd been judged unfairly in my life, never had it been by my own family.

"I want to wring their necks," Megan said. She had been on a royal diatribe over the news, and her strong reaction was validating. "Do they know what century we're living in? Where's their Christian tolerance and love?"

"It's an inner reflection, though, right?" I asked. "I've never openly proclaimed that I know the truth, but I've done it silently. I've judged people. Projected my insecurities. I've needed to be right. I'm pissed at my brothers for being like me."

"Well, we're all guilty of that. Guess that's partly why I've been so hot under the collar. Damn mirror," Megan laughed.

"I want to stop working so hard at being 'right,' and work on finding peace."

"Oh *Jule,* your brothers will give you practice with that! Whenever my family questions my character, I cave. You've talked me through a hundred of those times. Ultimately, you rest at the center of the whiplash where there's acceptance and surrender. If I remember to allow my spirit in, everything feels fine. Until the next go-'round."

Within a few days, my whole family knew. It was an unexpected blow, especially to my parents. Vacations together in Canada or at Christmastime would be impossible. Ethan and Dan said that they could not sleep under the same roof as Bill and me. Me versus them? Crazy! Although I had been growing apart from Ethan and Dan, I loved them so much. I always would. And there was nothing better than when the whole family got together. This new development seemed the most unlikely thing to happen to us.

I had many reassuring phone calls with Celia, Ray, and Kris. Ray, who had also converted to Catholicism years before, was an unexpected help. He understood Ethan and Dan's convictions better than any of us. One night, as he and I were talking on the phone, he explained, patiently, lovingly, some of the ins and outs of Catholicism, and Dan and Ethan's perspective. Along the way, I also learned more about Ray's complicated relationship with Dan. About the competition, the push and pull, the unspoken respect. I hadn't been as close to Ray as I had been to Dan and Ethan over the years. Ray had always seemed distant. But in the noisy clang of our family, maybe we couldn't hear Ray's quiet ways. Maybe I hadn't tried. Now, across the miles, he was the thoughtful voice of reason and faith. Leaning my tired head against the kitchen wall, listening to his soft words, warm tears slipped out. I missed this man I was now getting to know better. I could feel understanding returning to my heart. There was a love that was bigger than all this right-and-wrong business, which could tear people apart. Or bring them together. Two brothers stepped out of my life as the other stepped in.

Bill and I wondered what an annulment of his previous marriage would entail (only one wedding was in the Catholic Church.) We soon learned that the process would cost about a thousand dollars, but neither the money nor our wishes would guarantee that an annulment would be granted. Bill would have to go before two tribunals. Yikes. His ex-wife would have to complete a long personal questionnaire. It was unlikely that she would comply. Then the final kicker. According to one priest, our intention "to repair family unity," was not a justifiable reason for an annulment in the Church's book. We gave up when we realized we couldn't live the life that anyone else wanted for us. We were already living the life that we loved.

To my parents' credit, they quickly accepted the new situation. They would find ways to visit all their children and grandchildren even if we couldn't all be together. No matter where we stood, right or wrong, black or white, near or far, there was nothing that would ever shake their love. Nothing.

Cleaning up in the kitchen one Saturday morning, I saw a note that I'd put in Bill's lunch the day before. I'd written, "J.H. Loves W.G.," with a corny heart drawn around our initials. But Bill had since scratched out the H of my name and put a G in its place. Shivers ran up my arms. This wonderful man was imagining marrying me. Me! My bare feet smacked against the cold linoleum as I went to find him. Right then, he came around the corner.

"Nice note," I blushed. "What are *you* grinning about?"

"When I heard your footsteps just now, I was thinking: I always knew I'd hear the pitter-patter of tiny feet around my house, but I never imagined they'd be yours."

"I'm glad you don't mind."

"Mind? I love that you're different," Bill said with a hug. "You're a beautiful lady. I thought that from the moment I saw you."

"Oh, come on. You must have done a double take when you met me."

He cocked his head and looked at me for a second. "Do you know what first attracted me to you?"

Oh please don't say my boobs.

"It was your voice," he said with a smile. "The night we met, I heard you call out to Nancy, and I looked up to see who it was. There was such joy in your voice."

"But...what about the rest . . . the differences? The twitching is so ugly, and you have to look at me every day."

"The twitching doesn't bother me except when it bothers you. We all come with our quirks. You accepted me and my baggage."

He so warmed my heart. "You are so swee—oh hey, that reminds me, my first Botox injection is on Monday afternoon."

"My health nut is going through with the shots of botulism?" he asked.

"If it can help calm the spasms, it'll be worth it."

"I'll get out early from work so I can take you."

"Really? That would be great. The doctor suggested someone drive me home, but I figured I'd be okay. Actually, if the Botox works, I'll be more than okay, I'll be free!"

"You can be free, sweetheart, whether the Botox helps or not."

Botox wouldn't fix the physical condition, only mask it. Complications were possible too. It might look like I'd had a stroke all the time instead of fifty percent of the time. But as I sat in the neurologist's examination room, imagining my face calm and easy, it felt like I was propped up by pure sunshine.

"I must mix the proportions correctly, then we'll be ready," the doctor said, showing me a vial of Botox. He reminded me of Dr. Jekyll.

The thought of the injections was starting to make me sweat. Twelve jabs of Botox and the jumpy nerves would be paralyzed for months.

"In a few days you should notice some improvement. Takes a week or two for the full effect."

I could barely wait!

Dr. Yoder sat on a stool in front of me and gawked at the spasms. "This is the worst case of HFS I've seen." He actually laughed. I wanted to slug him. Maybe the Botox had paralyzed his heart.

"Do you have a ride home?" he asked as he put in the first needle. "Your eye may swell. It's better if you don't drive."

"My boyfriend is out in the waiting room."

The doctor sent in two more shots. "Is he handicapped also?"

The question went farther under my skin than the needles. "No, he isn't."

"Well, good for you." He sounded surprised.

He withdrew the last needle and handed me a tissue for the blood spots, all the while staring at my twitching, apparently unaware I was present. Then he walked me to the waiting room, no doubt to take a gander at the boyfriend. On the way home, Bill listened as I relayed the conversation.

"Julie, the man's a fool, and 'when you argue with a fool . . .'"

"I know — 'nobody can tell the difference.'"

"I'm sorry he's a jerk but it doesn't matter what he thinks. As long as you get some relief, I don't care if he's Mr. Hyde."

Thirteen
Two Souls, One Heart

I honor the place
where if you are in that place, in you,
and I am in that place, in me,
there is only one of us.
"Namaste"

I'd only had my hair cut and styled once before, a gift to myself before my first surgery four years ago. On this extraordinary April day, as I sat in front of Jane, the stylist, I felt like royalty.

"Easy on the hair spray," Tracy said. "Jules hates that ozone killer."

"We don't want the curls bouncing out of the wreath, though," Jane said.

"You're right. Let her have it. Your lungs will forgive you, Leibchen," Tracy assured me.

When I was through, Tracy sighed in delight. "*Dah*ling, your hair really is *fah*bulous!"

"You'd know hair." We laughed, remembering how Tracy used to scam me into curling her hair instead of doing homework. We drove to her house where my bridal party was getting ready.

"Your hair is beautiful!" said Casely, now a pretty young lady of ten.

"Cool curls," Zack added. He was seven, dressed in a shirt, tie, and colorful underpants.

"Ooooh. Can I have my hair up like that?" Sophie, my youngest goddaughter, asked Tracy.

"Sure, on *your* wedding day."

Bill, my parents, Ray, his wife Sarah, and their three kids were getting ready back at our house. Kris, her husband Greg, and their four kids were there at Tracy's; and Celia, her husband Jack, and their two girls were next door at the Coan Senior's wing of the big house. The air positively sparkled with electricity. People bustled this way and that, in and out of doors, barreling up and down stairs, all for Bill and for me. Everyone knit together again, like our summer vacations in Canada or Christmas at Mom and Dad's.

Caravanning to the church, my face was sewn up in a permanent smile. The only thing that made me nervous was making it down the aisle without any unbearable twitching. The last Botox visit had done a pretty good job. When I told the doctor about my wedding, he was intrigued. Me marrying someone "normal."

My dad and I stood at the back of the church with my wedding party — Tracy, Celia, Kris, Casely, and Sophie — lined up in front of us. The doors opened. I couldn't see Bill, but I smiled knowing he was there waiting. Just for me. The organ began to play, and as Simone Ramel's voice sang out across the rafters, the billowing notes held my breath on high. Amazing Grace.

"This is it, Juli-kins," my dad said with a proud grin, my arm curled around his like a vine. "Are you ready?"

"Yeah, Dad." I said, smiling with everything I had. His big blue eyes were lit up with unbounded love, with treasured memories of our years together. Like the time I came downstairs in my high school graduation dress and his whole smile raced to hug me before he could even get up from his chair. Or when he first saw my paintings after a summer at Rhode Island School of Design. I found him standing in front of them, speechless with pride and amazement. Or all the times he laughed so hard at one of my silly expressions. Or when he asked me if I wanted to go to Dunkin' Donuts, or the hardware store, or to get the Sunday paper with him. Or how we read the Sunday comics together. Or how he had always brought smiling flowers home for me every birthday. All the countless joys he had added to my beautiful bouquet since then. As I looked up at him, a lifetime of love blossomed from inside him like a spell. Like Home.

As my dad and I began down the aisle, so many loving faces held me fast in their light. Megan McWilliams, Judy Prescott, Trish O'Neill, Judi Hancox, Nancy and Dick Weber, and friends from every part of my journey were there to usher in my new life. My nine nieces and nephews giggled in their spiffy new clothes. Bill's sisters and brothers smiled as we walked towards the altar. I'd never felt so much love in one room. Their eyes said that I was special to them. That I was important. I belonged. I tried to memorize every single second so I could bottle it forever. At the front of the church, Celia, Kris, and Tracy dabbed away tears, their smiles barely containing the emotion bubbling up. For me.

Then I saw my mom. Glowing like sunlight through a prism, her cheeks were dripping with rain. She was full of color and joy and life. Like how she always laughed hysterically when she rode a roller coaster. Or the way she sat up with me night after night helping me write my first term paper in high school. Or how she woke me for school with her sweet "good morning" song. Or how she was willing to drive my friends and me anywhere—to the mall or the movies or someone's house for a sleepover. Or how she always harmonized when we sang the "Happy Birthday" song—and now, so do I. Always willing to give herself completely, she lived life with an optimism that eventually rubbed off on me. She had been there every day, teaching my heart to sing. My spirit to dance. I saw it as I walked by, deep in her eyes. I came from her. I came from that luminous love.

And there stood Bill, his white smile boosted up in a proud black tux. I'd waited so long to find him. Now I felt he'd been with me, every starlit night, all along. The loving and talented mechanic who had answered my troubled car-karma. He had dipped my soul in the chocolate-covered truth, an inner place that was more real than flesh. Long before this day, we had already kissed each other home.

When Bill and I were pronounced husband and wife, the church roared. Angels cheered.

At the reception, my family entertained us with fun songs and sweet songs, all dotted with harmony and synchronized dance steps. My nieces, nephews, and godchildren accompanied on every type of instrument and then brought down the house with their rendition of "So Long Farewell" from *The Sound of Music*. It was my family at their finest, dishing out their enthusiasm and generous love. Bill's older sister, Bernie, made a luscious spread of food for the entire party. Sadly, Ariel was back in California, unable to join the fun.

Ethan and Dan also missed the day, as they had indicated when I moved in with Bill. In years past, they sure would've enjoyed being a part of the show. As Trish and her husband James were cutting up the dance floor, I told her she was still the best dancer and looked gorgeous in her gown. "For what I paid for this dress," she grinned, "it should be able to dance by itself." My family and friends pranced and laughed until late into the evening, and when it was time to say good-bye, Bill and I held each other and looked out across the clubhouse floor. It was lit up with tiny white lights, not glittering chandeliers, and decorated with homemade bouquets, not fancy arrangements. It was not an expensive hall and we didn't have a five-piece band, but it was rich with love, laughter, promise, and the devotion of family and friends. And, of course, angels, who pulled open the heavens to celebrate our perfect night.

It was a brilliant beach day in Canada as Bill and I lounged under a forever sky. Kris and Celia were down at the edge of Lake Erie, sparkling in the water with their kids. They were taking turns throwing the ball for our wonderful yellow lab mix, Norman, whom we had adopted from a shelter a year earlier. Norm was a daily source of joy and fun.

"It's not our Caribbean honeymoon," I said, "but Silver Bay will always feel like home."

"Aunt Doodle!" Kris's youngest daughter, Heather, called from the water. "Are you coming in?"

"I'm on my way." I struggled to get up from the low beach chair for the hundredth time that day. My legs were pain-free, but still not particularly flexible, so I often used my arms to compensate.

"Easy does it, hon," Bill said. "Don't go breaking any records."

I waded into the marble blue lake, with Norm happily leading the way, as toys flew and rafts tipped howling kids into the water. Years ago, my little cousin, Kunji, had first dazzled my heart with the possibility of having my own kids. When Kunji and I met again, after many, many years apart, that old connection was still there; the family bond was as solid as her loving hug.

Watching my nieces, nephews, and godchildren grow up had cemented the longing. *But what if I'm too small to have kids? Too different?*

That night, I lay on the front porch couch, stretching my achy arms up over my head. This is the life, I thought, as the crickets song strummed the stillness. Bill came in with a snack, but when I sat up to join him, a painful stab shot through my right shoulder. "Ow! Oh, that hurt!"

"Are you okay?"

"I don't know. Ow! I can't move my arm!"

Bill came over to the couch. "Let me . . ."

"No! Don't touch it! It hurts when I try to move it. I think my shoulder's locked up." My elbows had often done the same thing when I was a kid. The nerve pain had been severe.

"Can you lie back? I'll get some ice."

I started to lean back but the motion sent the same pain down my arm. "Oh, God, it's really stuck." I stared at him, my eyes wildly pecking into his.

"Breathe, hon. Panicking will make it worse. Here, let's prop you up so you can relax. It's probably just a spasm." He arranged some pillows behind me and cautiously put one under my arm. "How's that?"

"Bearable, I guess. If I don't move." The evening wore on, the spasm did not wear off. "How am I going to sleep?" I whined.

"We'll do the best we can with pillows and ibuprofen."

"I hate taking drugs. They're just a . . ."

". . . Band-aid, I know. But without a medicine woman handy, we'll have to make do. You can gobble all the herbs and weeds you want later."

At night, I lay in bed unable to find a position where my shoulder didn't throb and scream. The painful darkness ran me backwards into frightening images: hospitals, naked photos, white-coats. *We just want to look at your pretty face. Would you mind standing on this table for us?* By three in the morning, I was sobbing and out of control. Everything that Bill tried was met with more tears and resistance. He stood by the bed, losing patience fast.

"Why won't you let me take you to the hospital? Maybe you have a fracture or something."

"They can't help me!" My face twitched. "I won't go!"

"Then take more ibuprofen. Please." Bill gave me the pills and turned on the radio. I focused on the music, trying to calm down. Finally, sleep won out. By morning, my arm was greatly improved. Gladness swept in. *Phew. It's all over.*

The following week, back in New Jersey, I got busy on a wedding job. After lettering only ten envelopes in calligraphy, I had to stop. I sat with an ice pack on my shoulder then took some herbs. *It'll be fine,* I told myself, *I just need to go slower.*

Bill massaged my shoulder every night. I used special oils and took supplements and homeopathic remedies, feeling sure I was making progress. But each time I'd try to work, the pain would return. So I'd get the ice, and sit and wait. I'd close my eyes and breathe, picturing angels and fountains of light. I'd smile into my bones and relax every muscle. Opening my eyes, I'd feel calm again.

The following week, after icing my shoulder, I went to push myself off the couch and the same pain ripped through my shoulder. *Don't panic.* I tried to stand to go put the ice pack in the freezer. Pain leveled me again. *I'm stuck here. I'm stuck! Go get the ibuprofen. No, don't move.* When Bill got home two hours later, I was a quaking mess.

At three in the morning, I was still awake, crying in pain.

"We're going to the emergency room," Bill said firmly.

"No!"

"You're not being rational, Julie. We've got to do something." An hour later, I gave in. What choice was there?

"I know you think doctors are ogres," Bill said as we drove, "but they might be able to help."

The X-ray technician eased me up onto the cold metal slab as I sniffled and cradled my arm. Every motion made me wince. The doctor arrived and examined me. "You have a lot of inflammation but nothing is broken or fractured. The X-rays show degenerative arthritis, but since you've had hip and knee replacements, I assume this pain is not a surprise."

"This felt more like an injury, though."

"You have a frozen shoulder," the doctor said as she read from her folder. "You probably aggravated it while swimming that day. I'll give you something for the pain and the swelling."

In desperation, I swallowed the big pink pill, the same one I'd befriended after my surgeries. As we drove home, I cried in exhaustion. Nothing was wrong but something definitely wasn't right. I managed to finish the big calligraphy job, but I sat with an ice pack every afternoon and every night, fighting with a grisly concoction of rage and sadness.

In the following months, my shoulder continued locking up, and the recovery time grew longer and longer. I started turning away calligraphy jobs, afraid to accept work and then leave someone high and dry. Bill wanted me to see an orthopedist, but I refused.

"They'll want to cut me open, Bill. Then I'll be in this pain every night for months! Maybe forever! Does that sound like a good solution?"

"Maybe they can go in arthroscopically and . . ."

"I can't do it! I can't!"

"It might be a simple procedure . . ."

"There's no such thing!" I screamed. "You have absolutely no idea what I went through during my surgeries! This is my right arm. What if they screw it up permanently?"

"You can't go on like this, though."

"I won't do it again! I can't!"

Bill bowed his head. When he was a kid, his mom hadn't taken him to the hospital when he was badly burned in the kitchen, or when he was stung by a swarm of bees. They finally went to the emergency room when he turned blue. In general, Bill's mom didn't reach out to friends, neighbors, or even doctors. She had never learned to drive. Because money was very tight, his dad worked two jobs and was rarely home, so there was no one around to whisk a child to the hospital. Plus, with five children, Bill's mom must have witnessed a whole lot of hard bumps on the head and worrisome accidents. She had probably learned to wait these things out. Way too long. So now Bill and I were on opposite sides of the medical coin—I'd always wanted to run away from the very thing he had needed.

Several weeks later, after a particularly bad shoulder episode, I gave in and went to an orthopedic surgeon. He took one look at my X-rays, saw the extensive degeneration, and recommended a specialist at the Joint Replacement Hospital in New York City. Two months later, after many wrenching discussions with Bill, I made the appointment. As we waited in the doctor's office, I drew my weapons, polished my armor. I wasn't about to allow arthroscopic surgery. The doctors' solution to everything involved knocking you out and slicing you up. But as we drove home after the appointment, I was reeling from the news.

"How can this be happening?" I sobbed. "A total shoulder replacement? It isn't fair! Just when my art was going somewhere. Just when life was falling into place!"

"I don't know, hon. I'll be right beside you, whatever the course."

"You mean surgery? God, Bill, I can't even think about the hospital without crying. I can't go through it again. It'll push me right over the edge. Shoulders are the most complicated joint, harder to recover from than knees and that was horrible. No way!"

It had been a year since the first shoulder incident. Every day I was afraid of causing a spasm with the slightest move. My only exercise was the regular use of my Wiffle bat, swinging it with my left arm, leaving it spent long before the rage expired. Months went by. I tried every alternative. Waiting. Looking. Hoping. Nightmares often woke me in a cold sweat. *How can I live like this? I can't give up my art! It's the one thing that makes sense. Wasn't I meant to be an artist?*

A week later, I finally put aside my calligraphy and watercolors completely. I discontinued advertising and referred customers to another calligrapher. It hit me immediately. Without something to contribute, I was lost.

My family was brimming with hard workers, and I was raised in its electric field. My dad gave an inexhaustible effort to his marketing job in New York City. He often brought work home on weeknights and weekends, spreading his impressive papers across our long dining room table. His face would lock in such serious concentration that no one wanted to disturb him. He wrote with such intensity that his pen shook the whole table. Attempting my homework at the same table felt like trying to needlepoint while riding a dirt bike. Everyone knew that Dad's commitment to excellence, to his family, and to his business was as sharp as lightning.

My mom was a dedicated real estate agent but with a more lighthearted approach. She enjoyed helping her customers in their search for the perfect home, a good school system, the right price. She celebrated when everything worked out, and she ached when things fell through. But she also worked long, unpredictable hours. She rarely said no to her clients, no matter what they needed, what time of night they called, or when they asked to see yet another house. She was a real estate therapist-advisor-lawyer all wrapped into one energetic ball.

My grandparents were also dedicated workers, and I have no doubt the work ethic went back much farther. So I wasn't about to be the first to break our long line of tireless workers. I had worked hard in school. Really hard. I had worked hard to understand my world. Really worked. I had worked hard at my art, a seeming contradiction as the work was meant to bring joy. I had worked hard to please others. *Please, please love me.* My single-minded concentration had cleaved two permanent vertical creases between my eyebrows. Work, work, work. Work equals goodness. Work leads to rewards. Tremendously hard work brings God-sized rewards.

Didn't Spirit expect hard work in order to solve life's riddle, find the code, make the grade? And to know the hidden God, something so awesome — well, I was sure *that* would take some major work. It would take the brightest, the smartest, the most diligent to stay the course, right? My meditation practice had fallen by the wayside since it seemed like time off that I didn't deserve. I was so hungry to understand the larger mysteries, and yet I mistrusted my soul when it spoke in quiet contemplation. Joy said to relax and breathe and feel the wonder.

That just sounds lazy. I can't relax! It will be my total undoing. I'll melt right into a blob of nothingness. I'll never amount to anything or accomplish anything. People will just laugh. I need to prove myself or I'll never be taken seriously. I have to work hard and pay my dues like everyone else. I have to measure up. No one gets a free ride. Especially not me.

I had always believed that the journey was full of necessary lessons and tests that everyone had to endure. No pain, no gain. Long years of school had hammered in that notion. After hard study and work, we would be given the coveted gold stars and granted release. But the hard work had become such an ingrained habit, a deeply worn groove, that absolution was no longer in my vocabulary.

I didn't recognize that in demanding perfection from my art, joy was often forgotten. Although I often admired my paintings or calligraphy when they were done, the process to get there was stressful. I'd worry and work and stew and press my nose to the grindstone. The price was now being paid. My shoulders had had enough with the tension and the held breath as I painted. With my stiff approach, art had become physically unmanageable. Unintentionally, I'd undermined a gift that was meant to uplift.

Again, I felt that my body was challenging my happiness. I'd found my unique artistic expression, and now it was being snuffed out. But I have Bill, I kept reminding myself. I have Bill, at last. I have what I always needed. *Always wanted. Bill. The One true thing. I should be forever happy. I should be so damn happy! Why am I falling apart with him there always willing to hold me up?*

But, of course, Bill couldn't fix me. Or my fears. If I chose to believe that my life was being spoiled, who in the world could convince me otherwise? If I chose to sink into despair, who could pull me out? There were so many people who had cheered me on and lifted me up, but there was only one little person who could make the big internal changes. Make the choice. It felt like a tall order that I'd never be able to fill. Not just yet.

"At Nancy's today, I ran into Judi, my old therapist. Remember her?" I asked Bill. "I'm thinking of going to see her again."

"That's probably a good idea, hon. I'm sure she could help you cope with everything. The twitching, your shoulder."

"Yeah. Could be my poor body has been deteriorating not only because of my genetics but also because I pushed it and hated it for so long. If I can get past my fears then maybe my shoulder can heal too."

"Or maybe Judi can help you to accept the inevitable."

Bill had unleashed the monster.

"It's not inevitable!" I yelled. "Back me up on this. Let me exhaust all other routes before I consider throwing myself on the mercy of the hospital again. The four other replacements have tied me to those damn doctors for the rest of my days! They don't know how long these plastic joints will last. Do you think I want one more artificial part that can go bad one day? I can't go replacing everything! My elbows and ankles next? My spine? What if I get nerve damage like I had in my left foot? I had to wear that awful brace and I couldn't feel my foot for four months. They didn't know if I ever would. And when the nerves did begin to heal, the pain was horrible. Excruciating. What if I lose the use of my arm completely? No, thank you!"

Bill looked beaten down every time I went into one of my crazy "what if?" monologues.

"Call Judi," he said.

I felt like a heel. "I'm sorry, I shouldn't yell. You've been so understanding. I'm scared, I'm not mad at you."

"It's okay. This has been a major setback. I know what pain can do to a person's outlook. You're patient with me when my back acts up and I get snippy."

"I try. You're really the first person that I've trusted enough to . . . yell at."

"I'm so glad," Bill said as he rolled up his magazine and bopped me on the head.

I tried to grab the magazine, but he pulled me off the couch and onto the floor. "You scare me whenever you do that!"

"That's the whole point," he snickered.

"I always think I'm falling, but you never let me."
"And I never will."

"I want you to close your eyes, Julie," Judi said. "Take several deep breaths. Picture a beautiful place where you can feel safe and peaceful. Imagine yourself as an objective observer of the feelings and events you're going to remember." She was quiet as I did my breathing. "Relaxed and centered?"

"Yes, I'm ready."

"Let yourself wander back to the first time you experienced the shame you're dealing with lately."

"Strange. I just thought of this field trip to the Space Farms Zoo."

"How old were you?"

"Seven or eight."

"Good, you're back at an early age when the feelings were taking hold. What else?"

"There was a snake pit. I felt bad that the snakes were stuck down in an ugly cement hole. Some boys were yelling and throwing sticks at them." I felt pain in my chest as I suddenly remembered the school bus. "When our class got to the zoo that morning, we had to walk past a busload of kids in the parking lot. I was slow and lagging behind with my friend, Judy Prescott. I heard laughter from inside the bus, and when I looked up, all these faces were staring and pointing. Several kids yelling, 'Look at that! Is that a midget? Hey! Are you a midget?' Judy was a little ahead of me and I didn't think she heard. I didn't want her or anyone to know how strangers saw me."

Judi put a tissue in my hand. "Okay, we're going to redo that scene so that you're the champion for that little girl in the parking lot. What would you have done if your adult-self had been there with her?"

"I guess I'd get her out."

"Try talking directly to that little girl as if she were in front of you. She's hurt and needs your comfort."

Oh, boy, this felt stupid. "Okay. I'd say, *I'm sorry those kids laughed. They've never seen someone . . . like you.*"

"Good. What else?"

"I'd tell her . . . *I love you. I like that you're different.*"

"What will you do to prepare her for the next time this happens?"

I felt impatient. "I don't understand how this helps."

"Children don't have the skills to cope with trauma. If no aware adult is available to help, the feelings go underground until the child is older and has the strength to—"

"I can't pretend to change that day. It happened. And a hundred other times like it," I snapped.

"Yes. We're changing your *perceptions* of that day by giving that little girl permission to grieve. Part of you is stuck back in time and still hurting over what was never acknowledged."

"I should be over this by now."

"That's a natural feeling," Judi reassured. "You've probably minimized your feelings your whole life, wishing they'd go away. Did they?"

I shook my head.

"What else does that little girl need to hear?"

The resistance inside didn't want to make it okay. "I'd tell her it doesn't matter how you look or what other people think."

"Do you believe that?"

She knew me better than I thought. "My family offered me that stupid consolation once in a blue moon. They'd say, 'Cheer up. You have a good heart.' I didn't know what was real."

"When feelings aren't addressed, they tend to make up their own reality and attract similar negativity."

As the months marched on, I held fast to my anger, which I mistook for strength. Hadn't it protected me when no one else could? I had eaten a lot of bitter silence since childhood, and now it crouched in my lungs waiting to breathe out the fire, the defenses, the years of self-judgment. Why would I trust a world that I thought was responsible for my pain? That had broken my spirit for good? That's what I told myself anyway. It made it dramatic enough so I could blow open my trove of fear and give myself permission to acknowledge the old pain.

The HFS was in its full glory again as the violent spasms pulled at my forehead, down through my face, and into my neck. I'd stopped the Botox treatments after discovering that drug manufacturers used mercury, formaldehyde, and other toxic chemicals in vaccines for infants. Did I trust them with botulism? In twenty years would they still say that Botox was safe? The only real "cure" was to accept myself as I was. But that idea made me shudder down to my core. I couldn't bear to have others see the spasms: wasn't it the penalty? I'd failed again by letting the HFS steal my confidence. Destroy my dignity. Then I realized I'd never had either. Only a good mask. A fake ID.

As I made peace with my deepest fears, the picture started to change. I began to understand that my body was reflecting a lifetime of anxiety, and the law of attraction was drawing similar events right to my side. The HFS and being a little person had brought out identical feelings: fears about being rejected, defective, unworthy. I hadn't been able to accept my dwarfed body; I thought it was my greatest failure. Maybe God felt the same way. Maybe I hadn't been strong enough, or good enough, or holy enough. Now I was being tested further. Or punished.

I had lived in that broken place for a long time, but now I knew that I was the only one sitting in judgment of myself. Perhaps the HFS and the SED were at the identical wavelength. The same source of shame.

Slowly, a little each day, I began to tear open my cocoon. I allowed others to see my contorted face, my vulnerability, my doubt. It was no small feat; I desperately wanted to sprint in the opposite direction. But the truth was waiting for me to face it. My soul loved me no matter how I quaked. So I stood still long enough to let the terror sink in. I let it have a voice. I let it kick and scream. And I listened. Because that's all it ever wanted. Just to be heard.

I read an article that explained something about my transformation. It involved an experiment with one hundred rabbits. Each was repeatedly injected with a carcinogen, and over several months all except ten developed cancer. The scientists scoured the data but found no common denominator other than the simple fact that the same lab assistant took care of all ten. When they questioned the assistant about the case, he said that he had not strayed from the strict instructions. However, he did mention that he liked to pet the rabbits every day. Sometimes twice. The bunnies who were loved, it turned out, had stayed cancer-free.

I could see it working. The love. The forgiveness. Peace and joy were natural healers, and my body was responding. The HFS remained unchanged. My shoulder, however, hadn't gone into spasm in over two months. And the pain was diminishing. Some days were better than others. But I no longer allowed myself to panic. My heart was relaxing into a new rhythm. A new openness. My metaphysical makeover was loosening my tight grip. Instead of treating my body as the enemy, I would now supply it with the very same life remedy that kept those bunnies bouncing.

"How'd your session go with Judi, sweetheart?" Bill asked.

"Pretty good. I ran into Judi's daughter-in-law. She had her newborn with her." I hung up my coat, deciding how to say it. "I've been thinking, hon, I know we've been putting off trying to have a baby because of my shoulder, but I'm feeling ready."

Bill looked up in surprise. "Really? I don't think you're in any condition to . . ."

"Maybe it's good timing. The last shoulder spasm was ages ago. Maybe I needed to just stop the calligraphy and relax. And I haven't had the Botox in a year."

"How are you going to carry around an infant, let alone go through a cesarean? That's surgery, you know."

"But it has a great ending and the recovery is much faster."

"Well, let's give this a little more time, okay? I don't want to jump into anything that could make you worse."

"It's the one thing that's felt really right in a while. Except for you, of course. You always feel right."

Fourteen
Medical Mercy

Through love
all pain will turn to medicine.
~Rumi

The whole morning was buzzing with excitement. Was I imagining it, or did something feel different? All my life, I'd wondered if I could even have a child. Now here I was thinking that I might be pregnant! At the grocery store, I forgot my keys. At the pharmacy, I walked away without the bag with the pregnancy test. I was drifting around like those first snowflakes of December, mindlessly being blown here and there, barely touching the earth at all.

Back at home, I ripped open the box, sat in the bathroom, and read the directions front and back ten times—and in Spanish too. Finally, I nervously used the stick, feeling like a dog peeing on a Lilliputian tree. My jiggly breath waited and watched the tiny windows of hope. I stared in shock when a pink plus sign miraculously appeared. I think I yelped and gulped all at once.

"We're having a baby! Bill!" I cried out to the empty room, "We're having a baby!"

I waltzed around for a while with our big dog, Norman, bouncing happily beside me. *Should I call Bill or wait until he gets home? No, I have to see his face.* It was three weeks before Christmas, so I dropped the little stick in a plastic baggie and wrapped it in holiday paper. "I'm pregnant!" I kept repeating, trying to believe it myself. "Grandma Bee, I'm pregnant!" I put my hand on my belly and imagined the beginnings of life inside. It now felt like hallowed ground. How incredible that my strange little body could do something so extraordinary. Was the baby's spirit around me? Had it always been? I took a deep breath and smiled. I felt honored. Everything was different. A child had picked me.

"Hi, sweetheart." Bill was home.

He looked at the two candles flickering on the dining room table with the small package in between.

"For me? It's a bit early for Christmas. Shouldn't I wait?"

"Go ahead. It's really, really small."

He opened the package and slowly lifted out the plastic baggie. After he studied the stick, he looked up in shock. "Are we . . . ?"

"Yup!"

Bill's laughter lit up the room. He threw his arms around me and spun us in a golden circle.

"Really?"

"Yes!" I cheered again.

"That's the best Christmas present!" Bill stared at me with so much love that I felt it could heal the whole world.

"The beginning of a brand new life," he said. "You know, I never thought my world would come together again after my separation. When I found you, I felt so lucky and so blessed. This is buttercream frosting on the cake."

Tracy patted her fashionable purse. "I have the mini-recorder right here so Bill can hear the baby's heartbeat tonight. I cried with all three of my kids."

"I wish he was here, but his new boss is a real stickler."

Molly, the nurse, came into the waiting room. "Hi, Julie. Congratulations! How have you been, Tracy?" She took us to the examination room, asked me to undress, and handed me a paper blanket. "The doctor will be with you soon."

I stripped down and got up on the table. "I'm so glad you found Dr. Mike."

"He delivered my three without a hitch," Tracy said.

The door swung open, and our OB/GYN strolled in. "Hello, ladies." He smiled warmly and shook our hands. "Congratulations, Julie."

The doctor proceeded with his exam and said everything looked good. He slathered cold gel on my belly. "At eleven weeks, we should be able to hear the heartbeat. Any morning sickness?"

"Yes. At about nine weeks, though, it was gone. Now, I feel great."

Dr. Mike was silent for a moment. "Why didn't you come in after you took the home test?"

"My husband changed jobs, and I wanted to get our new insurance squared away."

Dr. Mike prodded around for another few minutes. "I'm not getting it. Sometimes that happens. Still, I'll send you for an internal ultrasound. Why don't you get dressed. Molly will set it up." The door closed behind him.

"We'll get an ultrasound picture of the baby!" Tracy beamed. "They didn't do routine ultrasounds when I had mine. This is so exciting!"

I wasn't so sure. When Dr. Mike left, he didn't look me in the eye.

A half hour later, I lay on another table in a nearby radiology lab. When the technician finally arrived, she began the exam abruptly, using the internal probe like a gear shift. Tracy and I stared at the screen, trying to figure out what we were seeing. Tracy's questions garnered clipped answers.

"The doctor will be in to talk to you," the technician mumbled.

"Is everything okay?" Tracy asked.

"You'll have to wait for the doctor."

By this time, we were pretty sure that something wasn't right. We studied the growth chart on the wall. Shouldn't the fetus be bigger? Fifteen minutes dragged by until the doctor came.

"Dr. Mike wants to see you back at his office, Julie," he said, and he turned to leave.

"What?" Tracy demanded.

"Dr. Mike wants to..."

"Yes, we heard you. What for?" she asked.

"The doctor will fill you in," he said as he walked out the door.

"What's going on?" I whispered to Tracy as we got in the car.

"I don't know, Jule." Tracy sped back to Dr. Mike' office. We hustled inside and Molly waved us into the back. "I'm sorry. Dr. Mike had an emergency or else he would be here. You must have realized by now, Julie," she said solemnly, "that the pregnancy wasn't viable."

I stared at her in disbelief, waiting to wake up.

"I'm so sorry. The fetus only progressed to about the sixth week and then stopped. We don't know why this happens, but it is very common. One out of every three pregnancies ends this way. Perhaps more."

I sat frozen in my chair. Nothing was real.

"We need to schedule a D & C for tomorrow morning so when..."

"A what?" I asked.

"We have to remove the excess tissue."

"You mean under anesthesia?"

"Yes. You see, your body is still acting pregnant. It may not reject the tissue that needs to come out."

You can't touch me. You can't do this. "Won't it come out naturally?"

"Odds are against it. It can be very painful and go on for weeks. Infection is a concern. It's safer in the hospital."

This can't be happening. There's no baby. There hasn't been anything growing inside me for weeks? Now I have to check into the hospital? No! Oh please, no. The double shock was electrifying.

"I don't know what to do--I don't know what to say."

Tracy's eyes were glistening with tears. Pain slithered up my throat, but I knocked it back down. I didn't want to fall apart before the arrangements were made. I signed papers, Tracy next to me, her hand over her mouth as if to keep from screaming at God.

"Jule, I'm so, so sorry." Tracy drove with her sad eyes staring straight ahead, her hands clenching tight around the wheel. "I can't believe it. Oh God, I'm so sorry."

Bill's car was in the driveway. It had all taken so much more time than expected; he must have been wondering where I'd been.

"Do you want me to come in with you?" Tracy offered.

"No, it's all right. I'm so glad you were there today. I'll call you when I get home tomorrow."

"I love you, Jule." Tracy jumped out of the car to give me a hug. "Call me if you need to talk." Her eyes welled up again.

I walked towards the house, wondering how to tell Bill. As I reached for the door, it flew open. When I saw the concern in his eyes, I broke into tears for the first time.

"The baby didn't make it," I cried as he hugged me tight.

The following morning, Bill kissed me good-bye as they wheeled me towards the operating room.

"Hi, Julie, I'm Dr. Gates. I'll be your anesthesiologist this morning," a white-coat told me. He stood by my gurney and patted my hand gently. "Are you nervous?"

"Yes. Where's Dr. Mike?" I needed to see his face.

"Good morning, Julie," Dr. Mike said softly. "I was very sorry to hear the news. How are you feeling?"

"I'm anxious to get this over with."

The room was filled with busy, nameless people. I wanted to be introduced to every witness. They put my naked legs up in stirrups as frigid air swept over my skin. Dr. Gates sat down by my head. "Julie, when I start the medicine into your IV, you'll feel a slight burning. It will be over in seconds and you'll fall asleep. Are you ready?" He actually waited for my response.

"Yes." I closed my eyes and took a deep breath.

"Good, keep breathing just like that. Picture a beautiful blue ocean," Dr. Gates said in a soothing voice. "The waves are rolling in and out, with sunshine and soft breezes . . ."

For the first time, as I went into the blackness, I smiled. It seemed that only a few moments had passed before I came out of my drugged slumber.

"Julie, it's Dr. Mike. You're all done. Everything went well."

"Is Dr. Gates there?" I garbled, my eyes too heavy to open.

"Yes, I'm here," a surprised voice answered.

"Thank you," I said. "Thank you so much."

"You're very welcome," he answered.

I imagined my angels kissing him full on the lips. I was safe. Later, they wheeled me into the recovery area and I saw the worry on Bill's face.

"I'm okay!" I called out to him. "There's no pain and the nurse got the IV in on the first try! I kept visualizing this white tiger protecting me. And the anesthesiologist did a visualization too! Can you believe it? You would've been so proud, Bill. I kept on doing the deep breathing and I didn't panic."

Bill leaned over and gave me a kiss. "I never doubted you for a minute."

The days following the D & C were painful and long. Severe cramps left me doubled over. My initial thankfulness that my hospital experience wasn't traumatic waned as reality set in. I wasn't a mom. There wasn't a little baby. My belly was empty and the joyful pregnancy over. Megan arrived with a big bouquet of tulips the afternoon that I got home. Tracy brought over dinner and groceries. Judy and Trish talked to me on the phone as I cried. My family called and sent sweet cards. Judi came to the house for a few sessions. Nancy and Dick brought over supplements and herbs.

In time, the layers of grief unraveled. I wasn't afraid for the baby's spirit; I believed it could occupy a different body if the time came. But I worried that my own deformed body couldn't make a healthy little vessel. The wait to try again, to know for sure, felt like torture. I'd been so happy and diligent about my pregnancy, making healthy choices, rarely feeling negative. I didn't see the problem coming, and that shook me. Was I blind? Did I do something wrong?

The one thing I recognized was how my miscarriage had smoothed the way to the eventual C-section I knew I would have to have. Now, I wasn't as afraid of the hospital, of the needles, of the nurses, because I truly trusted Dr. Mike and Dr. Gates. These things gave the miscarriage some purpose I could see, but it didn't quite make up for the immense loss. Maybe I wanted to take the blame. Or the responsibility. In the past, I could see how my fears had created the very situations I'd wanted to avoid. This time, though, I couldn't understand my part in the drama.

Then I remembered something strange. When I'd first found out that I was pregnant, Bill was changing jobs. I'd waited to see the doctor until the new insurance was set. During that wait, I'd worried that my pregnancy wasn't legitimate because a doctor hadn't said so. My feelings of powerlessness against the world of medicine had quietly resurfaced.

I'd felt like a child again under the doctor's glare. Children don't have babies, and I was as small as an eight-year-old. I'd had the recurring fear that when I finally saw the doctor, he'd say, "There's no baby." In essence, that's what happened. By imagining a negative situation, I had been operating at that wavelength. I'd invited more of the same energy. Remarkably, the new perspective helped me feel better. Taking responsibility was no longer about punishment, sin, or blame. It was about choice, empowerment, and faith. As I rocked back and forth on the couch, a heating pad held to my abdomen, I realized that my journey wasn't negated because I didn't have a baby. *You did a good job,* I told myself over and over, and it helped me to cry, both for what was lost and what was gained.

Bill had faced an old nightmare too. The miscarriage had reminded him of losing his son at birth and the resulting end of his marriage. But this time, the ordeal strengthened our bond. We realized we weren't ready to try again, but in the meantime, we decided it was time to buy our own home. When you're a closet control freak like me, though, even good change rocks your boat. I loved the little ranch we found on a quiet, tree-lined street. The big back yard was loaded with lilacs, roses, tulips and a fabulous weeping cherry tree. But between the move, the miscarriage, my shoulder, and the HFS twitching, I was running to Judi every week. Then, miraculously, I found an acupuncturist who accepted my health insurance. My hopes soared. *This could be the answer to the HFS,* I thought. *This is it!*

Three months later, I sat in the waiting room with two other acupuncture patients. They were exchanging pleasantries and probably would have included me if I hadn't had my face wrapped in a magazine. *I can't let them see the HFS. They'll pity me. 'That poor midget, she's a nervous wreck,' they'll think. 'Has she had a stroke? Is she retarded?'* When I was young, I'd wrongly assumed that anyone who couldn't control his or her body in some way had a learning disability as well. Now I was cowering under that ridiculous assumption. *Are other people now thinking that about me? Why do I care?*

As the doctor began putting in the needles, I told him that there hadn't been any improvement. He said that nervous tics take a long time to heal. A nervous tic. He made it sound so trivial. Why had I let it tie me all in knots and put my life on hold? *Why?*

Over the last ten years, I'd tried every alternative therapy that I'd heard of or was suggested to me. Each time I put my faith in something new, I ended up despondent. I was feeling the blow again. Two steps forward, two steps back. After all my efforts, I hadn't been able to alter the HFS one iota.

When the acupuncturist left me alone to let the needles do their work, I sobbed quietly. Life felt unbearable. *Before the twitching, I'd at least been able to socialize, to show people that I wasn't so different. Now I can barely stand to be seen. I'm cursed with an affliction picked out just for me. Surely only God would know how to show off my pathetic weaknesses and force me to do better. No rest for me until I get the message! What else can explain it? Bad luck? Accidental defect?*

Many days I argued with myself back and forth, vacillating wildly between hope and despair. I recognized the healing ability of peace and love, and yet too often I still got caught up in panic and fear. I was as stubborn as the HFS. I knew my shoulder was getting stronger. But with the HFS getting worse, I often discounted the progress. The pressure I had long put on myself to be good, to be acceptable, to be loved, to conform to an impossible standard, was as plain as the twitch on my face. The powerlessness had gone straight to my head.

"Hi, honey," Bill called as he came home that night.

"Hi," I answered flatly.

"I think my brakes are going."

"Great."

"What do you want to do for dinner?"

"I don't care."

"How about eggplant parmesan?"

"Fine."

Bill got dinner ready as I set the table. After we'd eaten, Bill asked if I'd fed the dog.

"Aren't you going to ask about my day?" I burst out.

Bill looked surprised. "How'd it go?"

"Like you care. You're only asking now because I brought it up. Couldn't you tell I was upset?"

"Sure, but you weren't saying anything so—"

"Why can't you ever ask me first?"

Bill was silent, which made me angrier. "You knew I was upset but said nothing. How am I supposed to interpret that?" I demanded.

"I don't know," he said sheepishly. "Tell me then, how was your appointment?" Of course, that was no longer the subject.

"You're avoiding the point, which is what you always do when it gets difficult. You pretend like every thing's fine." If Bill hadn't felt so blindsided, he might have realized that I was describing myself. And maybe my parents. I'd never been sure whether they, or I, had wanted to know, or could really handle the real me, so we'd played the "everything is fine" game. Had they known I was suffering? Did Bill understand now? I couldn't hear anything over the voice of my own shame. I was busy recreating the only drama I knew.

I wanted to crush him with my seething silence, my favorite weapon, and wait for him to slither back to me in guilt and beg forgiveness. Wouldn't that mean he loved me? The temptation was hard to fight, but deep down, what I wanted more was to change. If Bill wasn't going to prod me with questions, "proving" his love for me, I had to do it myself and speak up even when every bone in my body was saying, "No one cares." I began telling Bill about my doctor's visit. The waiting room panic. Feeling defective. Boston.

"You're not a defect," Bill said.

What I heard was, "Don't feel that way."

"Why do you always say that?" I yelled. "Your opinion of me doesn't change all the *stares* and *laughter* and *humiliation!* I feel like a defect and you're saying that I shouldn't feel that way!" I paced as the frenzy thrashed inside. "After I've been subjected to a *trillion* faces that proclaimed me unacceptable and funny-looking and *deformed*, do you really expect me to believe in your one solitary voice that says that all of those other people were *wrong?* All the doctors were *wrong?*"

Bill had seen me explode before and had said that my attacks made him feel inept, afraid that anything he said would upset me further. Speaking up in his own family had only been met with ridicule, leaving him tongue-tied like me. He wanted to take away my pain. He was in the fix-it business, after all, and he could diagnose a car at a hundred paces. When it came to me, though, the repairs seemed far more complicated.

"Those other people were wrong," he said, "You aren't a defect and—"

"Are you *trying* to shut me up? Or make it all better before I can even *express* myself? I already *think* and *feel* these things. I need to say them out *loud!*" I was crying and shouting at the same time. "It's not just my past. I'm afraid you won't *ever* understand why I feel the way that I do! As a kid I swallowed my painful feelings and now that I finally have the nerve to speak up, I don't want you trying to stuff them back down again by telling me my feelings are *wrong!*"

"I didn't say you were wrong. I only want you to know that I don't see you as a defect. I never have, and I never will."

Something in his eyes stopped my tirade. Maybe he didn't understand, but he wanted to. I had to quit lashing out at him and let him try. Why did I demand to be right about my drama? As the anger retreated, I sat down and cried harder.

"I'm not angry at you," I sniffed. "I'm sorry you're getting the brunt of something that has nothing to do with you."

"So . . . who *are* you angry at?"

I took a deep breath. "I'm angry at the world, and the doctors, and my family, and myself, and at God. Everyone." Bill took a while to respond. His silence reminded me of the lack of communication with my parents', causing my fear to spike into anger again. "I'm baring my soul and you just sit there with nothing to say?"

"I want you to see yourself the way that I see you," he said.

"Have you been listening to me? Look at the *huge* amount of evidence to the contrary. In my first therapy session with Sylvia, she said that naturally I would've felt frightened as a child, not only by the world but also by my family's silence. That validation was such a relief — to know that I wasn't *crazy.*"

Bill leaned over to hold me, and I bawled into his chest. I'd spent so many years believing that I was an idiot for not being able to "get over it." Bill was the first person I'd let see that I wasn't well-adjusted at all. I was used to arguing for my limitations in my head; I'd spent so much time trying to change them, but it took speaking them out loud to finally begin to truly hear their tired story.

"You're not crazy," he said.

"I know. Can you see, though, how I'd think I was?"

He paused for a second, afraid at first to confirm my sadness. "Yeah. No one prepared you for the challenge of being a little person."

"It felt like an impossible responsibility to figure out who I was, what was wrong, and why people treated me unfairly. I thought that I was expected to fix the problems myself. But I was too little to know what to do. Then I blamed and hated myself for not knowing."

"Let it all out, honey," Bill said quietly as I cried.

I felt sorrow gasping deep in my chest. My heart had been closed for a long time, but my soul was eagerly waiting to realign. Yesterday's story now had a safe exit, leaving a trail of mourning in its wake. Happiness rehearsals were gearing up in the wings.

Days later, nervously unpacking boxes in our new house, pain shot down my arm, asking me to stop. *Stop what?* I wondered. The depressing thoughts I'd been battling for three decades flooded back. *I'm at the mercy of a defective body. It'll only get worse.* Then I remembered something in one of Bernie Siegel's books: *God is redirecting you.* This mess must have a reason. Angels are looking out for me. Strength comes out of the most difficult situations, right?

I noticed an old journal in the box and leafed through. March 1993. After hip surgery and right before knee surgery. I read on. *Whoa.* I sounded so desperate, so bitter. I thought I'd moved past that depressing drama. I closed the journal and saw my art doodles on the cover. *I can't even do that anymore. I'm not making money. I can't unpack the house. I can't paint the walls. Without my right arm, I can't do much of anything.* I thought about journaling again to relieve some of the frustration, but writing with my left hand was slow and aggravating. The more I focused on my growing family of complaints, the more they multiplied, drawing in their cousins and relatives.

The mail that day had an envelope from my dad with photos from the summer in Canada plus an ad for a computer. He wrote in the margin, "Offer still stands, Juli-kins! *Aloha nui loa,*" Hawaiian for "lots of love." My dad had long encouraged me to learn computer graphics and had offered to loan Bill and me the funds for a computer. We'd only have to pay him back when, or if, I made money at it. Nice deal. I was intimidated by computers, though, and scared to replace the familiar brush with a mouse. Of course I could barely hold a pencil now, so I had no more excuses. With a keyboard, I wouldn't have to use my right arm. Hmm.

The very next weekend Bill and I brought home a little iMac, without the first idea of what to do with it. Bill poured over the manuals and in no time we were up and scrolling. It didn't take long for me to fall in love. Not with the graphics, though—with e-mail. Its immediacy was a salve for my disconnection. In my left-handed hunt-and-peck method, safe on the other side of the screen, I reached out to friends and family, told them about my struggles, and felt less alone.

Then I began writing to myself. After two years of missing my art, I realized that I could still paint a three-dimensional world, but one splashed out in words instead of colors. My inner canvas was full of creative material. Thoughts and feelings spewed out like water over a dam, dashing for freedom before the floodgates closed again. Writing down my feelings helped me truly face them, in a way I'd never done before. I could finally see that the events of my past had been surmountable. It was the denied feelings that had become a powerful disability. Now they'd be held fast in paper, not flesh. Peace was only a new perspective away.

My parents were the next hurdle. Wouldn't they be disappointed that, at thirty-six years old, I wasn't well-adjusted at all? Was it only my happy facade that they'd loved?

> Dear Mom and Dad,
>
> At last, the new house is coming together, but I'm so discouraged about my shoulder. I feel like I'm not much use around here, although Bill assures me otherwise.
>
> Lately I've wanted to share some things with you, but I've been afraid. I know how much you hurt when your kids hurt, and I don't want to add to your pain. The crux of it is this—because I've always wanted you to be proud of me, I've been covering up my real feelings. I often appear to be doing okay even when I'm not.
>
> A few months ago, I asked you both why you never spoke about Ethan's and my dwarfism, and why we never even used the word. When Dad wrote back, he seemed angry. He asked pointedly, "Have you forgotten how you withdrew from discussions about your short stature? How you didn't want to join the Little People of America?" I hated myself for not having the courage, for not being able to speak up. But since you weren't talking, I assumed it was an uncomfortable subject to be avoided. With the teasing all around me, I was pretty sure that being a dwarf was a bad thing. Then, somewhere along the way, I started to blame myself. I not only look wrong, I thought, but I am wrong.

I want to believe that my fears aren't real, they're just very loud. I adopted them thinking they would keep me safe; if I was careful about what I said and what I did, and tried to be the person that other people wanted me to be, then I could keep others from rejecting me. Little did I know that I had to stop rejecting myself first.

I hope you can understand why I interpreted things the way that I did. I'm not writing to blame you for your choices; I'm writing so I can stop blaming myself. I want you to love me just as I am.

Do you ever feel that the universe is testing you? I don't know. I used to think I was barely passing, but maybe I was the one who was giving out the F. Maybe Spirit always hands out A's.

Write back soon,

I love you.

~Julie

I reread the letter and winced. I emailed it to Tracy first to see what she thought. Her reply came a few hours later.

My dearest Leibchen,

What a heartfelt letter. It made me cry, anyway. I wouldn't be surprised if your parents did the same.

You once told me that when you were born, and your parents brought you home from the hospital, your mom and dad sat at the kitchen table and cried. Had they known then the person whom they love and cherish today, they never ever would have shed a tear. Before all else, you were their child, and they grieved for your future without knowing the beautiful person you would become. If we could only go back in time and show them that, in the end, despite the heartaches, you would be just fine. Wonderful actually. Hey, we all have things that we think are unacceptable and peculiarities that we want to hide. Your "scars" happen to be visible, but you know that you're not so different as you sometimes feel.

Oh, Jule, I've said this before, and I know it's what your parents feel as well; if I could carry around some of the sadness in your soul, I would do it in an instant. If I could minimize some of your fears in the world, and let you live in peace, there would be no greater gift for me. I know there are struggles you face each day that I really can't imagine, and all I can do is be grateful that I know you, and that my kids have grown up in your glow. You are a wonderfully crucial part of my life that keeps me young, grounded, secure, and validated when I need it most. You may think you're a mess, but I know better.

Leibchen, the truth won't hurt your parents. Send the letter. And remember, for all their decisions, they definitely did something right. The world got you.

Let me know what they say.

i lub u, 4-ever

xo Trace

I wiped away the tears and stared at the "Send" button. Would my parents be mad? Shocked? I said a prayer and hit the button. I tossed and turned that night, knowing that my dad would be on the computer early the following day.

In the morning, I quickly opened my e-mail and saw a reply from my dad. I gritted my teeth and opened the message.

Dear Julie,

I have been wondering what I could say to make you feel better about yourself and your lot in life. Because you really should feel good despite all your worries, which are real, I know.

Julie, you are one of the most well-adjusted people I know. Believe it. Furthermore, you have a delightful personality and are an attractive young lady (just ask Bill). Sparkling eyes, big smile, and ready to laugh, giggle or tee-hee at the slightest provocation. You have an exceptional understanding of people and you have so many friends, which is a testimony to your goodness.

Please don't ever hesitate to talk with us about your physical problems. Clearly we erred; but we felt there was no point dwelling on your differences.

Mom is still at the office but plans to call you tonight. I'll call tomorrow to talk things over, okay?

All our love, Dad

My breath popped like a balloon. He thought I was well-adjusted. I shut my eyes and cried.

That night, I had a dream. A young girl with scraggly blond hair and small odd-looking limbs was perched high above me. She wore thick glasses over her crossed eyes. Although she looked unstable and lost in her own world, she was giggling and smiling brightly. I gaped at her for a while, a mix of anger and pity washing my insides. *Why is she smiling? Doesn't she know how awful she looks?* I was surprised to find that it was my dad holding the girl steady while she sat on Mom's shoulder. They stared at the child with heartbreaking pride and joy. While still dreaming, I began to sob and woke up in a lake of tears. My parents, unaware of my distorted view of myself, hadn't known I was suffering. Maybe they had always loved my reflection. Maybe they had always seen what mattered: the real me, the soul of me. They'd seen me with love and assumed I'd see myself the same way. Until now, they'd been wrong. Eventually, they were right. The love was getting through. It was finally getting through. My parents hadn't pretended or ignored the truth. They *felt* the truth; I was as valuable, beautiful, and lovable as anyone else.

The doctors had once put me up on a table, on display. I had dutifully stood like a soldier allowing the enemy to examine my flaws. I'd learned to hide my fear even during a surprise attack. I wanted my mom and dad to be proud. I wanted the world to like me. I wanted the doctors to approve, so I smiled when they took naked pictures, and I smiled when I was on display, and I smiled when they told stupid jokes. When I was dying on the inside, I smiled. When I finally realized, as an adult, that I'd betrayed myself as a child, I desperately wanted to go back in time and stand up for myself. Speak up for myself. I couldn't go back in time, but I could start doing it now.

That day I wrote a lot, and I wrote for many weeks after, reviewing and redoing the life I thought I'd known. My right hand started jumping into the typing mania and my shoulder grew stronger. They say that you can't change the past, but it was changing for me. Somewhere during the excitement, my woeful tirade transformed into a long love letter from my soul. The revelations were cathartic as my heart broke wide open. The doctors weren't evil, they were unaware. My parents weren't unloving, they just didn't know what a good actress I'd become.

The anonymous computer screen became a place to put all my pain. Then, somewhere along the way, it started to put me in my place. I began to see that no matter what the situation, my fears were generally the same as they'd always been. Each new problem was the same old addiction, cleverly disguised in different packages, still waiting to be unwrapped once and for all.

I was born with certain physical limits, but after a time, my fearful response had taken charge. I'd been subconsciously using my body as a gym excuse from the universe so that no one would expect me to accomplish as much or be responsible for as much as "normal" people. I went over the heartaches of my life. I wrote them out, gave them a voice. Dwarfism. Bullies at school. Jeering from the Canadian neighbor. The family silence. Josh. Chase. White-coats. Boston. Surgery. I'd felt forsaken, but angels had watched over me the entire time, knowing that from where spirit stood, the story was perfect. It was illuminated, purposeful, and part of my path home.

As the hurt and self-pity diminished, it dawned on me that my problems had served my own inner design. My loyal body had followed my fears like a manual and would stay in line with those directions until I drew a grander picture for it to follow. All my life, I'd been asking for healing and love, yet I'd been preparing for pain and disappointment. The universe had been providing a neutral illustration of what I'd expected.

In seeing my intriguing creations, the self-judgment started to fall away. The lies and the "I'm not good enoughs" were just worn-out patterns. I kept forgetting everything I'd learned, and then I'd remember again. And Love forgave it all.

Life was far more glorious than I had allowed. It wasn't a bad hand, I just had to play it differently. Happiness couldn't catch my eye unless I looked in its direction. I decided to make my target nothing short of joy.

Months passed and Bill grew accustomed to a nightly review of my day of writing. One night, something new surfaced. I wasn't complaining; I was reporting. I was becoming the objective observer that Judi, my therapist, had always talked about. As I stood talking to Bill, somewhere beyond myself, beyond the drama, I suddenly saw an intriguing story. It was my story.

"All those years, I was so sure I was a freak. I felt I didn't deserve a full, happy life."

"I think everyone feels that way at one time or another," Bill said.

"Exactly. You know, I've been selling myself short for so long that . . ." Then something awoke inside of me, as I stared into space. "Hey, that could be the name of a book. Bill, I'm writing a book! Up until now, I had refused to believe anything good could come of my arthritis. But I never would have done all this writing if my shoulder hadn't given out." Relief tackled me to the floor. The desire to share the purposefulness of my sob stories was encouraging me to finally leave them behind and move beyond them all. I had something to give. It was me. It didn't matter how short I was, or whether I could paint, or if my shoulder hurt, or how well I walked, or if I was nice, or if my face looked funny. The convincing smoke screen had fooled me for a while, but slowly, after the clearing in the fog, I found something real underneath.

I'd been lost on a mesmerizing merry-go-round that had been circling home base all along. The instant I thought I could help others learn to stop it, it stopped for me. My intention swung back around and took me with it. In wanting to give, I realized that I actually had something to give. All the metaphysical teachings suddenly came alive. My life became bigger than my separate little self and I felt connected and renewed before I'd even changed a thing. The old bumper stickers on my car were now real. "We Are One." "Namaste."

Over the years, I had strayed about a million miles from myself. Now I was making my way back. My body hadn't been in my way; it had shown me the way. All at once I felt like an honored guest in my own life. My soul, who had been patiently waiting, was inviting me inside again. Although I'd been gone a long while, I immediately knew my way around. As the wheels of fortune clicked into motion, and new life greased my worn-out joints, I began to walk in joy.

Fifteen
Short Doesn't Mean Squat

Angels fly high because they take themselves lightly.
~-G.K. Chesterton

"C'mon, hon, we better get going," Bill called from the kitchen.

"I just put the computer to bed," I answered, as I wobbled towards him. "Guess what? I have seventy-five pages written on my book."

"Can I read it yet?"

"It's a really really rough draft. Maybe once I've edited a bit more."

In the car, I talked during the entire trip, trying to ignore my bladder's plea. I'd had to drink three large glasses of water for the test. We sat in the waiting room for ten minutes as I squirmed in my seat.

"You'd think that they'd know about the loaded bladder and take me right in for the ultrasound."

Bill nodded, crossing his legs in sympathy.

A good-looking couple came in and sat down opposite us. I overheard the woman, who appeared about as pregnant as I did, asking the receptionist if they could take her right in for her ultrasound. I smiled in sympathy, but she didn't see me. She was slender and pretty, wearing a balmy yellow maternity shirt that showed off her round belly. She made pregnancy look beautiful. I suddenly felt like an ugly tree stump in my oversized turtleneck and stretchy sweatpants. I wondered if Bill ever thought the same thing. I glanced over to find his face wrapped in *Parents* magazine. I smiled and took a deep breath. As I leafed through a magazine, the baby pictures brought a wave of worry. The chances that Bill carried the same recessive gene for my type of dwarfism was 1 in 100,000. If he did, as both my parents did, the chances were 1 in 4 that our baby would be affected. Whenever I mentioned those slim odds to anyone, they breathed an enormous sigh of relief. I hated that.

One of Bill's coworkers, after seeing me once, had told Bill that it wasn't right to pass my genetics on to another generation. Wow. As if there was nothing else good in me to pass on. How many others worried for my unborn baby, or for Bill and me? Every silent wish that my baby would be "normal" felt like a slap in the face. Years back, in Boston, one doctor had queried my mom about her pregnancies with Ethan and with me. We had been sitting in an open waiting area as he fired off the questions.

"Did you take vitamins? Did you smoke or drink? How was your diet? How were you feeling? Did you exercise? Did you take any medication? Did you do anything unusual?"

"Nothing out of the ordinary," my mom responded quietly. "I didn't expect any problems. After all, Ethan was my fifth baby and Julie my sixth."

"The other four children are all normal?"

"Average height," she said, looking very young.

The doctor wanted something that my mom didn't think she had. He wanted clues to solve the mystery of how to prevent the likes of Ethan and me. My dad was sitting quietly, wringing his hands red while Ethan read a comic book. Ethan was twelve and I was ten. I looked nervously around the waiting area, hoping that no one was listening. I hated Boston. But even through my burning anger, I felt a twinge of sadness for my parents. Something in their manner hid a pain I rarely saw. A pain I thought I'd caused.

Now, years later, I understood the difficulties my parents had faced. It would be hard to have a child like me, not because my differences were intolerable, but because it was too easy for the world to focus on those differences. I had always believed that it mattered deeply what other people thought, and that I couldn't live fully in a world where babies like me were born into pity. Where doctors quietly imparted the bad news and nurses went home to kiss their healthy children. Where relatives sent flowers that reeked of sadness and friends brought gifts wrapped in fear. I had believed that the collective dread had opened a hole and thrown each flawed baby in. I'd learned how to shovel the dirt in on myself.

Could I celebrate my baby no matter what form he or she took? I wanted to feel confident because I was different, not in spite of it, and to pass that along. I wanted to teach the world to welcome differences. As my eyes fell on Bill, my shoulders relaxed. My baby would have a great dad, a great life. Who better to raise a little person than one herself? Wouldn't it be incredible if Bill and I carried the same rare recessive gene and had somehow found each other in this big world, just as my parents had? Wouldn't that be a miracle instead of a mistake? The thought lifted my eyebrows in revelation. I think several strands of DNA started to uncurl their tight fists. I had grasped so tightly to the victim mentality that I couldn't see I'd had a choice all along. Isn't it remarkable what an open heart can change?

If our souls help to choose their own circumstances, wouldn't my baby's soul be taking the same opportunity? An eager volunteer? A brilliant co-creator? Still, I felt torn. A part of me mourned the misfits. Did I want to revisit my struggles and watch my child enduring the same gauntlets? Not really. I was ashamed that I couldn't proclaim complete acceptance of myself and release my mind from the past. I hadn't found every spiritual gem that my little chickadee form offered. I had found enough understanding to brighten my path, to give it purpose and breadth. But for my own child? Could I teach her the beauty of being different? Could I remind him that the gifts would outweigh all else? Could I pee soon?

"Julie?" the nurse called.

At last. Bill and I walked back to the exam room where I got up on the table. The technician, Joe, proceeded to slather the cold gel on my belly, down where the baby's heart and mine were now sweetly entrained. *What if . . . what if . . .*

"Do you want to know the sex?" Joe asked.

"Yes," we said together.

When the pictures began coming up on the screen, we were spellbound. We saw the head! Then the profile of the face, the arms and legs, the pearly spine, even the four chambers of the heart and the two hemispheres of the brain. All this miracle growing inside my tiny nest. This extraordinary mystery taking shape in the heat of me, just out of my sight. A baby! My worries were suddenly flattened like a freckle.

"It looks like . . ." Joe paused for dramatic effect, "you have a boy."

"A boy?" I squealed.

"A boy," Bill sighed.

I hovered above the table in sheer enchantment, riveted by the images on the screen. "A boy," I kept repeating. I didn't care one way or the other, but now the baby seemed so much more real. There he was, right under my skin, a sweet paisley curl, breathing my blood, sweeping my soul.

"Congratulations," Joe said after all the measurements and pictures were taken. "Everything looks great."

Great? Could he tell whether the baby was a dwarf? I didn't want to admit that I cared. The baby was healthy, as far as the ultrasound could tell, and that felt wonderful.

Bill and I floated down the hall.

"Good luck," I said to the woman in yellow with the very full bladder. All at once, I felt I looked as good as she did.

"We're having a boy," Bill said.

As we got in the car I realized I'd forgotten to use the bathroom, but my bladder no longer seemed to care. Joy made more room for everything.

~~~

My left hand tapped on the keys as my right hand rested on my beach-ball belly, sitting in my lap like a prize. Such promise and light inside the darkness.

Only three more days until I could hold my baby. I hadn't resolved how I felt about the possibility that my child was a dwarf, but the worry was small and the delight had grown as large as I had. Actually, I'd only gained ten pounds, but on my frame it looked impressive. I got more stares than usual, but I was growing proud of them. Proud to be a mom.

Being responsible for a baby had me feeling more determined and more alive. The life force that had been wrapped up in other people's opinions was now coming back to me, energizing me. The differences that had blinded me were paving the way to a clearer vision. Whatever difficulties my son would encounter in life would deepen his capacity for love. His ability to choose. His decision to align with his source. The trials would set him free.

Staring out the open window, a bright cardinal gazed at me from his usual perch. A breeze wafted inside and gently lifted my chin. The weeping cherry's skirt started to sway. Squirrels chattered and birds sang. Flowers and fairies harmonized as my baby danced under my skin. The syncopated peace closed my eyes. We were dipping our toes into the same stream. The same united spirit, temporarily broken into pieces. Each tiny hologram living by its own design, reflecting the larger truth. The separation is a game, an illusion, a sleight of Mother Nature's hand. Our triumphs, no matter how small, will resonate through the universe. We are eternally connected. Always One.

There had been long lonely years living in my forgetful flesh. When I kissed them good-bye, it felt like they'd lasted only a moment. The agony was small once the understanding returned. It had all been so simple and good. I'd always been whole. *Tomorrow I might forget again, but today, for now, I know it's true. In the big picture, life makes sense. It's like heaven right here, and over there, and in me, right on earth.*

It was Friday and the C-section was scheduled for Monday morning. This was the last open weekend for Bill and me before the stork's delivery. As we were getting ready to walk out the door for dinner, the phone rang. Something told me to take the call.

"This is Dr. Langdon from Morristown Memorial Hospital," said a gentle voice. "May I speak to Julie?"

"Yes, this is Julie."

"I have you scheduled for a C-section on Monday, is that correct?"

"Yes, that's me," I answered happily.

"Congratulations. I'll be working with Dr. Mike as your anesthesiologist. I wanted to check some of your information. I see on your chart you've had bilateral hip and knee replacements due to degenerative arthritis. I'm wondering if . . . you have good flexibility in your spine."

"I have some stiffness, but nothing like the other joints."

"Okay. Um, I also see here that . . . you're four feet four inches tall."

"Correct."

"The reason I ask is that to do an epidural, we'll need adequate room between the vertebrae. Your height and the arthritis pose . . . certain considerations. Tell me, can you feel space between each vertebrae?"

"Oh, I can't reach that far. Can you hold on?"

I waved for Bill to come and check my back.

"My husband thinks there's space but not as much as in his own back."

"Okay." Dr. Langdon sounded apologetic. "I should have had you come in for a checkup. Unfortunately, I only read your file tonight. Your chart says that during your surgeries, intubation was difficult."

"Yes. They couldn't get the tubes down my throat. I guess I have a narrow opening. For the second surgery they used pediatric tubes and they did the intubation while I was partially awake. It wasn't fun."

"Well, I'm afraid that if we can't do an epidural, we'd have to put you under general anesthesia, which would mean your husband could not be present, and we'd have to intubate."

"What? No, no, please. I really want to be awake for the birth. I'll do whatever I have to do. Please."

"We'll try our very best to make that happen."

"Why couldn't Bill be with me?"

"Hospital rules. With local anesthesia, they allow it. Not with general. I'm sorry to throw this into your weekend, but I think it's better if you're prepared. So, we'll see you Monday morning?"

"Yes. Thank you. Bye."

My stomach had quickly curdled in concern. "I don't want to be asleep when the baby arrives!" I cried to Bill. "And you couldn't be there! They'd have to put those tubes down my throat while I'm awake!" I could feel myself stumbling back, ready to entertain the old victim again. She was beginning to fuss and whine and plead her case.

Bill knelt down to hug me. After a shaky few minutes, I decided I wasn't going to let my old terror carry the day. My husband, my pregnancy, and the writing I was doing had me seeing my life from a higher perspective. Although fears occasionally caught my attention on their way to some unknown catastrophe, I wasn't going to hitch a ride today. I'd done enough moaning over these issues; the air was finally starting to clear.

"It'll be okay," I told Bill, as the twitching took over my face. "I'm going to focus on the joy of being awake. If I have to, I'll accept being asleep. Whatever it takes to have our baby safe and sound."

"And you too," Bill said.

"I'll be fine. You'll still go with the baby, wherever they take him, if I'm under general, right?"

"I won't leave him either way."

~~~

Bill and I drove to the hospital at six in the morning and signed in. I put on my hospital gown, was strapped down to a baby monitor and an IV. My doctor looked cheerful as he shook Bill's hand. "Good morning, Julie. All set?"

"Of course!" I said.

"We're very ready," Bill said nervously.

Dr. Mike looked at the curly scroll charting the baby's heartbeat. "Everything looks good." We'll see each other in a half hour or so," he said. As he left, another white-coat replaced him.

"Hi, Julie Genovese?"

"Yes?"

"I'm Dr. Langdon, your anesthesiologist. Can I take a look at your spine, Julie?"

The doctor gently parted the back of my oversized hospital gown and pushed on my vertebrae. "As we talked about on Friday, we'll try for the epidural, but if we can't get it started, or if the baby goes into distress, we'll have to put you under general anesthesia."

"Okay." The reality of surgery suddenly slapped me silly.

"See you in a little while," the doctor said.

Bill looked over at me tenderly. "We'll hope for the best, sweetheart."

"I'll be awake. If I'm not, you'll go with the baby, right?" I felt compelled to confirm our plan again.

"Right."

Barbara, my kind nurse, came in to say that Dr. Mike had to perform an emergency C-section, so we would have to wait a little longer.

I closed my eyes and tried to relax. I told the baby I loved him and that I'd miss carrying him inside. I thought about the baby's first movements when I was four months pregnant. That initial strange bubble, which had felt like a tiny flip-flopping fish, had captured my complete attention. *Was that . . . was that the baby . . . or just gurgling gas?* In the following days, when those decisive bubbles had continued, I knew it was magical life. With every small pop, I would grow very still, suspending my breath, waiting for an angel. I'd hold my stomach in anticipation of the next teeny hello and when it came, my whole body would chuckle in giddy surprise. Those moments were enough to make anyone a believer.

After a quiet half hour, Barbara returned with a grin.

"The other baby is doing fine and Dr. Mike is ready for you. We can take you to the OR now. Do you need help or can you walk with the IV?"

"She could drag a silver-backed gorilla right now if you asked her to," Bill said.

The time had arrived. I practically ran with that IV down the hall. Barbara brought a stool over so that I could climb onto the operating table. After I was settled, Dr. Langdon began to prepare my back for the epidural. "You're going to need to arch your spine like a hissing cat so we can get as much room as possible between the vertebrae."

I leaned forward on Bill and did the best Halloween cat that I could.

"Here we go." The needle pierced deep into my back as I squeezed Bill's hands.

"Tell me if you feel any pain going into your hips," the doctor said.

"There's sharp pain in my left hip," I said.

The doctor retracted the tube. "Okay, we'll try again."

After the eleventh attempt, Dr. Langdon was concerned, and I began to shake out of control. Then my shoulders froze up in pain.

Barbara draped a warm towel over me. "It's just a reaction to the local anesthesia. It'll pass."

In spite of my best efforts to dismiss it, fear began to gnaw at me.

"Take deep breaths, sweetheart," Bill said.

I closed my eyes and tried to relax. As I pictured light and angels, the shaking subsided.

Dr. Mike came in and he and Dr. Langdon had a quick, quiet discussion.

"Julie, do you want me to continue or . . . ?" Dr. Langdon said.

"Yes. I know you can do it."

Bill's hands, resting on my thighs, were shaking. He was remembering the child who had died in his arms, and a marriage that had died as a result. I looked into his eyes and smiled. "It's going to be okay this time."

Dr. Langdon continued with a few more attempts. "We may want to opt for general anesthesia. You must be getting tired of being a pincushion."

"A few more tries," I said calmly. "I know it will work. I'm going to hear my son's first cry."

After twenty jabs, faith and destiny locked arm in arm and the epidural went in.

"It's working," Dr. Langdon said in relief. My heart did a triple half gainer.

I lay down on the table and the nurses draped a curtain across my chest. Dr. Mike went to work.

"It's almost time," I whispered to Bill.

"The grand opening," he said.

"You'll stay with the baby?"

"Wild unicorns couldn't drag me away."

I tried to move my toes just to see what it would feel like. It felt like—nothing. Just as it was supposed to.

"How are you feeling, Julie?" Dr. Langdon asked.

"Fine," I said in amazement, "but my hands are going numb."

"That's because the epidural is up so high on your back. It will be the first to wear off when we stop the medicine." The doctor talked to me for a while as Bill watched over the curtain.

"I think I see . . . is that the baby?" Bill asked excitedly.

All at once, everything grew large. People were talking and moving quickly, purposefully. A universal pulse guided the room. I was a slow feather spiraling towards hallowed ground, a part of a sacred passage. A holy moment. Trumpets sounded. Cherubs sang. God laughed.

"There he is!" Bill cried.

"It's a boy!" Dr. Mike said.

With happy tears, I squeezed Bill's hand and watched the scene unfold through his glistening eyes. The enchantment on his face was worth ten thousand pictures.

"He has lots of black hair, hon!"

I pictured my grandparents doing wild cartwheels.

"Congratulations," Dr. Langdon said softly. "You did great."

Then I heard what I'd been waiting for. Spencer cried.

"I hear him!" That was the moment when I knew about my son. Maybe it was the drugs, or maybe it was something I'd known all along. He was a little person, yes, but not a dwarf. I didn't feel relief, as I had expected. I just felt the privilege of having him.

Bill looked at me full of love. "He's here. And he's big!" he said proudly. "I'm going to cut the cord, okay?"

"Okay." Breathless joy closed my eyes. I sent love across the airwaves to Spencer.

"Six pounds eight ounces," Dr. Mike said as Bill's camera flashed.

"Nineteen inches."

The pediatrician talked quietly to Bill, explaining that the baby needed to go to the neonatal unit for observation. *Did he say the baby wasn't crying enough?* I smiled. I knew that my little boy was fine. I pictured my grandma popping cigars in the mouths of every angel in the place.

Barbara swaddled Spencer and brought him over. "Oh," I gasped through my lens of tears. "Hello, sweet boy."

"Congratulations, Julie," Barbara said.

"Thank you," I whispered through my tears, as Bill's camera went off again.

"Look at his pretty hazel eyes," Barbara said.

What did you know? My grandmother's name was Hazel and she had hazel eyes.

I gazed at the tiny godsend and for a moment Spencer stopped crying and looked back at me. Then the nurse whisked him away and Bill followed close behind. I lay quietly as Dr. Mike finished. I'd gotten through the epidural and the surgery, and I was okay. I was better than okay! Only a scar from the C-section would remain. Each of my scars would tell a story about where I'd been; they couldn't change who I was.

I was waiting in the recovery room when Bill wheeled in a bassinet. Spencer didn't have to go to the neonatal unit after all. My chest pounded with excitement.

"He's so tiny!" I said as Bill laid the baby in my arms. I felt swept away. I stared into Spencer's pink face as he nuzzled, ready to nurse. He latched on easily, as I watched in astonishment. He's here at last, and he's eating! I was quenched by life, empty of fear. Bill leaned in close with a look that said everything I wanted to hear. Bill had always known how to speak to my soul without a word.

There was a mystical haze when Spencer was born and a throng of gossamer angels dancing at the end of my bed. I wondered if the baby could still recognize them by sight or if he now had to remember them by heart.

I smiled and silently thanked the staff and the two gentle white-coats who'd placed this miracle in my arms. They were a powerful part of my full circle and our love story of opposites.

Sixteen
It's All in Your Head

Our deepest fears are like dragons guarding our deepest treasure.
~Maria Rainer Rilke

On December 4, 2002, and January 29, 2003, two and a half years after Spencer's birth, I underwent brain surgery. I know, it sounds horrible. After a sixteen-year odyssey with HFS, though, I was willing and desperate enough to ask the white-coats for help. Again.

When the spasms first started, they came and went for about a year, worsening every time they returned. Three years later, when the strange contractions settled in for good, I started fighting hard. I knew a battle against my body was futile, yet I waged one anyway. *Surely, if I get angry enough*, I thought, *I can change it. Or God will.*

A compressed nerve in my brain was causing the continual jitterbug under my skin. My face was jerked into spasm about every five minutes, then it twitched for five minutes, subsided for five minutes, then repeated the cycle. All day, every day. The HFS contracted all the muscles on the left side of my head, from the top of my scalp down through my neck, and bolted my left eye closed. It woke me each night and pulled my mouth so taut that my pillow was covered with drool. I felt struck down, once again, by my appearance—my Achilles heel. My feelings swung back and forth: HFS could be a curse or an opportunity.

I searched for ways in which the HFS had served my soul. My first realization was that, compared to the spasms, being a little person was a cakewalk. In fact, it rarely bothered me at all anymore. Amazing. The HFS had shaken me up, turned me upside down, and helped to empty out every insecurity I'd ever had, and then some. The adversity began to spur me on. It helped to focus my energies and define my dreams.

As I lay in bed one night, listening to Bill's soft breathing, I smiled . . . and twitched. I felt so thankful for the wonders in my life. Tonight, instead of regressing into my old "please please help me God" prayer, I was calm, and I was open. I'd stopped demanding a solution from the Universe and started believing in one. I closed my eyes and suddenly, out of the blue, I remembered it. My first neurologist had told me about an experimental surgery for HFS. He said it was dangerous and successful only fifty percent of the time. The surgeon would need to drill a hole the size of a quarter into the skull, then go to the brain stem and cushion the blood vessel that was compressing the seventh cranial nerve. Back then, I'd shuddered at the thought. Never in a trillion years, not my skull. Now, thirteen years later, I lay in bed and realized that great strides might have been made with this surgery. Excitement and relief squeezed me tight. I went to sleep with a huge, spastic smile. The HFS woke me twice that night; hope lulled me right back to sleep.

The following morning, my eyes opened wide at six. Well, only my right eye, of course. I jumped out of bed and flew to the computer, knowing I had some time before my day officially began. I quickly found an online support group, the Hemifacial Spasm Association (HFSA.) Why on earth hadn't I done this sooner? Had I been that oblivious to the fact that others endured this condition? Had I been so ashamed of the HFS, that I somehow edited out all solutions? In blaming myself, I'd felt that the responsibility of a cure was entirely mine. I'd felt so alone that I couldn't imagine anyone understanding. In the same way, I'd felt isolated in my dwarfism, even though my brother Ethan was in the same family, in the next room. The Little People of America was in every state. Once again, right at my finger tips, the answers had been waiting. I was ready at last.

What I read was thrilling: "Our Circle of Friends are current or former HFS sufferers." *Former?* "You don't have to reinvent the wheel about what you are going through. We experience many of the same symptoms (or did until MVD) and we really do know what it is like to try and live a 'normal' life while in the clutches of twitches and spasms. We have walked in your shoes so nothing shocks or surprises us. Even all the things you've hidden from family and friends are familiar to us. We accept and we understand. Welcome, you have made a wonderful contact. Bet you thought there was no one else in the world who was suffering like you are."

Tears raced each other down my cheeks. Microvascular decompression (MVD). I read about the surgery that could set me free. At present, the success rate was ninety-five percent. I clicked on every link and read every journal from members who'd had the surgery. Some had posted pictures of themselves with their faces twisted in ugly spasms. I stared in amazement. I'd never seen another soul with HFS. That night I told Bill about everything I'd learned and said I wanted to have the surgery.

When I sent the MRI of my skull to Dr. Kassam, he noticed something rare, an Arnold Chiari malformation (ACM). He said that he would have to remove a chunk of bone from the base of my skull to improve the odds for a successful MVD. After the first surgery to correct the Chiari, there was a waiting period of two months before the MVD. Two brain surgeries? Two big scars? Two recoveries? I felt I'd been kicked in the stomach.

My dad e-mailed links to Chiari web sites, and I read through them and wept. The World Arnold Chiari Malformation Association said: "In Chiari Malformations, an excess of cerebellar tissue known as the cerebellar tonsils extends down through the foramen magnum into the upper portion of the spinal canal. In so doing, the cerebellar tonsils put pressure on the brain stem and spinal cord . . ."

My brain was overcrowded, under pressure. That sounded about right. The HFS and ACM were all in my head. I'd known that for years too. I had another rare syndrome to add to my list: spondyloepiphyseal dysplasia (SED), HFS, and now ACM. One in every 6,000 people are born with ACM; one in 100,000 are born with SED; one in 100,000 are born with HFS. Of those who have HFS, less than 1 percent are affected before age thirty. Mine began when I was twenty-three. I'd definitely won the genetic lottery.

That night, I went online to the chat room and found that one other member had the Chiari surgery and a successful MVD two years earlier. I wasn't alone. I decided not to pity myself anymore and to keep moving ahead. Whenever I felt down, Bill patiently reminded me that I'd endured the spasms for sixteen years. I could do this too.

The next hurdle was my insurance company. It took five months and two appeals but they finally granted authorization to go to University of Pittsburgh Medical Center. Fortunately, my parents lived an hour outside of Pittsburgh, and they'd take care of Spencer while I was in the hospital. There was no one I trusted more. But Spencer, at two and a half, had never been away from me for more than a few hours. The hospital stay would be three to five days, more if there were complications. How would I go that long without hugging him? How would he feel without me?

Spencer pitter-patted into the room where I sat at the computer. He climbed into my lap for a cuddle, and I smiled clear down to my monkey toes.

"Having fun with your trains?" I asked.

"Brid fall part," he said, in his sweet crackly voice.

"The bridge fell apart again? I can fix that."

Spencer scrambled down and ran out to the living room. I put the bridge back together and sat watching as he played with his wooden train set. He looked like Bill and also a little like my brother, Ethan: brown hair, high forehead, and big hazel eyes. Some days, I saw Ethan all around me, in the movement of my own hands, the bend of my elbow, the gait as I walked. Our similarities were no longer objectionable, though; I'd learned to accept the reflection. In the mirror, I could see Dan's slightly crooked smile on my face; sometimes I could hear him laughing at one of my jokes or singing a song we loved. I hadn't seen my two brothers in years, but they were with me every day. I had recently called Ethan at the hospital after his shoulder surgery. Knowing of his years of pain and limitation, it was great to hear him in such good spirits. We laughed together, and I smiled long after I hung up the phone. My brothers had once said that their difficult decisions and actions had been out of love for me. Given their beliefs, I finally could feel it was true. Only time would tell where the love between us would lead.

Spencer proudly showed me his long line of trains. My boy. My prize. He was life beating in all its fullness. He was the rainbow in soapy bath bubbles. The dewdrops of autumn. Joy leapt from his toes and giggled through every leaf pile. With Spencer shining so brightly in his truth, Bill and I just couldn't help but stand in our own. Our son had us sailing old childhood delights out of a forgotten bay. He slowed our pace, as we watched every butterfly, felt every breeze, noticed a world renewed. And yet he was also the quickening of time. The years had never thrown us so decidedly forward, into love, into change. Becoming a family was the most wonderful, challenging, and important journey we'd ever charted. Was I crazy to put my brain under the knife?

My moments of doubt were short-lived compared to the peace that had won me over since I'd decided on surgery. Over the years, I'd tried many alternatives to quell the nervous plundering. My spirit felt the healing, and yet the HFS wasn't cured. Typical of the condition, it kept getting worse. Finally, I was willing to put my metaphysical pride back on the shelf and allow the white-coats to turn off the problem that I had turned on.

Three months later, Bill, Spencer, and I headed for Pittsburgh. We spent the first day at the hospital for preadmission testing. Dr. Kassam's head nurse, Lois Burkhart, treated me like an old friend. Dr. Kassam, a legend to the people he had cured, was warm and kind. He talked quietly and showed pictures of his young sons. When violent contractions clamped down on my face, he looked past them and talked to the heart of me. My knight in a shining white coat had arrived.

The hours of marching around the hospital for tests were exhausting. As Bill and I drove home, we argued over directions and rush-hour traffic, avoiding the real issue. The next day was Chiari surgery. We were quiet for a while until Bill finally spoke. "I'd be lost without you."

"I'm not going anywhere," I answered stiffly.

By morning, I was sobbing in Bill's arms. I cried when I hugged Spencer and my parents good-bye. I was still crying when Bill kissed me and they wheeled me towards the OR.

The doctors would make a five-inch incision down the back of my head and into my neck to remove a two-by-four-inch section of skull, as well as some of my uppermost vertebrae (called a laminectomy); they'd also take a look at my brain. This would take three to four hours if all went as planned. That night, I'd be in the intensive care unit. Oh boy.

The neurosurgeon's work area during a MVD is about the size of the head of a tack. However, because of my Chiari malformation, the work area was even smaller. Dr. Kassam would be removing some of my skull in order to decompress my brain. Put that way, it actually sounded kind of good.

They brought me to the pre-op waiting area and I clung to a piece of paper with affirmations inspired by mind-body researchers like Dr. Bernie Seigel and Dr. Christiane Northrup: "After the operation you will feel comfortable, safe, and pain-free. Your operation went smoothly and you will heal very well." Would the anesthesiologist agree to read them as I went under anesthesia and as I came out? Maybe he'd think I was nuts.

When I met Dr. Carol Rose, she promised to talk to me, and said that she did so routinely. I was in great hands. She kept me partially awake during the intubation, but I didn't panic. I went under anesthesia and woke up again without fear. The first thing I heard was groaning. It was me. A nurse asked how I was doing. I told her that it felt like I had a steel hat nailed on, which was ten times too tight, and I could barely move my neck—but, hey, I was okay. I was talking and even smiling. Bill came in, enormous relief on his face. That night, I worried about being alone. But when I woke up every hour or so, I was relaxed and the pain was tolerable. It was a far cry from my bilateral hip and knee replacements.

Three days later, I was released. I could hardly wait to see Spencer. Over the next several months, he'd often say softly, "I miss you 'ospital." The feeling was mutual.

A week later, home in New Jersey, my mom took me to my local doctor to have the seventeen stitches removed. Before we left, I looked at the back of my head. Frankenstein had nothing on me.

Eight weeks flew by as I recovered from Chiari surgery. Then Bill, Spencer, and I headed back to Pittsburgh for my MVD. I was so excited at the thought of having a pain-free, peaceful face. I'd decided the universe wanted me to win. The angels were rooting for me. I wasn't bad, and I wasn't being punished. I didn't have to fix it all by myself, and I didn't have to be perfect to be cured.

Mark Shelton's book, *Working in a Very Small Place: The Making of a Neurosurgeon*, documents Dr. Jannetta's development of the MVD procedure. Shelton writes, ". . . the configuration of blood vessels around the base of the brain causes a blood vessel, generally an artery but sometimes a vein, to press against one of the 'cranial nerves,' the twelve pairs of nerves that arise from the brain and control our sight, hearing, taste, smell, the movements of the eyes and face."

As a result, my nerves were short-circuited and on constant high alert. The way I had led my life had become imprinted on my physiology.

Dr. Kassam and Dr. Horowitz would be making a five-inch incision behind my left ear and drilling a hole into my skull about the size of a quarter. With an endoscope, they would go to the brain stem and insert bits of Teflon between the bothersome blood vessel and the cranial nerve. It was a sophisticated operation in one of the most dangerous areas of the brain called the cerebellopontine angle. Some possible complications included facial paralysis, cerebral spinal fluid leak, hearing loss, vertigo, and stroke. As with all surgeries, there was always the chance I wouldn't wake up. Gulp.

At eight the following morning, I was on my way to pre-op. I was ready. I'd done the inner work and had swept away as much negativity as I could. The rest was in the hands of doctors and angels. Next thing I knew, I was in the recovery room, feeling completely drained of life. I saw Bill's smiling face but had no strength to keep my eyes open or talk. Lights, sounds, and movement aggravated the pounding in my head. I was moved to the ICU where I noticed some twitching. I wanted to slip away. When I woke next, my bed was surrounded by blurry white-coats. I brightened a little when I saw Dr. Kassam. He held up four fingers close to my face and told me that all four arteries which could have been involved in the problem were involved in the problem. My head now had quite a bit of Teflon in it.

I didn't eat for several days because everything kept coming back up. Whenever my head was thrown forward by the retching, I worried about the stitches. Somehow, everything held together. I was still whole. I barely remember talking to Bill, though I somehow realized he was worried. So was I. Four days in the hospital and I could hardly walk. It had snowed so hard that Bill and my parents hadn't visited in two days. I didn't notice.

On the fifth day, I resolved that I was going home no matter what. I had to see Spence. I ate some crackers and drank a little. It all stayed put. Then I realized there was no twitching. *Wow!*

None? I tried to whistle, a sure trigger for the spasms. Nothing happened. My face remained calm. *Fantastic!* I smiled at Bill even though I felt like a compost heap. Perhaps eight weeks hadn't been enough recovery time between major surgeries. As Bill packed my things, I took a Percocet but neglected to eat more than a cracker. Bad move. I signed papers, thanked the kind nurses, and we hightailed it out of the hospital. About a half hour into the car ride, my stomach burned like an angry tandoori oven. I arrived at my parents' house covered in puke. They were so happy to see me that they barely noticed.

At home, I lay around like a rag doll for six days until my post-op appointment. As my dad pushed me in a wheelchair back through the hospital, the habitual fear and nervousness stirred. Then I remembered I no longer had to hide. I started smiling at everyone, everywhere. In the elevator, down the hall, into the office, I just beamed like a xenon headlight. What a wonder to be free! After the stitches were removed, and Lois offered a good progress report, my dad and I headed home. My mom, Bill, and Spence were waiting with lunch. After two bowls of chicken broth and rice, I could feel myself returning. Warmth was peeking out from every cold corner. How perfect that my parents, whose love had called me into this world, were there to welcome me back to life.

Three weeks later, I received a copy of a letter to my local doctor from Dr. Kassam. It had been written one day after MVD surgery.

> Dear Dr. Greenbaum,
>
> It was a pleasure speaking with you today. Julie underwent her microvascular decompression for Hemifacial spasm. The surgery went quite nicely despite being a very crowded posterior fossa. She had a complex series of pathology involving the vertebral artery, posterior fossa cerebellar artery, anterior communicating artery, and a small arterial loop as

well, causing a fairly dramatic compression. We were able to relieve the lateral spread completely which is an excellent indication of Hemifacial relief.

Again, we really do appreciate the trust you show in allowing us to care for her.

Sincerely yours,

Amin Kassam, M.D.

Michael B. Horowitz, M.D.

The world of medicine had changed, and so had I.

The years of loss made the restoration indescribably wonderful. Life felt fabulous. The SED, the HFS, the ACM, the arthritis, the surgeries, and the white-coats had each set a part of me free. My nightmares were dreams in disguise.

I'd had two knees replaced, two hips replaced, and two craniectomies (brain surgeries). But the pair of surgeries that gifted me most were my two C-sections. The second one brought our wonderful son, Kyler, into the family. On that first day, as he lay beside me, a new little planet orbiting my heart, I felt an infinite expanse around us. Although he was tucked in a tiny body, in a small room, we were part of a big dream. In the everyday hospital world, nurses streamed in and out, the phone rang, the food came, but the miracle remained in the smell of his hair, the sweetness of his yawn. Wrapped up like a baby burrito, his life was all warmed up and raring to go.

As Ky was waking from his nap one afternoon, Spencer lay snuggled up in my bed next to him. "Everybody gets softer after they sleep," Spence said with the sweetest smile. "Especially babies." My family has softened my hard edges, unwound the old restrictions, unleashed the rainbows.

I still have a lot to unlearn, but when I occasionally dabble in the old darkness, the kids help to snap the light back on. They are teaching Bill and me more than we can sometimes sop up. As they grab our hands, laughter curls around their small fingers. They remind us to live inside the wonder. To keep a box of crayons in our heart. To design our own Eden. They have come to rescue us from our own forgetting.

The early chapters of my life read a bit like fiction these days. I barely recognize my old self who drew big generalizations from little understanding. Somewhere along the way, I realized that my spirit, not my problems, was the center of my universe. Feeding the difficulties just helped them to grow. I didn't invent suffering, loneliness, and rejection, but I took them as companions for years until I chose differently.

A few months after my last surgery, as I read through a hospital bill, I stopped at an interesting sentence: "Suboccipital craniectomy with C1-2 laminectomy and duraplasty . . . small posterior fossa . . . repair skull *defect*."

I waited for the pain; there was none. I read the word again. Defect. But the sad story was really over. Gone. A smile crossed my life.

I went to the living room and pulled out a small piece of paper from a hidden pocket in my wallet. It was the wish list I had written years before at a New Year's celebration. "A loving relationship," was written in tiny scrawl. *My Bill.* I could definitely check that one off. Second on the list was, "A free vacation to Hawaii." *I got a lot more than that.* Next came, "A pain-free body." *I'm getting closer.* Then I read, "I release anger, fear, and judgment. I choose joy." That night, ten years earlier, I'd been too embarrassed to write that I desperately wanted a cure for the twitching. As it turned out, releasing my anchor of negativity was a part of the healing. The HFS was a reminder that as long as I was aligned with happiness, the physical stuff was like wrinkles, or scars. Only skin deep. Every wish on my list had been answered. The only thing that had been standing in the way of my dreams was my own disbelief.

One morning, when Spencer was six and Kyler was two, I found them happily rummaging in my closet. Suddenly, Spencer emerged triumphant, holding a dented yellow Wiffle bat. The sight of it made me laugh.

"Mommy, can we pway wif it?" he asked excitedly.

"Sure, I don't need it anymore," I answered. It had been a long time since I'd madly mauled my bed with that old bat. The raging fear, which had once dictated my world, had been released. Years ago, I'd have thought it impossible. Shows how much I knew.

Those who I thought were my enemies became my allies. Pain moved towards healing. Hate turned to love. Fear to joy. I'd once judged my life as inadequate, but from my soul's perspective, it had always been magnificent. It turns out that in the great celestial card game, there's no such thing as a bad hand. The full circles of life had brought me Home. Being born different was not a curse in the end; it was magic.

ACKNOWLEDGMENTS

I feel so grateful for the many wonderful people who have been an essential part of my life and the completion of this work.

My very biggest thank you goes to my best friend and husband, Bill Genovese, for his extraordinary love, determined support and tenderhearted care. I love you beyond measure.

To my amazing sons, Spencer and Kyler, who bring the joy and wonder out of their hearts and into every day. I love you to the moon and back (a bazillion times.)

To my sisters and brothers, angels since birth, who honor me with their love and friendship.

To my talented agent, Stephany Evans, who believed in my story from the start and has been a wise teacher and advocate through the whole process.

To my priceless publisher, Lynn Price, for her enthusiasm, perfect wit, and tireless work.

To my jewel of an editor, Erin Stalcup, whose gentle clarity brought the manuscript new life.

To the magnificent Dr. Wayne Dyer who has been my greatest inspiration, and whose generous and majestic spirit helped bring this book to the public.

To Dr. Christiane Northrup, Alan Cohen and Dr. Bernie Siegel for offering their fantastic endorsements before the manuscript had a publishing nibble.

To Dan Millman for taking the time to offer valuable advice and insight.

To the visionaries who opened the door and set me on my path; Dr. Wayne Dyer, Esther and Jerry Hicks, Louise Hay, Dan Millman, Dr. Christiane Northrup, Dr. Bernie Siegel, Pat Rodegast, Neale Donald Walsch, Jane Roberts, Drs. Helen Schuchman and William Thetford, Dr. Deepak Chopra, Richard

Bach, Susan Page, Jan Phillips, Martha Beck, Sue Monk Kidd, Elizabeth Gilbert, Marianne Williamson, Dr. Caroline Myss, and Doreen Virtue.

To Edna Farley for your remarkable generosity, thoughtfulness and for going the extra mile for me.

To Sonya Oppenheimer and Anne Amerson for reading one of the first rough drafts of Nothing Short of Joy with such enthusiasm and grace.

To Hazel Dawkins, for editing the second really rough draft with a talented eye, light heart and terrific sense of humor.

To Julie Maloney, an exquisite writer, mentor and gorgeous soul who unlocks magic.

To my writing sisters at Women Reading Aloud for sharing your empowering voices and contagious light.

To my fellow homeschoolers and their families who have inspired me to grow and learn alongside my kids.

To my grandparents, Hazel and Howell Bond and Adeline and Marshall Rey, who continue to guide me from the other side.

To my fabulous circle of friends who have held their light up for me with such love; Tracy Coan, Judy Prescott, Megan McWilliams, Simone Ramel, Lisa Delchamps, Dawn Quirk, Joslin Fields, Maureen McCormick, Judith Hancox, Nancy and Dick Weber, Kimberly Newsome, Anastasia Werner, Juanita Kirton, and Renie Garlick.

Finally my deepest gratitude to my extended family and community of friends near and far. You know who you are. Thank you for years of friendship, fun and a deep connection that reminds me I'm never alone.

Although this is a true story, various names have been changed for reasons of privacy. The people, dialog and events recorded in *Nothing Short of Joy* were, naturally, viewed through my own subjective lens. So I offer my apologies, in advance, for any unintentional misrepresentation. I have tried to tell my truth to the very best of my recollection.